TALES AND TORTS

Stories of a Country Lawyer

ROBERT B. KEARL, BA, LLB

ILLUSTRATIONS BY JANE CONRAD

◆ FriesenPress

One Printers Way
Altona, MB R0G 0B0
Canada

www.friesenpress.com

Copyright © 2022 by Robert B. Kearl
First Edition — 2022

All rights reserved.

No part of this publication may be reproduced in any form, or by any means, electronic or mechanical, including photocopying, recording, or any information browsing, storage, or retrieval system, without permission in writing from FriesenPress.

ISBN
978-1-03-915728-6 (Hardcover)
978-1-03-915727-9 (Paperback)
978-1-03-915729-3 (eBook)

1. BIOGRAPHY & AUTOBIOGRAPHY, LAWYERS & JUDGES

Distributed to the trade by The Ingram Book Company

To my mother, may your memory and legacy live on inside the pages of this book as it does in my heart. You are a true inspiration of kindness, love, and the storyteller's art.

To my children, who always wondered what I did all day.

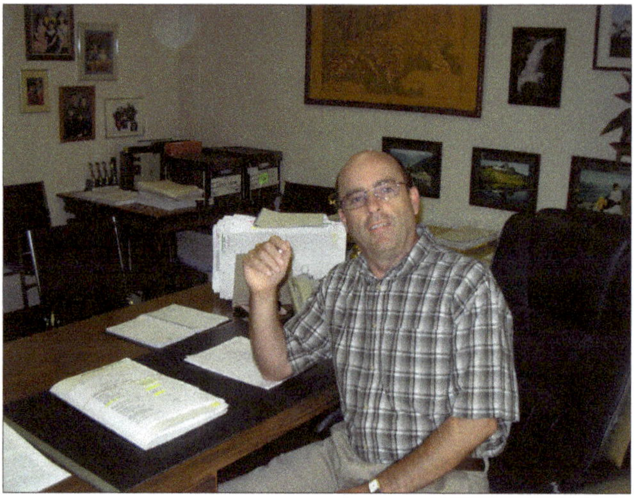

TABLE OF CONTENTS

Preface: The Storyteller	ix
Introduction	xii
Chapter One	
The Trilogy That Led to Becoming a Courtroom Lawyer	1
Chapter Two	
The Country versus the City	16
Chapter Three:	
An Ironic Twist	22
Chapter Four	
The Case of the Missing Moustache	30
Chapter Five:	
Politically Correct	43
Chapter Six:	
Marriage	52
Chapter Seven	
The Supreme Court of Canada	63
Chapter Eight	
The Rhyme of the Ancient Farmer	76
Chapter Nine	
The Jewish Russian Tenor	80
Chapter Ten	
Was It Murder?	88

Chapter Eleven
    Odds and Ends   95
Chapter Twelve:
    Was the Gift Perfected?   110
Chapter Thirteen
    A Modern Legal Don Quixote   115
Chapter Fourteen
    The End of the Road   119
Chapter Fifteen
    The Tongan   124
Chapter Sixteen
    The Dog Was Worth More than the Man   134
Chapter Seventeen
    The Luck of the Irish   142
Chapter Eighteen
    Fort Langley: Historic Birthplace of British Columbia   148
Chapter Nineteen
    Pilgrimage to Paisley   159
Chapter Twenty
    Greed, Like a Swarm of Locusts   165
Chapter Twenty-One
    The Long and the Short of It   175

Chapter Twenty-two
    The Love Triangle   203

Chapter Twenty-three
    Spare the Rod and Spoil the Child (Proverbs 13:24, 29:15)   223

Chapter Twenty-four
    Ethylene Glycol Intoxication   230

Chapter twenty-five
    Fort St. John in Winter   234

Chapter Twenty-six
    Premenstrual Syndrome (PMS)   239

Chapter Twenty-seven
    Toby the Bull   244

Chapter Twenty-eight
    Evil   249

Chapter Twenty-nine
    Volenti Non Fit Injuria   262

Chapter Thirty
    The Farmers and the Fort Langley Floodplain   266

Chapter Thirty-one
    Tragedy on Chinese New Year's Eve   271

Conclusion   **285**

Acknowledgements   **287**

PREFACE: THE STORYTELLER

Storytelling is the bedrock of human connection. Stories, whether told orally, visually, or in written form, connect the past to the present to the future in a looping chain where histories, geographies, and identities overlap and intertwine. From curious hand paintings on cave walls to cultural origin myths to tall tales repeated tiresomely at the family dinner table, sharing stories creates a special relationship between storyteller and story reader. What novel ideas or cautionary tales can the storyteller pass on? What power can the storyteller hold if there is no one around to absorb and interpret their words? We may not realize the truly magical reciprocity of this relationship until time and experience compel us to reflect on the legacies we leave behind; however, as children we understood this beautiful interchange well.

At bedtime when I was a little boy, Mom always read stories to me. Two of my favourites were *Winnie the Pooh and the Blustery Day* by A.A. Milne and *Mother West Wind Why Stories* by Thornton W. Burgess. Burgess wrote his enchanting stories on the banks of the "Smiling Pond." Each story begins with a question posed by the Merry Little Breezes or Peter Rabbit to the very old and very wise Grandfather Frog. Why is it that Jimmy Skunk never hurries? Why does Jerry Muskrat build his house in the water? Why does Miner the Mole live underground? Now Grandfather Frog knows all about the days when the world was young. Sitting on his big, green lily pad in his usual way with his hands folded across his white and yellow waistcoat, his big googly eyes twinkling, he begins with a deep, gruff voice, "Chug-a-rum!" Like Peter Rabbit pleading with Grandfather Frog for another story, I also begged Mom to read another chapter.

I do not remember a time when I did not love stories.

It is this love of stories that led me to my love of the law. Each legal case in law school starts with a collection of facts and witness statements formed into "stories," either by the victim or the perpetrator. As a lawyer, every client I met with had a story to tell, which resulted in me feeling empathy for them and their problem. While initially my role was to listen, absorb, and interpret their words, soon I, myself, transformed into the storyteller. Using legal principles which I applied to the facts, it was my job to achieve justice for my clients by unravelling complex and compelling narratives. Each person is unique and has a story only they can relate. I found it fascinating to be in a position to hear so many varied experiences in life by so many individuals with distinctive and critically important legal problems to be resolved that represent the intricacies of human existence.

Helping all these people solve their problems is the story of my law career. For this reason, I decided to write about a few of my more unusual experiences practicing law in this book, *Tales and Torts: Stories of a Country Lawyer*. As the axiom states: "Sometimes the truth is stranger than fiction." In my legal sketches, this certainly proves to be true. Each story I recount is based on a real case found in public record. As you can imagine, in some of these cases, my clients experienced the highest and lowest moments of their lives. Their pain, trauma, joys, and triumphs are deeply personal and real. For this reason, many names have been changed to protect the identities of the innocent and save them any further trauma or embarrassment. Moreover, as time has gone on, I have found myself reaching back with the tendrils of my memories and wondering about the finer details of their lives—details I was not then privy to in a hard case file, witness testimony, or purpose-driven interview. In these cases, I have used literary licence to fill in gaps in the narrative with my own suppositions about what these individuals might have been thinking, feeling, or seeing in the course of their unique cases.

I hope you enjoy reading *Tales and Torts: Stories of a Country Lawyer* in the same way that I enjoyed curling up on a chilly night, warmed by the lilting voice of my mother, curious about the adventures, calamities, and lessons my favourite characters had yet to experience on this wild ride of life. Keep in mind, however, that the characters I introduce, along with their legal woes, are much more complex and deserving of our empathy than Miner the Mole. Their stories, interwoven with a bit of fancy and a body of fact, are as real as the stripe on Jimmy the Skunk's back.

Robert Bruce Kearl

INTRODUCTION

I didn't always want to be a lawyer. Even though the stories I so admired as a child involved characters whose adventures occurred in their own idyllic backyards, I wanted to travel the world. So, in May 1977, with a fluency in French, a Political Science degree from the University of British Columbia, and nothing but the spirit of adventure in my back pocket, I planned to become what I thought encapsulated my talents and attributes the best: a Canadian Global Ambassador. To what country? I had no idea. Certainly, my adventures would extend beyond Grandfather Frog's "Smiling Pond" or Christopher Robin's "Hundred Acre Wood."

Little did I know that a grander adventure than I had ever imagined would befall me, and that was becoming a husband and a father. I met my wife, Beth, and the world, indeed, fell at my feet as we planned to welcome our first child together. Visions of globetrotting and galas in far-off cities dissolved merrily into the idea of tickling tiny toes and walking hand-in-hand with my love on the beaches of English Bay.

In a spur of the moment decision—one that would change my life forever—I applied to law school. Unlike my peers, who wisely planned out their education with much forethought and preparation, I wrote the law school entrance exam without studying! I was fortunate enough to obtain a high enough mark, when combined with my fourth-year grades at UBC, to be accepted to all four law schools that I applied to. With my young wife, it was time to decide whether I wanted to go to Saskatoon, Calgary, Edmonton, or Vancouver.

Since spring arrives early each March with the blossoming of the Japanese cherry trees in Vancouver, it was an easy decision. With Edmonton, Calgary, and Saskatoon locked in winter with the cold wind howling, blowing the snow around at twenty degrees below and a lovely warm breeze off the Pacific Ocean in Vancouver, I decided on UBC. In addition, Vancouver was, and remains, a magnificent port city with lovely beaches on the Pacific Ocean, along with Stanley Park's giant red cedar trees and exquisite views of the North Shore Mountains across the harbour. The setting for the City of Vancouver is incomparable.

Law school was very interesting as each case told a story. I love stories. I learned that the outcome of each case was decided on the facts, or what I have called, the story. Legal principles are applied to the facts to arrive at a just decision. Examining each case to determine the reason for the judge's decision was fascinating. The three years of law school flew by. I obtained my Bachelor of Laws Degree from the Faculty of Law at UBC in May 1980.

However, I still could not practice law. I had to complete one year of articling with a law firm and pass the bar entrance exams. Driving from Vancouver to Calgary each year to visit Mom, Dad and family in Calgary, I happened to notice a pretty little sign on the highway that read "Langley." Langley was just a forty-five-minute drive up the Fraser River Valley from Vancouver—close enough to the big city in which I attended school, but perhaps far enough away to be a safe and quiet place to raise a family. In the seconds it took to flash past the sign, I had already decided; I would article and practice law in this town called Langley. I had never been there. I knew nothing about it! However, if life had taught me anything so far, it was that I needed to trust my gut. Like my decisions to marry, create a family and go to law school, something inside told me that Langley held the key to my free-spirited, yet homespun sensibilities.

I interviewed with a small country law firm in Fort Langley (population 3,400), which I later learned was the historic birthplace of British Columbia. It was (and is) a tiny village on the Fraser River, surrounded by dairy farms, cranberry and blueberry fields, and the clean smells of the country. I met with Don Nundal, senior partner of Nundal, Cherrington & Easingwood, who was dressed in a brightly coloured shirt and casual blue jeans, an old, black lab laying at his feet in his cozy office.

I was surprised and delighted by the quaint picture this law office, and Nundal, himself, painted. It was quite the contrast with the formality of the big downtown Vancouver law firms at which I had previously interviewed. There, I heard stories of new lawyers packed into cubicles like robotic minions preparing cases for senior lawyers to go to court, obsessed with billable hours and climbing the corporate ladder. While I admit this may be an unfair portrayal of these colossal firms, at the time, the contrast between the tucked-away, warm, wood-trimmed office in the country and the metal, cold, high rises in the bustling city was a stark one.

I wanted to run my own cases and have the freedom to act independently. I liked the small town of Fort Langley, the countryside, the less formal attitude, and Don's winning personality. We really hit it off. The decision was clear to me, and I decided I would article in Fort Langley and settle my family, which had grown to include an energetic little boy and beautiful baby girl, not too far away in the burgeoning suburb of West Langley (later called Walnut Grove). This turned out to be the best decision my family and I could possibly have made to start my career on the right foot.

Indeed, the country is where the legal stories of my life began, and soon, like Winnie the Pooh and Peter Rabbit, I had but to step outside my back porch to be met with beautiful and tragic characters, conflicts, and experiences that would bring meaning, wisdom, and incredible learning to me professionally and personally.

Instead of representing my country to the world as a global ambassador would, my clients brought the globe to my doorstep. Their stories, rife with political and personal intrigue, obliged me to "travel" to various locations unique to their circumstances and personal histories in order to understand their particular predicaments. From an opera tenor escaping persecution in Russia, to the misadventures of a Tongan tourist, to the plight of orphans in war-torn Haiti, the stories of my clients represent the universal struggles of humanity. By representing them and exploring the intricacies and legalities of their conflicts, I journeyed abroad and also explored, as Shakespeare relates, that "undiscovered country" of the self.

Fort Langley

Built in 1827, Fort Langley was a Hudson's Bay Company fur trading post located on the banks of the Fraser River and part of a trade route for the British Empire at the centre of a large population of Indigenous peoples. The Indigenous peoples were partners in business and marriage—trading furs and fish for blankets and other goods—and to strengthen its position, the Hudson's Bay Company encouraged its men to marry Indigenous women.

In 1858, gold was discovered on the Fraser River, which changed everything. As thirty thousand miners came calling, Fort Langley went from being a modest trade and provisioning post, to becoming the centre of a gold rush. Fearful of an American takeover, the British government, on November 19, 1858, had Governor James Douglas proclaim the Colony of British Columbia.

The Kwantlen First Nation administers an Indian reserve on McMillan Island across the Bedford Channel from Fort Langley. It is thought the first traces of people living in the Fraser Valley date from four thousand to ten thousand years ago. The Sto:lo, meaning "people of the river," called this area their traditional territory. The Kwantlen are a Sto:lo people.

Our office was a small bungalow converted into a law office, located at 9067 Church Street, the street named after the historic St. George's Anglican Church (opened in 1901) just a half block to the north. My articles consisted of two extremes: John Cherrington would work systematically, step by step with me, through each legal problem, while Don Nundal would just bring a client into my office, plunk the client in front of me, and tell me to figure it out myself. It was a good combination. I was successful in many small claims trials during my articling year.

While working full time, as part of my articles, I was required to study the law in many areas, such as Criminal Law, Constitutional Law, Tax Law, Tort Law, Family Law, Contract Law, Company Law, Civil Litigation and Procedure and others, and then write an exam at the end of each course. At the end of the year, I had passed all my exams, and in addition, Don Nundal and John Cherrington reported that I had completed a year of legal work to their satisfaction.

The day finally arrived. The Law Society of British Columbia certified that Robert Bruce Kearl of Fort Langley, BC, was, by the Benchers of the Law Society of British Columbia, on Tuesday the twelfth day of May, A.D. 1981, duly called to the Bar of the Province of British Columbia, and at that date declared a member of the Society in good standing.

TALES AND TORTS: STORIES OF A COUNTRY LAWYER

The Fort Law Office—front entrance and north side

CHAPTER ONE

The Trilogy That Led to Becoming a Courtroom Lawyer

What is the difference between the facts and the truth? In life, we often use these terms interchangeably, yet they are quite distinct from each other. Facts are generally understood to be realities that cannot be disputed and are unaltered by belief or subjectivity. For example, as children we are cautioned that if we touch the hot stove, we will be burned. This is a fact. A child simply holding the *belief* that they will NOT be burned will not change the outcome. They will be burned. Truth on the other hand, is a much more mercurial concept to define. A perception or belief can feel true to one person based on how they experience a moment. For example, individuals are often applauded for "speaking their truth" or "speaking truth to power," which leads one to believe that truth, indeed, is a matter of perspective or experience.

That being said, not all truths are as valid as others—even if the way one feels in the moment is. And so, the cold, hard facts must be relied on to conserve truth when two parties disagree. What would happen if someone told you that touching a hot stove would not burn you? What if they said it with great confidence? What if they shook your hand and promised? What if you agreed, relying upon their "truth," and were consequently burned? While the analogy is not perfect, the interplay between fact and truth is explored in all of my cases, yet most memorably in the first three cases I ever tried.

The Doctrine of Part Performance

Warren Sherk was known by all of his friends as "Dutch," so that is what I called him. The nickname connotes courage or determination, possibly because early German immigrants were perceived, rightly or wrongly, as obstinate or strong-willed. Dutch was a strong man, six-foot-two-inches tall, 194 pounds, with big hands, made even larger as a result of repetitive manual labour. Dutch had green eyes, light brown hair, slightly olive skin, a strong jaw, high cheek bones, a straight nose, deep-set eyes, and a sloping forehead. Most would say he was handsome.

Dutch had entered into an agreement with Mr. Hartshorn to develop a large acreage in Aldergrove (an area on the east side of Langley) over a period of ten years. In return, Mr. Hartshorn would give him a half interest in the land. Nothing was put in writing. It was strictly an oral agreement. Dutch was a man of his word and expected everyone else to be the same.

At the end of the ten years, Hartshorne did not give Dutch his half interest in the land, but rather served him with an eviction notice. I started an action in the Supreme Court to right this wrong. I knew that Dutch was telling the truth. The facts were on my side; however, how could I overcome the Statute of Frauds, which declares that in order to enforce an agreement regarding an interest in land, the contract must be made in writing and signed by the person giving up that interest?

I conducted extensive legal research at the courthouse in Vancouver where I discovered the leading case I could rely upon to solve this problem. It was a decision of the House of Lords in England in 1883: Maddison v Alderson. In that case, Maddison alleged the deceased Alderson had made a verbal promise that if Maddison worked as a housekeeper without wages for several years, then Alderson would make a will, leaving Maddison a life estate in the property. The deceased had signed a will leaving Maddison a life estate, but the will failed because it was not witnessed properly.

Maddison relied on the oral agreement, performing her part by working for the deceased without wages for several years and abandoning other prospects for advancement in her life. The trial judge found Maddison had established part performance of the contract, thereby making it enforceable despite the Statute of Frauds. The test was adopted by the Supreme Court of Canada in a case in 1907, stating that: "The acts relied upon as part performance must be unequivocally and in their own nature referable to some such agreement as that alleged."

To succeed, I had to demonstrate Dutch performed his part of the agreement and prove that these acts established such an agreement regarding an interest in land, not any other agreement. I knew the courts did not wish to allow the Statute of Frauds (intended to prevent fraud) to ironically become an instrument of fraud.

It was an uphill battle. The defendant's lawyer insulted me constantly, calling me an inexperienced idiot, because I failed to recognize this was a case that could not be won. He emphasized that I was in my first year of practicing law, while he had twenty-seven years of experience. He would place his hands on his hips and then look down his nose at me in a gesture of pure arrogance.

He insisted any actions on the part of Dutch simply established a tenancy agreement.

I just ignored him and plowed ahead. In my mind, I pictured the victory of David, the little guy, going out to battle with Goliath, the giant. Dutch deserved such a victory. I was hungry for it.

The trial required ten days of evidence presentation, as I had Dutch describe every detail of the work he performed with his two sons and two daughters, who grew up working alongside him on the property. He explained how he cleared the land, built bridges over the large ditch to get access onto the land, constructed a horse training track, other outbuildings, and many other improvements. My argument was simple. Why would Dutch do all this work to improve the land over a period of ten years? It could only relate to the oral agreement that he was to receive a half interest in the land. Attributing such intense work to mere tenancy made no sense.

Dutch was a large, tough working man. In contrast, he was married to a petite, French-Canadian named Noella. Each day in the public gallery of the court, Noella would be reading her Bible in French. She was hoping God would be on our side—as was I. During the trial, I reviewed with Dutch some of his evidence on a point that could be used against him. He asked me what he should do. I advised him that he was under oath to tell the truth—the **whole** truth—so he should tell everything precisely the way it happened. He did. This will become important, as you will see later.

After ten days of evidence, we started the argument. By now, I knew that the judge, Mr. Justice Dryer, by his comments and questions, was smarter than I was. I proceeded for two days with my argument, explaining why Dutch told the truth and the reasons he should come to the conclusion that Hartshorne was a liar. Of course, Hartshorne denied the agreement. Now the pressure had shifted to the arrogant lawyer for the defence, as it did not appear that my argument was facing a closed door.

The longer I made submissions, the more it appeared the judge liked what I was saying, as he would nod approvingly. He also posed many tough question to the defence lawyer, indicating he found his answers unsatisfactory. On the third day of argument, the defence lawyer collapsed and was taken to the hospital. Accordingly, the trial was adjourned.

No doubt, the arrogant defence lawyer had told his client he would easily obtain a dismissal of this case. However, the trial was not proceeding as he had planned, and the stress had now shifted from me to him. The pressure was too great for him to continue, which resulted in a delay of two months.

Finally, we returned to court to finish the argument, at which time the judge reserved. This meant he would not give oral reasons for his judgment from the bench but would provide written reasons later, which he did.

A few months later, the written reasons arrived, at which time I met with Dutch and his family in my office in Fort Langley. It was a joyful meeting due to the fact we had won! Mr. Justice Dryer ordered that Dutch was entitled to a half interest in the land. Noella, Dutch, and their four kids danced throughout the office shedding tears of joy; ten years of work would not go for naught.

In a portion of his reasons for judgment, there was a finding of fact that Dutch was a credible witness who could be relied upon to tell the whole truth. He even cited the example Dutch and I had discussed of some evidence that could be used against him. The judge was impressed that Dutch did not word things to his advantage or leave things out; he just told the truth. Of course, the twelve reasons I gave for why Mr. Hartshorne was a liar helped.

Hartshorne obtained new lawyers and appealed. Mr. Justice Seaton, the senior appellate court judge, made short shrift of that appeal. On behalf of the three judges, he declared the appeal didn't have a chance in hell. It was dismissed.

Dutch, Noella, and the rest of their family became my lifelong friends. Dutch has gone on to the next life where, I understand, telling the whole truth matters as well.

Unconscionable Bargain

Do you remember the moral to the stories of the "The Boy Who Cried Wolf" or "Little Red Riding Hood"? In each story, the wolf represented some danger of which to be cautious, whether it be lying or trusting strangers. Like these childhood fables, my second case also includes a "wolf" - a wolf in sheep's clothing. It cautions us to beware of those who clothe themselves in the guise of goodness yet use their power to trick and betray.

One sunny morning, I received a phone call from the manager of the Langley Lodge, a long-term care home in Langley. He felt that an elderly woman staying there had been taken advantage of, so he wanted me to come down to provide her with some legal advice. I met with "Little Miss Milligan," as she was called, in her small room in the home.

The first thing that struck me quite forcefully as I entered Miss Milligan's room, and caught sight of her standing at the head of her bed, was how frightfully thin she appeared. I tried to hide my shock at seeing someone so angular. As I moved forward, introduced myself, and shook her hand, I became aware of how frail she was due to a loss of muscle mass. I was careful not to press her hand firmly for fear I would crush it.

As I glanced over her room, the odd thought occurred to me that maybe it was fortunate she was so thin, as there wasn't much space between her bed and the drab walls. Her room was sparsely furnished with a single bed, dresser and night table on which I noticed a well-worn King James version of the Bible and a small, green lamp. At the foot of her bed stood a dresser with six drawers that I supposed contained all of Miss Milligan's possessions in this world. Beside the dresser was a white door leading into her private bathroom.

As my mind wandered back to her, I thought about the reasons why a body could be so underweight. That led me to wonder when she lost her appetite and her sense of taste and smell? When did eating become a chore, not an enjoyment? How could anyone give up their love of chocolate?

Next, I observed the deep furrows in Little Miss Milligan's brow. I wondered if every wrinkle could tell a story about her struggles and survival. I could tell that Miss Milligan was shy and feeling uncomfortable, as she was blushing, somewhat speechless, shaky, and breathless.

I sat down at the foot of her bed with my pen and notebook in hand and began to ask her questions. It required a great deal of patience, but finally her sad story came out in a voice as quiet as a whisper.

Her prior wolfish lawyer, Joe, and a predatory businessman friend of his from Edmonton had met with her in her room. She had signed documents, but she didn't know what they were. She was worried as she didn't know what she had done. She was alone without anyone to advise her.

I learned that Miss Milligan did not have any family, was never married, and didn't have any children. Before coming to the Langley Lodge, she had lived a solitary life on her dairy farm in Glenn Valley, just east of Fort Langley, on the Fraser River. There, she avoided other people and turned into a virtual recluse. She was taken to the Langley Lodge when she could no longer take care of herself. The old farm house remained vacant. The acreage was uncared for and lay dormant.

I did a search on the title to Miss Milligan's farm in the Land Titles Office in New Westminster. Sure enough, there was an option to purchase recently registered against her land for a fraction of its value. Jim (another associate lawyer in the firm) and I brought a legal action in Supreme Court to set aside the transaction as an unconscionable bargain.

Again, the leading case came from England. One of the most famous judges of all time in the common-law world had brought some threads of the law together to establish the law of Unconscionable Bargain in Lloyds Bank Ltd. v Bundy, a decision of Lord Denning in 1974. He wrote: "Old Herbert Bundy was a farmer. His home was a yew tree farm. It went back three hundred years. His family had been there for generations. It was his only asset. But he did a very foolish thing. He mortgaged it to the bank; up to the very hilt."

His son, Michael, owned a business that was in financial trouble. Mr. Bundy had guaranteed the loans to the business with the mortgage to Lloyds Bank. The bank knew about the financial difficulties, but did not tell Mr. Bundy. Lloyds foreclosed on the house when the money was not paid. Mr. Bundy had a heart attack in the witness box at trial.

The issue to be determined was whether the contract leading to the repossession of the house was voidable. Lord Denning held that the contract was voidable owing to the unequal bargaining position in which Mr. Bundy had found himself vis a vis the bank. He held that undue influence was a category of a wider class where the balance of power between the parties was such as to merit the interference of the court. Mr. Bundy had, without independent advice, entered the contract, but it was very unfair.

My case involved Little Miss Milligan, an elderly recluse in bad health in the Langley Lodge, vis a vis Joe the lawyer and his business friend from Edmonton. Clearly, this was a prime example of unequal bargaining between the parties. The second step was to determine if the bargain was unfair. Undoubtedly it was, since the option to purchase was for less than fair market value.

Lord Denning's case was followed in the courts of British Columbia, which clarified the law for the case of Miss Milligan.

The trial lasted about a week. Its climax was when Miss Milligan testified that she signed the document because the duplicitous lawyer told her to "just sign it." Intimidated, she thought she had no choice but to sign it. This lawyer had done her will, which is how he had learned about the farm. When the judge heard that evidence, he ordered the transcript be sent to the Law Society, which eventually resulted in the lawyer being disbarred – his true wolfish nature laid bare for all to see.

Of course, we won, which resulted in Little Miss Milligan obtaining title to her farm again. Although aging had affected her cognitive ability, Miss Milligan still understood what had happened. At ninety-two years old, her movements and reflexes had slowed, her hearing and vision had weakened, but her understanding of right and wrong had not changed.

Miss Milligan recognized that the two men she sued were consumed by the insatiable hunger of greed. They preyed upon her vulnerability, pretending to have her best interests at heart while concealing their savage urge to devour. After this unfortunate series of events, her great desire was to benefit people worthy of her help, so she left her dairy farm to the Children's Hospital upon her death two years later. Although she never had any children of her own, she felt great joy knowing the good she could do for children in need.

Rescuer Law

The third case in the trilogy began with a tragedy. There are many dairy farms in Glenn Valley located immediately east of Fort Langley, along the Fraser River. A terrible calamity occurred at one of them when three men entered through the top of a one-hundred-foot-high silo and later were all found dead. It was the greatest tragedy to ever occur in Glenn Valley and the Fort Langley area, so the circumstances of these deaths garnered a lot of attention among the local people, and the catastrophe was front page news throughout British Columbia.

Under normal circumstances, dairy farming has a peaceful, regular rhythm. Using modern milking systems, it takes about five to ten minutes to milk a cow. Cows are typically milked twice a day—once in the early morning and again about twelve hours later. Dairy farmers rise early to prepare the cows for milking, as each cow is individually cleaned and inspected. Cows are natural grazers, preferring to eat five to nine meals a day, so dairy farmers must provide access to fresh food and water throughout the day. As ruminants, cows spend a lot of time chewing and digesting their food—four to seven hours a day.

Cow feed usually consists of a mixture of the farm's own grass and crops such as corn, oats, or barley. Thus dairy farmers spend a great deal of time in the spring, summer, and fall growing and harvesting these crops and then storing them in silos so they can be fed to the dairy herd during the winter rains.

News of the death of the three men spread like wild fire throughout the farming community, upsetting the natural tranquillity of the countryside. The experts determined the cause of death. The silo was filled with corn stalks to feed the dairy cows in winter. As they decomposed, a gas heavier than oxygen was released, which displaced the oxygen. If anyone entered the silo, they would die in minutes, because there was no oxygen to breathe.

The experts formed the opinion that the father went into the silo first for some unknown reason. He knew that a silo must be vented before entering, so they concluded that he fell in by accident, as he had not vented the silo. Next, his adult son came along, perhaps looking for his father. He found his father in the silo and jumped into the silo to save his father without thinking about whether the silo had been vented. The father was already dead, and now the son was too. The father and the son were the owners of the dairy farm.

Finally, the son's friend, who was visiting the farm, found the two of them and jumped in to rescue them, but was overcome within seconds and died within minutes. It was not expected that the visitor knew the standard procedure of venting a silo before entering.

The friend was not married and had no children. He used a portion of his money every month to support his mother in Germany. When the mother came to Fort Langley to learn what had happened to her son, we brought an action on her behalf under the Family Compensation Act, which provides for recovery of financial loss on the death of a spouse or child.

Legal cases in British Columbia supported the policy decision of the Provincial Legislature in Victoria to protect rescuers where possible. The friend, who entered the silo last, was seen as a rescuer. He did not know about the need to vent the silo. The father and son, however, knew this was the normal practice among dairy farmers in Glenn Valley. I travelled through the valley and interviewed many dairy farmers who told me this was the case. I called a few of them to give this evidence at the trial. The owners of the farm carried insurance. If we won, the insurance company, not the father and son, would pay the German mother.

It was another victory, this time for the bereaved mother. The recovery was the amount of money the mother in Germany would have received over her lifetime if her son was not killed in this tragic accident. The reason we won was simple. The farmer's son knew that if he put himself in a dangerous position where he would require a rescuer, then he could reasonably foresee that a rescuer might suffer harm. The father and the son were negligent in not venting the silo. The danger was foreseeable by the owners of the farm, who carried the insurance.

This trilogy of cases, along with some others, was won in my first year of practicing law. In Vancouver, these were the kind of cases that only lawyers with over twenty years of experience would handle because of the complicated nature of the facts and the truth. I suppose all those years of absorbing stories that I cherished left me with quite a knack for collecting and interpreting the stories of others while weaving my own. Don Nundal, John Cherrington, and R. Henry (Hank) Easingwood were impressed. I was immediately offered a partnership. I accepted. The law firm in the small village of Fort Langley became Nundal, Cherrington, Easingwood & Kearl.

At this time, we bought out a law practice in Langley, Scarlett & Baker, because the two lawyers had been appointed judges of the Provincial Court. Hank worked at our office in Langley City, but with this purchase, Don went to our Langley city office as well. The senior partner's office now became my office. At the time I interviewed with Don for an articling position, I never could have imagined in my wildest dreams that I would become a partner and that the office where I was interviewed would become my office—all within a year of being called to the bar to practice law in British Columbia.

Some years later, Don retired, and the firm became Cherrington, Easingwood & Kearl. I remained in that same office in Fort Langley for thirty years. At the height of our expansion, we had a third office in Aldergrove with twelve lawyers working for us in the three offices. At that time, we were the largest law firm in Langley and maybe in the whole valley. The last few years we downsized to Fort Langley with the three partners and two associates: Tim Grier from Saskatchewan and Erin Easingwood, Hank's daughter.

Some years later, Hank passed away from colon cancer, and John wanted to retire, so John and I merged our law firm with a larger firm with offices in Langley and Vancouver. I finished my last ten years practicing law at LK Law in the Langley office located on the fourth floor of 8621-201 Street.

My office had a magnificent view of the mountains to the north and, in particular, the highest peaks in the area, with an elevation of 1,716 metres, called "Golden Ears." The summit of these twin peaks is a spectacular hike—for both its beauty and its challenge—that always makes for a memorable day. I amused many of my clients with stories of the unbeatable views in all directions from the summit, as well as the difficulty in completing the twenty-five-kilometre round trip as a punishing day hike, which I did the numerous times I climbed to the top.

After practicing law for forty years, another year articling, and three years at law school, amounting to forty-four years at the law, I retired on December 31, 2020.

ROBERT B. KEARL

Bachelor of Arts, May 1977

Bachelor of Laws, May 1980

CHAPTER TWO

The Country versus the City

As I mentioned before, one of the reasons I decided to article and later join the partnership at the small country law office in Fort Langley was Don Nundal, the senior partner. He was quite the character. Energy just seemed to burst out of him. This kind of enthusiasm was magnetic and drew people to him. He could leave the office, walk down Glover Road, the main street in Fort Langley, to a coffee shop, like Wendell's Bookstore and Cafe, and then return a half hour later with three more legal cases from folks he befriended along the way. Everyone seemed to know him or know of him, which was one of the delightful qualities of working out of a small township.

Don was an ex-RCMP officer. He quit the RCMP and went into the law because he was tired of fighting drunks in small towns in

Northern Saskatchewan. He spoke the language of the farmers and fishermen, the rural people. His father, Elford Nundal, was a farm veterinarian, so he knew everyone who owned a horse or had a dairy herd. There were an abundance of horse and dairy farms in Langley, which meant Elford was known by almost everyone. The Township of Langley was mostly a rural community at that time. His dad worked with these families, understood them, and was elected by them to be the Mayor of the Township of Langley, making Nundal a household name.

Don loved to hunt and fish. He would take a few weeks off in the summer to head up to the Cariboo, an area in the interior of British Columbia, to hunt. He would fish for the big ones in the Pacific Ocean. He was well known for his guns, his dogs, and his fishing boat. I was just a city boy from Calgary, so I had never even fired a gun in my life. I did work on my Uncle Russ' ranch in Southern Alberta for the summer when I was thirteen and fourteen, so I knew a little about country life. Uncle Russ had horses, sheep, cattle, hogs, chickens, and dairy cows. We had to bail a lot of hay in the summer to feed all of his animals in the winter, so I learned how to work hard on the ranch. Sometimes I would tag along with Don on some of his fishing trips, but I never did see the appeal of hunting.

The kind of fishing I had experienced growing up was high in the Rocky Mountains just south of Waterton Lakes National Park on the border with Montana. Dad would lead me and my two brothers, Eldon and Brent, up Lee's Creek for miles, always in the shadow of Old Chief Mountain. We would then fly fish all day, moving our way down the stream to our camp to join Mom and our two sisters, Kathy and Jean. We caught many fish like rainbow and speckled trout, but they were all minnows compared to the giant salmon, halibut, and lingcod Don caught.

But Langley was changing. City folks were flocking to the country, drawn by the clean air and wide, open spaces. They didn't mind all the lovely strawberry, raspberry, blueberry, and cranberry fields in Langley, but what they didn't like were the smells, the dirt, and the noise of animal farms with cattle, dairy cows, chickens, and hogs.

John Deacon owned a feedlot on an acreage in Langley. He had operated that feedlot legally for many years. It was the sole support for his family. He was proud of his labours. It was good, hard, and honest work. Each year he brought feeder calves down from the small hamlet of Barriere, located just north of Kamloops, at the confluence of the Barriere and North Thompson Rivers.

Halloween night, 1978, changed everything for John. The cattle truck arrived from the long haul down the Fraser Canyon, exiting from the Highway at Langley. The seventy-seven feeder calves were bawling, anxious to get off the truck. It was around 10:30 at night when they arrived at John's feedlot. The truck driver, David Morgan, was tired. John and David were anxious to unload the calves. However, they were surprised by a group of men and women obstructing John's driveway. John Deacon confronted the crowd. He knew these people. They were his neighbours. They objected to the smells and noises of his feedlot. These were the city folks who were the new arrivals to Langley. Most of them worked in Vancouver, but lived on small hobby farms in Langley. It was the classic conflict between country and city.

John Deacon and the neighbours shouted and argued, but the neighbours would not move. It was impossible to unload the truck. Someone called the police. The RCMP arrived. The Langley bylaw enforcement officer also arrived. The police officer listened to the complaints of both sides. He did not know what to do. The bylaw officer surrendered to the mob, ruling that a noise bylaw had been violated and turned the truck away. The vigilante neighbours shouted out with glee; they had won, they had shut down the smelly feedlot. They raised their voices and fists in triumph.

John Deacon was angry. He was a farmer just doing what he had always done. It was how he put food on the table for his family. There was no question about the zoning; it was a legal farm operation. A tired David Morgan was forced to head down the highway to find some place to stay for the night. The calves would be forced to stay on the truck.

The next morning, David returned with the calves. They were unloaded into John Deacon's feedlot, mixing with his cattle that were already there. During the next few days, John noticed that the calves were not looking healthy. In fact, the whole herd looked sick. He called in a veterinarian who made the diagnosis that they were suffering from pasteurella pneumonia, commonly called shipping fever. Many died; the others were stunted in their growth. However, this was not all, for the feeder calves had infected the rest of the herd. All the cattle that survived had to be sold at a large discount. It was a huge loss for John, one that he could little afford. John consulted with Don Nundal. An action was commenced by John Deacon against the obstructionist neighbours in the Supreme Court. This would be my first Supreme Court trial. Only cases with a monetary value of twenty-five thousand dollars or less commence in Provincial Court which is sometimes called Small Claims Court. All major cases are commenced in the Supreme Court of British Columbia. I was an articling student and I was excited to be a junior supporting Don and helping him prepare for the trial.

Don's expert was a veterinarian who was also a professor at the Western College of Veterinary Medicine at the University of Saskatchewan in Saskatoon. The expert was of the opinion that the extra stress of the stay overnight in the truck caused the shipping fever. Don was ready for trial. Don gave an excellent opening statement, after which, the judge requested that the lawyers meet with him in his private chambers. The judge said that Don "was an impetuous young man with a monkey for a client." This shocked me because Don was an experienced lawyer and the judge had not even met our client yet. He told the lawyers to go settle the case.

Of course, with the judge saying what he did, it was impossible to settle. We proceeded with the trial the next day. Throughout the trial, the judge interfered with everything Don did. It was terrible. I asked Don how he could put up with such disrespect, but he replied that it was all good for the appeal. Don just plowed ahead, putting in all the evidence he would need in the Court of Appeal. In all my forty years of practice, I never experienced a more hostile judge. Later, I learned that this judge died a short time after this trial of a brain tumour, which could explain his outrageous conduct. In my career, I found Supreme Court judges to be intelligent, patient, and for the most part, respectful.

We lost at trial. I wrote the factum for the Court of Appeal, which set out the facts, the law, and the argument. The trial judge was wrong in finding that the bylaw enforcement officer was the cause of the damages. The loss would not have occurred but for the actions of the neighbours. Furthermore, the bylaw enforcement officer had no right to stop the truck from offloading the calves because the noise this caused was the result of the operation of a farm in an area zoned for agriculture. Don argued the appeal. The Court of Appeal agreed with our submissions. The appeal was allowed. John Deacon was awarded damages against his neighbours. They paid for all losses including interest and legal costs. The neighbours never bothered John Deacon again. Justice was finally done.

Don lived with his wife, Elly, in a unique octagonal home constructed on a small acreage in a rural part of Langley called "Strawberry Hills." Due to a medical condition, Elly could not have children. Elly was like the grand lady of the Fort Law Office. She would come down to visit quite often. All the staff loved her. She was naturally very slender, but tragedy struck in the form of cirrhosis of the liver, which was triggered by a bug she picked up travelling in Costa Rica. She became a wisp of a woman, with yellow discolouration of the skin and jaundiced eyes. Death should have come to an old lady in her sleep, but it came early with great pain for Elly.

The death of Elly was devastating for Don. For a long time, Don ceased to regale us with his funny fishing and hunting stories. He was unusually quiet and sad. They say that time heals all wounds, and I suppose this is true. We hired a new lawyer, Marion, who was single with one child. To my surprise, I learned that Don was dating Marion, a devout Catholic. Even more surprising, Don started to go to church on Sunday instead of fishing and hunting. Don and Marion were married in a nuptial mass in the Roman Catholic Church, in Latin, with Gregorian chants and incense. It was great, although I thought I was revisiting the medieval period.

Marion and Don had two children to add to the one Marion brought into the marriage. I had always thought Don would be a great dad, and he was. Don was a damn good lawyer. He lived a long and fulfilling life. I can still hear him reciting, from the other side, two famous sayings among lawyers that were displayed on his desk: "Sue the Bastards" and "When in Doubt, Sue Everyone."

CHAPTER THREE:

An Ironic Twist

The general practice of law is like juggling. There is the constant pressure of keeping all of the balls up in the air. At all times, I had 125 to 150 cases on the go. Each case had stages when work had to be done, then periods when it was necessary to wait. Each required step was recorded in a diary system. I was fortunate enough to have an amazing legal assistant, Sharon Montgomery, who made sure I was in the right place at the appointed time, except for the instance when she mistakenly sent me to Northern BC for a discovery. A discovery is a pre-trial procedure where parties of the case gather to examine the other side under oath in front of a court reporter who records all the evidence. The evidence and witness admissions can then be used by either side at trial. Discoveries are a bit chilly at the best of times, but this one would take place in the middle of a freezing winter…or so I thought.

There I was, at the greatest greasy spoon in Quesnel in the Billy Barker Hotel, with my client, having bacon and eggs, when a rather harried sounding Sharon called to say the other lawyer and his client were in Kelowna. In some comical oversight, Sharon sent us almost six-hundred kilometres away from the actual location the discovery was meant to take place! I always tease her about that one. Apparently, the staff had to calm her down at the time by adding Irish whiskey to her coffee, she was so upset. Despite her one mistake, everyone in the office still thought of her as Mary Poppins—"practically perfect in every way."

Sharon's family originated from Bangor, Northern Ireland but moved to a small acreage in Langley before she was born. She looked Irish at five-foot-three-inches tall, 120 pounds, with brown eyes and shoulder-length dark hair. Sharon had an amazing capacity to remain cool, calm, and collected when bedlam ruled all around her. In a busy law office, her characteristic composure was essential and allowed me to do my job to the best of my abilities.

Sharon had an amazing memory. She always remembered everyone's name, and it was a big joke around the office that I was always asking her, "What is that guy's name?"

Sharon functioned with professional precision, like a human filing cabinet with every legal document carefully organized into its proper place. We worked together for almost forty years during which time I admired her loyalty, capabilities and honesty so much so that she became like another sister to me.

The majority of my practice was composed of civil litigation, disputes arising out of corporate law, commercial transactions, real estate contracts, construction disagreements, personal injury claims, administrative law, and insurance claims. It was a general practice, so I did almost everything except family law and immigration. The balance of my practice consisted of criminal defence work. The criminal case I will now recount involves such an unusual ironic twist that I would not have believed it, if it did not happen to me.

Friends and family often tease me about my penchant for exaggerating stories, but this story does not need the tricks of the storyteller's trade—it stands on its own as a prime example of how reality can be stranger than fiction.

Ed was a large, bombastic man, about six-foot-two-inches tall and weighing around three hundred pounds. At forty-three years of age, he had not done much of anything in his life. He lived alone in a trailer on the wrong side of town and was the type of person that people would call "white trailer trash." He did have an on-again, off-again kind of lady friend named Marie, who lived on the top floor of a three-storey apartment about five kilometres away. Ed came to see me, because he was charged with "pointing a firearm."

The police particulars disclosed that Ed had a fight with Marie at the pub, so Marie fled home to her apartment with Ed following her in his car. Fortunately, he couldn't get into the locked building because Marie would not let him in. He shouted up to her apartment, which created quite a commotion and caused a small crowd to gather on the street below.

Marie came out onto her third-floor balcony and shouted back, turning their private fight into a very public, raucous shouting match. Ed was mad. He retrieved his rifle out of the trunk of his car, waving it around like a madman. Someone in the crowd called the police, who arrived within minutes and arrested Ed without any resistance. The police seized his loaded rifle.

I researched the law and found a case in the Supreme Court where the judge wrote that to convict on the charge of pointing a firearm, there must be evidence of actually pointing the weapon at someone. The trial proceeded in Provincial Court, which is a lower court. There were plenty of witnesses to the event, but not one of them could testify that Ed pointed the rifle at Marie or directly at anyone else.

At the end of the Crown's case, I moved to have the charge dismissed, citing the legal case I found in my research. The judge was bound by the doctrine of *stare decisis*, a Latin term meaning "to stand by that which is decided." Another term for *stare decisis* is precedent. The case I cited was a precedent for judges deciding similar issues later. The decision was from a higher court, so it was binding on the lower court judge. If it was from the same court level, it would merely have been persuasive.

The judge did not want to dismiss the charge, but he had to follow the law. It was obvious to me from the beginning that the Crown made a big mistake in laying the wrong charge. There was plenty of evidence to convict Ed of dangerous use of a firearm, which would have resulted in the rifle being permanently confiscated, as well as an order that Ed would not be permitted to own, have in his possession, or purchase any firearm at that time or in the future.

If there is one thing that you must remember in understanding the ironic twist in the second half of the story, it is this: because the charge was dismissed, Ed got his rifle back.

Many months later, a young man came into the office first thing in the morning. He did not have an appointment, but he told the receptionist that it was a life or death situation. He insisted he had to see me right away, and as she could see how frightened he was, she convinced me to see him. I learned his name was Tom.

Tom started out by saying he had witnessed a murder just the day before. His whole body was shaking. I told him to start from the beginning and to just tell me what happened. Tom said he had been at his friend Larry's place the previous morning, at which time Larry told him he was upset with his mom's boyfriend, because sometimes he would beat her. Larry told Tom he wanted to visit this man to tell him to stop. He didn't want to go alone, so he asked Tom to go with him, and Tom agreed. Larry and Tom drove to where the boyfriend lived. Larry knocked on the door and the boyfriend answered. Larry explained that he wanted to talk to him, at which point they were invited into the trailer and sat down at the kitchen table. Larry and Tom were on one side, the boyfriend on the other.

Larry began to tell the man how upset he was that he was beating his mother. He told him he had to stop. This was his mother. No one was allowed to hit his mother. Suddenly, Larry got up and walked down the hall behind where the boyfriend was sitting, while the boyfriend talked with Tom. There was a rifle standing in the hallway. Larry picked it up. He walked back with the rifle. He stood behind the boyfriend's back, pointed the rifle at the back of his head, and from about thirty centimetres away pulled the trigger. The man's brains splattered all over the kitchen table.

Tom said he was in shock. He was terrified. He had no idea such a thing was going to happen. He was now afraid for his own life, as he thought that Larry would shoot him next. Larry told Tom they had to hide the rifle, so they found a good hiding spot in the woods and then split up. Tom didn't know where Larry went, but Tom went to a friend's house just across the Fraser River for the night. It was a terrible night. Tom came to see me to find out what he should do.

It was clear that Tom was not part of a plan to kill the man. It also seemed obvious that he only aided in hiding the rifle to protect his own life. I told him he should turn himself in to the police, and I didn't think he would be charged with anything, but there was a slight risk. However, it was certain he would be the main witness for the prosecution. Tom agreed to follow my advice, so I called Crown counsel to explain the situation. This resulted in the police being sent to obtain a statement from him in our library.

In my discussions with the police, I finally learned the identity of the dead boyfriend. Tom had never seen him before that fateful day. He didn't know his name. No doubt, you have guessed it by now. It was Ed. The fact that the dead man was Ed was quite the coincidence, but this was not the ironic twist. The ironic twist was that Ed was killed with the same rifle he was waving around when he was charged with pointing a firearm. It was only because the charge was dismissed that the rifle was returned to him. It was then used to kill him.

Tom was never charged with an offence. He did give evidence at a trial a couple of years later, where Larry was convicted of manslaughter. I am not sure, but I think he was sentenced to six years in jail, but got out in four for good behaviour.

Perhaps the sentence was light because of Larry's legitimate concern for his mother, and no doubt there were other factors presented before the trial judge that I am not aware of and that mitigated the sentence. Reports in the news are often distorted as important facts are often overlooked, sometimes causing unjust criticism of judges for handing out what appear to be lenient sentences.

Some people ask me how I feel about defending the "Eds" of the world, but I explain that it is up to the Crown to prove beyond a reasonable doubt each element of the charge against an accused. It is fundamental to our system of justice that an accused is innocent until proven guilty. I feel good about upholding our system of justice. Although I play a small part, it is an important part—especially to the person accused of an offence, as you will learn in my next story, "The Case of the Missing Moustache."

Sharon Montgomery in my office (circa. 2000)

Sharon Montgomery at her desk (circa. 2000)

CHAPTER FOUR

The Case of the Missing Moustache

Sometimes one detail can make or break a case. While they say, "the devil is in the details," sometimes you can use the details to catch a devil. This was certainly true in a crime that involved a waitress named Julia.

Julia worked at the 50s Diner on Main Street in the Village in Fort Langley, which had a statue of Elvis Presley out front. It depicted the "King of Rock and Roll" with a microphone in his hand, swivelling his hips like he was doing the twist to the song, "Jailhouse Rock." The restaurant was on the corner of First Street and had windows down the side that looked out to a park with a large green space, picnic tables, and a playground that was always filled with young mothers watching their little children.

There were about twelve booths by the windows, each seating at least four adults. At the counter there was a row of softly padded stools, turquoise in colour to match the décor. On the wall, above the second booth was a framed poster of James Dean in *Rebel*

Without a Cause, a cultural icon of teenage disillusionment and social estrangement. Above the next booth, was the even more celebrated image of Marilyn Monroe in a white dress, standing above a subway grate with the air blowing her dress suggestively above her knees.

In the middle of the row of booths sat the most revered mechanism of the 50s—the jukebox. For only a quarter, the baby boomers in the diner could listen to their much-loved songs, reliving their favourite memories to the sounds of "I Only Have Eyes For You" by the Flamingos, or Bill Haley & His Comets' "Rock Around The Clock," or "Don't Be Cruel," by Elvis Presley. The boomer music even spilled into the early 60s with the greatest rock band of all time, The Beatles. They talked about where they were when The Beatles were a sensation on *The Ed Sullivan Show* in 1964, singing "All My Loving" and "She Loves You."

Julia was voted runner up to the "Spirit Queen" when she graduated from the local high school. She thought about being a runner-up quite often. She felt it was a great moment in her life. She frequently wondered what it would have been like if she had won. As soon as she graduated, she applied for a job at the diner. The owner quickly hired her. He could imagine how attractive she would look in a poodle skirt with bobby socks, saddle shoes, and an eye-catching blouse. Julia really fit in with the baby boomer crowd. Her pay was not that far above minimum wage, but the tips were very generous. The baby boomers were certainly bighearted.

Julia had plans to advance her education. She anticipated going to a local college to become a dental assistant, or a paralegal in a law firm, but time passed by without her ever taking any steps to make her plans a reality. Before she knew it, she had been working at the diner for seven years. For her twenty-fifth birthday, she met with her old girl friends from high school. It was fun talking about their high-school days, but sometimes when the girls were gone, she felt down and wondered if being the runner-up for the

Spirit Queen would be the highlight of her life. It wasn't that she didn't attract attention from the boys—she did, with her long, dark brown hair. They often told her she was pretty, but the boys all seemed so shallow. She was not interested.

When her shift was over at the diner, Julia walked down Main Street past the shop displays and then jaywalked across the street to enter a small alley lined with a row of maple trees on one side. At the end of the alleyway, she turned right onto the street where she lived, in unit #5 of a succession of tiny, timeworn row houses. It was not pretty, but the rent was cheap.

There was a pub a couple of blocks down Main Street from the diner. The owner of the pub told Julia she could work there as a barmaid anytime she wanted. When she worked at the pub, she had a completely different wardrobe. She wore a tight, short skirt that barely covered her bottom and a low-cut blouse that barely covered her top. She knew by experience that this style of dress was indispensable to obtaining the most generous tips.

One night when Julia was working at the pub, there was a table of young rowdies that were ruder and cruder than she had ever experienced before. A middle-aged man, a customer at the bar, soothed her with comforting words, telling her that everything would be alright. The tone of his voice was so distinctive and reassuring that it calmed her. She never forgot him, or his voice, so warm and rich. His voice was quiet and gentle in contrast to the raucous noise from the loud voices at the table nearby.

Julia was pleased to take his order of a well-known local cider brewed from fresh, local ingredients grown on Langley's abundant farms and orchards. When she returned with his order, she was greeted with his pleasant and polite voice.

Many months later, after finishing a shift at the pub, she walked home. The row housing where she lived consisted of ground-level, 650-square-foot units, complete with a kitchen, living room, bathroom, and one bedroom. The bedroom window faced onto the street. It was a scorching day in the middle of August, so the window was open to let in whatever cooling breeze there was. Thick clouds had rolled in that night, blocking all light from the stars and the moon. The only light was from a street lamp half-way down the block.

Julia was exhausted, so she quickly took off her clothes to go to bed. It was two o'clock in the morning when she lay nude under a single bed sheet, which was her custom during the summer months. It didn't take long for her to fall asleep.

Suddenly, she was awoken by a man on top of her, holding her body forcefully. A hand in a tightly fitted leather glove covered her mouth. She could not move. She could not scream. At five-foot-two-inches tall, 120 pounds, she had no chance to overpower her attacker. He whispered into her ear soothing and comforting words. "You will be okay. Everything will be alright. I will not hurt you." The voice was quiet and gentle, warm and reassuring. Then he raped her.

When he was finished, he jumped out the bedroom window and disappeared into the night. Julia was traumatized. She was so shocked that she ran into the street naked, calling for help. Her neighbours immediately came to her aid. One called 9-1-1. The female neighbours helped her go back into her flat to get dressed and tried to comfort her. The police arrived in minutes.

The police dog squad was called in, but the German shepherds found no trace of the attacker. The police helicopter was unable to search the area due to dense, low-lying cloud cover. A caring female police officer spoke with Julia, attempting to provide comfort and a feeling of security, while she elicited from her the particulars of what happened. After she made careful notes of every detail, the officer drove Julia to the hospital for treatment, where an experienced female doctor conducted a full physical examination and gathered evidence of the sexual assault. She carefully noted that there was no outward evidence of a physical struggle—no bruising, cuts, wounds, scratches, marks, or abrasions of any kind. The only physical verification of rape was a large amount of semen, which was discovered during the course of the internal examination. Everything was recorded in a report to be sent to Crown counsel, a female lawyer who specialized in sexual assault cases. This crime occurred long before DNA testing, which would have determined, without any doubt, the perpetrator of the crime.

With true compassion, the female officer wondered where Julia wanted to stay for the night, since she probably feared returning to her flat. Julia explained that she didn't have any family in the area, so she asked if she could be taken to the home of her best friend from high school. Subsequently, the officer drove her there with the arrangement that she would pick Julia up the next day around noon. She reassured Julia that she was not alone and told her she would arrange for her to see a counsellor.

The feeling of being alone had hounded Julia from the time she was twelve years old when her father passed away unexpectedly from a heart attack. As she was an only child, it was natural for her mother to smother her with attention, always anxious that her only child would come to some premature end. For some strange reason, this kind of devotion only caused her to feel more isolated. This explained why Julia got a job and moved out of her childhood home as soon as she graduated from high school, and why she told the officer that she did not have any family in the area, when her mother did live nearby. It would not be possible, she thought, to endure the pressure and high anxiety caused by her mother's intense fretfulness, when all that Julia needed was rest and sympathy.

The officer returned, as she promised, taking Julia to the police station to look at books of photos, mugshots of convicted criminals, to see if she recognized her assailant. She spent several exhausting hours studying the ugly faces of men she had never seen before. Abruptly, she began to tremble all over. Jumping up from her chair, she cried out, "This is the man! This is the man!" The shaking increased. She was sweating profusely as she continued to cry out, even louder, "This is the man!" She created such a commotion that several police officers rushed into the room to see what the uproar was all about.

The person identified in the photo was William Harris, who found himself in the book of mug shots because of a conviction for impaired driving. He was an ordinary-looking, forty-six-year-old man, who was five-foot-ten-inches tall, 180 pounds, and had short brown hair. He lived a twenty-minute drive from the scene of the crime. The police obtained a warrant for his arrest, as well as a search warrant for his house and car. They were eager to arrest this man and carry out the search, as they had been hunting for months for a notorious criminal dubbed, the "Gentleman Rapist," who was terrorizing the valley. This criminal had escaped capture following fourteen assaults over a period of more than a year.

The modus operandi was well established; the Gentleman Rapist would enter through an open bedroom window, leaving no fingerprints because he always wore tight-fitting leather gloves. The victim was always a young woman who lived alone, which meant he must have followed each victim home in advance, carefully planning the crime. He always broke in around two o'clock in the morning when the young woman was asleep. He would overpower his victim, and then whisper into her ear with a soothing, comforting voice: "You will be okay. Everything will be alright. I will not hurt you." It was a contradiction of terms, but it was his soft words and gentle way, as narrated by each of his victims, that led to his infamous title devised by newspaper and television reporters.

I am sure every woman and all good men are offended by the title "Gentleman Rapist," created by the press, as rape is a brutal, dehumanizing and violent crime. There is nothing gentle about rape, and it is absolutely contrary to the ethics and morals of all true gentlemen. As such, the moniker is disgusting.

The police were certain this was the breakthrough they were looking for, as it seemed they had finally caught the serial rapist who had eluded them for so long. Six police cars pulled into William's driveway with sirens blaring. William was arrested in full daylight, on a Saturday, in front of all his neighbours, while the police searched his house. After telling William the reason for his arrest, the officer told him that he was allowed to speak privately to a lawyer of his choice, as soon as possible, if he asked to do so.

The officers placed him in the back of the police cruiser with his hands cuffed behind his back. William complained that the cuffs were too tight. It hurt, but the police ignored him. He repeated again and again that he didn't understand any of this, because he didn't rape anyone. Confused and in a state of sheer terror, William said the right thing: "I want to talk to a lawyer." Now, the police could no longer talk to him or manipulate him to extract a statement that they could use against him later.

William was taken to the police station, where mugshots and fingerprints were taken. He was still in a state of shock and panic when I received his telephone call at the office. I asked if he was in a private room where we could talk. He said he was, and then he tried to explain what had happened to him. I couldn't make much sense out of what he was saying, other than, "I didn't do it! I didn't do it!"

We knew each other, as I had spoken on his behalf at the sentencing hearing when he entered a guilty plea to the charge of impaired driving. Little did we know at that time what trouble he would get into because of the mug shot taken when he was arrested. It was the only blemish on his record. I thought it was doubtful that he would have committed such a serious crime, since I remembered what I learned about his character when I spoke in court on his behalf. After graduating from high school, he attended BCIT in Burnaby, where he completed a four-year course in business. Graduates from BCIT are highly regarded, which led to a job in the insurance industry. While working at an insurance agency, he met the woman who became his wife. He was a member of the Rotary Club, where they helped many families in need. In addition, I remembered that he coached boys soccer and baseball for many years, all of which gave him a stellar reputation for community service.

As I thought about all the things I knew about William, it confirmed my belief that he would not intentionally harm anyone—let alone rape a woman. However, I understood that a rapist can come from good stock or be a pillar in the community. I thought to myself, *Does anyone know what a rapist looks like, anyway?* I told him to say nothing to the police, as anything he said could be used against him. I drove to the police station where we talked, but there wasn't much more to discuss. He didn't know anything except that he was innocent, and I believed him.

William was held in jail overnight, and then brought before the court the next day, where I appeared on his behalf to obtain his release until the trial. The Crown did not have enough information at that time, so the issue of his release was adjourned for two weeks, and he remained in custody. I received the police particulars, which disclosed that nothing was found in the search of his house or his car that incriminated William, including the fact that they did not find the leather gloves. The experts dusted the scene of the crime for prints, but they were not surprised when none of them matched William, as the assailant wore gloves.

In the end, the only evidence identifying William as the dreaded criminal known as the Gentleman Rapist was the assertion of the victim. There was no physical evidence, nor was there any corroborating testimony from any other witness. William was not a flight risk, as he owned his own home, did not have a criminal record (other than the impaired driving conviction) and did not have any ties anywhere other than in British Columbia, so he was released on bail pending the trial. Important to remember is that one of the founding principles of our system of justice is that an accused is presumed innocent until proven guilty. The second is that guilt must be proven beyond a reasonable doubt. In light of these fundamental legal doctrines, the court would normally release the prisoner, unless there was strong evidence the accused was a flight risk, and the case was extremely strong against him. It was reasonable, given all the circumstances, that William be released pending the trial, so the judge ordered his release.

The next step in the legal proceeding was to make an election as well as set a date for the preliminary inquiry, which is when a Provincial Court judge reviews the evidence to decide if there is enough to have a trial. Since this was a serious offence, William could elect to have a jury trial or elect to have a trial in front of a Supreme Court judge alone. The rule of thumb, among lawyers, is that if the case for the defence is weak, choose a jury, but if it is strong, elect a judge alone. I thought we had a strong defence; accordingly we elected a judge alone.

William was clean shaven when I saw him in lock-up at the police station, as well as when I had represented him regarding the impaired driving charge. Consequently, he was clean shaven in his mug shot. I happened to ask him whether he had always been clean shaven, which is when I learned that in the past, including when the offence occurred, he had a giant handlebar moustache that was particularly lengthy, with a long downward curve that extended the full length of his chin. I told him to get me some photos of him with the handlebar moustache, especially the ones taken at, or around, the time of the rape.

Talking with William, I learned that on the night of the crime, he was playing poker with his neighbours until around 1:00 a.m. He was getting tired of losing, so he told his neighbours that he was exhausted and going home to bed. This caused the party to break up, and they all went home. The poker game was at the house immediately next to his, with an open window from the kitchen overlooking his driveway, where his car was parked. I spoke with the neighbours, a husband and wife, both of whom confirmed his story. They said they went to bed shortly after the game broke up, at around 1:15 a.m., so they thought they didn't fall asleep until around 1:30 a.m. Their bedroom window, on the second floor, was on the side of the house next to William's house, so they said they would have heard the car leave before they went to sleep, as it was a hot day in August and their window was open. They did not hear him leave with the car.

The offence occurred at around two o'clock in the morning, so it was possible for William to get to the scene of the crime—only a twenty minute drive away—but it didn't seem likely, as there was a very short window of opportunity. Unfortunately, William did not have a complete alibi, because he was separated from his wife and living alone at the time.

The day of the preliminary inquiry arrived. William was sitting beside me, clean shaven, at the counsel table. The Crown called their witnesses—the police officers, the doctor who did the examination, and the complainant, Julia, who pointed to William beside me, identifying him as her assailant. The crucial point in the preliminary inquiry finally arrived, which was during my cross examination of the complainant, when I asked, "Was your assailant clean shaven, or did he have a moustache?" The complainant answered, "He was clean shaven." I followed up with a further question. "How did you know your assailant was clean shaven?"

She replied, "I saw his face. There was enough light from the street light that I could see he was clean shaven, and his face touched my face and lips when he kissed me, and I could feel he was clean shaven."

I continued, "Are you certain he was clean shaven?"
Her answer: "Yes."

The defence never calls evidence at the preliminary inquiry, as it is an opportunity to review the Crown's case and cross-examine the Crown's witnesses, which provides essential information to the defence about how to prepare for trial. When I finished my cross examination of the complainant, the Crown closed its case, and the judge ruled there was sufficient evidence to go to trial.

The trial took place in the Supreme Court in New Westminster a number of months later. We were ready. I made an admission at the opening of the trial that the complainant had been raped, telling the court that the only issue was the identity of the assailant. I told the court my theory as to why the complainant was honest, but mistaken. I explained that after the sexual assault, as she was going through books of mug shots at the police station, she finally recognized someone. It was the customer at the bar in the pub when she was being harassed by those crude rowdies, who spoke to her with a soft, calming voice and told her that it was okay, to calm down, and that everything was going to be alright. It turns out that calm customer was, indeed, William. Once William was shown a picture of Julia in pre-trial preparations, he was amazed that he did, in fact recognize Julia, the pretty waitress from the pub (though he didn't know her or even her name at the time). He was shocked that they would ever cross paths again in such a grievous fashion. To her, the voice seemed to be the same voice, and William had said similar words to what the Gentleman Rapist had used. She had come to the mistaken conclusion they were one and the same person. Julia honestly believed she was raped by William, but it was not true.

Of course, I arranged my witnesses well in advance. I had William's boss, who owned the insurance company where William worked as the manager; then, there was his girlfriend; his ex-wife; and finally his neighbours. The Crown proceeded to call the police witnesses, the doctor, and then the complainant. My only cross examination was of Julia, when I asked the same questions that

I had posed at the preliminary inquiry about her assailant being clean shaven, and the reasons why she knew, for certain, he was clean shaven. She gave all the same answers. The Crown closed its case. Now it was my turn.

My first witness was the accused, William, who vehemently denied committing the offence. He gave lots of background about his life, his work, his divorce, his present girlfriend, and the game of cards with the neighbours on the night of the offence, among other things. He also provided a photo of him, with the big handlebar moustache, taken near the time of the offence. Of course, he testified he still had a huge handlebar moustache when the offence was committed.

My next witness was one of the neighbours, who reported about the card game and William saying that he was tired and going home to bed. Also the evidence was given about the bedroom window looking down on the driveway where William's car was parked, and that it did not move while the neighbour was still awake, which was until about 1:30 a.m.

The boss, the ex-wife, and the present girlfriend all testified that William had a huge handlebar moustache at the time the rape occurred. The credibility of these witnesses was unassailable. I closed my case.

After the closing argument by the Crown, Mr. Justice Hogarth looked down at me and said: "Mr. Kearl, I will not need to hear from you. How could she have missed the moustache? Case dismissed."

As you can imagine, my client was ecstatic, jumping for joy and hugging me. The accusation that he was a rapist had hung over him like a dark cloud for almost eighteen months. It is a grave injustice to be charged, hauled off in handcuffs in front of your neighbours, held in jail, and dragged through court, all while being innocent. Imagine the greater harm when innocent people are convicted of crimes they did not commit. I think about how William's life would have been destroyed if he was wrongly convicted. Even with the innocent verdict, there were, no doubt, many of his acquaintances who thought he only got off because of some technicality thought up by his sharp lawyer.

Nearly a year later, I read in the newspaper, the front page story of the capture of the Gentleman Rapist. It was a fluke. A police officer happened to be driving by, when he saw a man crawling out of a window at around two o'clock in the morning. The officer had stopped the man, who was wearing tight leather gloves, when he heard cries coming from inside the house. In the end, the Gentleman Rapist confessed to all his crimes, including giving details, that only the assailant could know, concerning his rape of Julia.

Finally, there was complete closure for my client, William. I never met Julia again after the trial, but I suppose she thought William did it, even after he was acquitted. She must have thought that justice was not done, and the rapist had gotten away with it. She probably obsessed over this supposed grave injustice and continued to suffer. When she learned the truth, I hope she finally found closure, as did William, when the real criminal confessed and went to jail for his crimes.

CHAPTER FIVE:

Politically Correct

Mounted in the foyer of our office in the Fort, behind the receptionist's desk, above the many old company seals, is a portrait of the Queen. It is the classic photograph of Queen Elizabeth II when she was young. Displayed on the wall beside her is a large, framed copy of the Magna Carta ("Great Charter"), guaranteeing English political liberties. The Magna Carta was drafted at Runnymede, a meadow by the River Thames, and signed by King John on June 15, 1215, under pressure from his rebellious barons.

The first office down the hall, behind the receptionist's desk, is that of my partner, John Cherrington. Our offices sat side by side, with large floor-to-ceiling windows opening toward the mountains to the north. It was only fitting that our offices were so close together, as we worked hand in glove for thirty years, without so much as a serious disagreement between us. John did the solicitor's work, commercial transactions, real estate deals, wills and estates; while I did the barrister's work, the work done in courtrooms.

I always joke that John is more British than the British. Entering his personal office, the first thing to be seen is a large, bordered portrait of Winston Churchill hanging on the wall. It is clear that Churchill is John's greatest hero, as he named his cat "Winston" and his dog "Churchill"—or is it the other way around?

Churchill did resemble a bulldog. However, John is a bulldog. Since John was an academic in school, he attracted some attention from the bullies, just like his hero Winston Churchill, who was bullied without intervention. This only made both of them stronger. Undeterred by their taunting, John thrived. Later at UBC, he graduated with history as his major, writing his first non-fiction book, *Mission on the Fraser*.

Like an Englishman, John is well educated and ambitious, as he successfully aspired to build a prosperous law firm. He is adventurous enough to walk across England and search the sand bars of the Fraser River for gemstones, which he is able to polish in his tumbler at home to display for ornamental purposes. Stereotypically, a well-read Englishman is often described as somewhat anti-social, because he prefers to read his large collection of books rather than interact with others or take interest in his surroundings. However, John is both an intellectual and a people person, whose capabilities and strength of character helped him build a large clientele.

John has short brown hair and is a strong presence beyond his size of five foot eleven inches and 175 pounds. Due to the certainty he evokes when speaking, he creates confidence in his clients. He is gentlemanly, like the British, clear in speech and logical. He has the ability to "keep calm and carry on." He looks the part of an Oxford history professor, as he always wears a shirt and tie in the office, accompanying a tweed jacket with leather patches at the elbows.

John and his lovely wife, Dorothy, had a clear division of labour that I still often joke about, but it worked very well for them. Dorothy did all the labour at home, including the outside yard work and painting, while John toiled at the relentless volume of work at the office, which was necessary to build a successful law firm, plus support their family, which included three children.

The outside work was substantial, as the Cherringtons lived in a large house on ten acres on Bradner Road in Abbotsford. The community boasted the Bradner Flower Show since 1928, displaying fields of bright yellow daffodils and red tulips in the spring. A green thumb and DIY landscaper herself, Dorothy cut the large area of grass on their property on a brilliant green John Deere riding lawn mower. Dorothy insisted that John was not allowed to mow the lawn because he was not as adept at handling "her" machine. She feared he would, no doubt, smash it into a tree or damage "her baby" by hitting some roots protruding above the ground. It was a match made in heaven, as this suited John just fine.

John and I played tennis every Friday afternoon at the tennis court located on his property. It was about a twenty-minute scenic drive from the office, east along River Road beside the Fraser River, passing the dairy farms and blueberry and cranberry fields. Then it was a climb up a very steep slope to Bradner Road, on the high ground, with a great view of Glenn Valley, extending all the way to Fort Langley. Every tennis match was a titanic struggle, as John always played with dogged determination, even though he could rarely brag about a win.

We worked so closely together that I could hear John in his office at the end of each day telephone Dorothy, who would suggest the three things she could prepare for dinner that evening—fish, salad, or chicken. I would jokingly phone my wife, Beth, to ask what my three choices for dinner were. She quickly replied, "Grilled cheese, grilled cheese, and grilled cheese with a pickle."

John was the glue that held the law firm together. He was always there to hold down the Fort. While working full time as a lawyer, he wrote three more books: *The Fraser Valley: A History, Vancouver at the Dawn,* and *Walking to Camelot.* As well as being an excellent solicitor, he is also an outstanding historian and writer. We developed a close friendship.

Around our law office, we did not stick to the politically correct view. John was an outspoken critic of socialist policies, and I agreed. I think we were true to the view of libertarians—those that strongly advocate that government should get out of the way, leaving the greatest range of freedom for the individual. Individual liberty was our battle cry.

We championed the cause of individuals in every walk of life, without regard to race, colour, ancestry, place of origin, religion, marital status, physical or mental disability, sex, sexual orientation, or age. In fact, we were proud to advocate on behalf of all of our clients, regardless of education, language, wardrobe, tattoos, piercings, hair colour, body size and shape, personality, or income. It didn't matter if they were ugly or handsome, had abilities and talents or none, or had beliefs or doubts. We even advocated for the ones that smelled of alcohol or tobacco smoke and had lots of facial hair…which leads me to my next story.

A lady, five-foot-nine-inches tall, with long, wavy, black hair and an attractive face came into the office to see John. Mary was seeking legal advice about her common-law husband's estate. The main asset of the estate was a clear title home worth roughly two million dollars, located on two acres in Victoria, on Vancouver Island. The entire estate had a value of nearly three million dollars. John advised her that it would involve litigation, and since he was a solicitor, his partner, Robert Kearl, would take up the cause. John assured her that justice would be done. He arranged an appointment for her to see me the following week.

Mary arrived on time at her scheduled appointment, entering my office with panache, wearing a brightly coloured print dress with flowers in her hair. After John's assurances, she was convinced I could almost walk on water, so I was the man for the job. She explained that her husband, Ted, made a will before they met, providing for his entire estate to be bequeathed to one of the most famous environmental foundations in the country—possibly the world—headed by a man legendary for his political correctness. The foundation assured the masses in writing: "We are nature. All people and all species. We are interconnected with nature and with each other. What we do to the planet and it's living creatures, we do to ourselves."

Mary continued to unfold the story to me. Ted was married for twenty-two years and had two daughters. His first wife died tragically from cancer about ten years ago. The two daughters were now adults, married and living in Victoria. Ted did not leave anything in his will to his two daughters. His will was prepared by a lawyer in Victoria, who also prepared a detailed and lengthy addendum to the will, outlining the reasons why he disinherited his daughters. The addendum indicated that the daughters were violent thieves who would break into his house, steal anything they wanted, and beat up their father. The two of them rode motorcycles, so I christened them "The Biker Mammas."

The Biker Mammas took outrageous advantage of their aged father, who had no means to defend himself. He did call the police on several occasions, and the particulars, as well as the police file numbers, were set out in the addendum. Since the Biker Mammas were cut out of the will, they hired a lawyer in Victoria to bring a legal action to vary the will, under the Wills Variation Act, which allows a child or a spouse (including a common-law spouse) to challenge a will in court if the will is inadequate or unfair.

Mary now related her background. She was transgender as she did not identify with the sex that she was assigned at birth. She sought medical assistance to transition from male to female; accordingly she identified as transsexual. Beginning from an early age, she suffered from gender dysphoria, the distress she felt due to a mismatch between her gender identity and her sex assigned at birth. Depression, anxiety and confusion occupied her mind as she acted out female behaviour in her childhood. She remembered that she would say, "I'm a girl, not a boy," and feel upset or angry when she was called a boy. The response she received was so negative that she suppressed her feelings.

Later, to prove to the world she was manly, she married and had children. Furthermore, she chose the most masculine occupation to hide her true feelings and joined the military and subsequently the police. In the end, after her family was raised, she admitted to her wife her true feelings. Fortunately, after the initial shock, many discussions, and a detailed study in scientific journals, his wife came to understand the truth about her husband, which led to a very amicable divorce. Mary began to weep as she described how her children came to accept her, just the way she was.

At the age of sixty-five, she began the medically assisted physical transition, during which time she met Ted, who was a seventy-five-year-old widower. They fell in love. They lived together as husband and wife for five years in a home in Victoria, owned by Ted. Sadly, Ted became seriously ill with heart disease, and Mary took care of him until he died six months later.

Mary loved their home in Victoria, and the time they had together. She also loved the time she devoted to her large flower garden, growing tulips, daffodils, red roses, purple hydrangeas, deep blue lobelia, pink begonias, and vivid reddish-purple fuchsias and daylilies, ranging in color from yellow to orange, with diverse shades of scarlet, tomato-red, maroon, and pale pink. I gave her the moniker, "The Flower Girl." It seemed clear to me that her heart beat to a different drum; nevertheless, it was warm and loving just the same.

I commenced a legal action to vary the will, acting on behalf of Mary, the common-law spouse. The claim by the Biker Mammas was joined together with my action. It was now a dispute between the environmental foundation, the Biker Mammas, and the transsexual common-law spouse over who would inherit Ted's estate, or how his estate would be divided among them.

I met with the lawyers acting for the foundation in Vancouver, on a warm Friday afternoon, on the twenty-second floor of a large office tower overlooking English Bay. The view was breathtaking. I elucidated my position that it would not be wise for the foundation, which relied on numerous donors concerned with environmental issues, to oppose the claim of a transsexual common-law spouse. It would not be politically correct. I continued that should this lawsuit proceed to trial, it would garner an enormous amount of publicity across Canada, the United States, and perhaps the world, since the fact pattern was so fascinating and exceptional, and thereby might adversely affect charitable donations to the foundation. Moreover, I didn't think the celebrated head of the foundation, renowned for his political correctness, would wish to oppose my client, the transsexual common-law spouse. We adjourned the meeting to allow these lawyers to get instructions from their client.

Two weeks later, I received a telephone call from the lawyers, explaining that the foundation would give up any claim to the estate to my client, but not to the two daughters. We decided it would be an undisclosed agreement, leaving me to deal with the Biker Mammas. I took out an appointment to examine the Biker Mammas under oath at a court reporter's office located in downtown Victoria. The day for the examination for discovery finally arrived. I certainly had plenty of ammunition, as provided in the addendum to the will. Mary told me that she didn't want me to leave her alone with the Biker Mammas, as she was afraid of them. However, I privately thought that she could have taken them down if she had wanted to, considering her military and police training, and the fact that she was significantly larger than I was.

It was a lovely day in September, so I decided to fly from the harbour in downtown Vancouver to the inner harbour in downtown Victoria by seaplane. The flight was only thirty minutes, saving me time while I could be enjoying a breathtaking aerial view of the twisting coastline. I particularly appreciated flying over the delta that is about fifty kilometres wide, where the Fraser River empties into the Strait of Georgia near Vancouver. There, the muddy fresh water mixes with ocean water to form a thin plume of buoyant brackish water, which looks like chocolate milk from the air.

Landing in the harbour in Victoria was very convenient, as it was just a five-minute walk to the office building where the court reporter was waiting, along with the two daughters, their lawyer, and my client. I immediately started my cross-examination. It lasted all day, as I had the inside story on every evil thing these two women had perpetrated on their father, chapter and verse, from the police reports. At the end of the day, they threw in the towel, giving up any claim to the estate of their father. Their lawyer finally realized there would not be a judge in the land that would give them anything after all they had done to their father.

My client was ecstatic. Justice was complete. Mary started with nothing, and then wound up with the entire estate. The common-law wife happily cultivated her flowers in her Victoria home for the remainder of her days. Perhaps cultivation of flowers was like a self-cultivation and self-realization, as a garden is more beautiful when different species and colours are included and given space to grow.

TALES AND TORTS: STORIES OF A COUNTRY LAWYER

Linda Baber, receptionist (circa. 2000)

John Cherrington at his desk (circa. 2000)

CHAPTER SIX:

Marriage

Some lawyers and judges are married to the law. I am married to my wife, Elizabeth Ann (Anderson) Kearl, known as Beth, whom I affectionately call "Dearie." We met on campus at the University of British Columbia (UBC) during my fourth year in the Bachelor of Arts program in the fall of 1975. Beth was in the Education program, with a major in English and a minor in Music.

I noticed her while attending a religion class at UBC. She was very cute: five-foot-three-inches tall, with an attractive figure and weighing 120 pounds. She was the perfect size for me since I was five foot-seven-inches tall and 135 pounds. Beth had medium-length, dark brown hair, which she kept hidden under a kerchief. I guess she spotted me as well, since she invited me to a Sadie Hawkins Dance, which was our first date.

In order to go on the date, Beth and I travelled on the bus from UBC to her home in Richmond, where I met her father, mother, four sisters, and one brother. At that time, I was a poor student with only a ten-speed bicycle for transportation. I paid for room and board with a family just off campus. Every day, I had a fifteen-minute cycle, along a scenic bike trail lined with massive oaks, maples, and cedar trees, on the University Endowment Lands, to my classes at UBC. The stunning campus is located at the western tip of the Point Grey Peninsula in Vancouver, surrounded by forest on three sides and ocean on the fourth.

Beth went upstairs to shower and get ready for the dance, while I chatted with her mother in the kitchen on the main floor. Beth liked to hide under a kerchief so she didn't have to wash her hair every day, because it rained a lot, and her hair would go all frizzy. I remember the next moment as if it happened yesterday, when Beth descended the stairs, then came around the corner into the kitchen—it was love at first hair wash!

At the dance, we jived, double time, to the old rock and roll tunes of the 60s, like The Beatles' "She Was Just 17." We amazed everyone at the dance with all our fabulous moves. We also looked pretty good dancing the fox trot and the waltz. It was unusual for me to be so possessive, but I kept Beth close to me all night. Right after the dance, I dropped my Friday night girlfriend and my Saturday night girlfriend, as now I only wanted one girlfriend—Beth.

The next week, I took Beth skating at the indoor rink on campus where I displayed my strong skating prowess, having been raised in Calgary where I would skate each winter evening on a rink in the park at the end of the street where we lived. Beth did well, but her ankles began to hurt. However, this was not a problem for me, as I was happy to hold her up and keep her close to me.

Our third date was a long walk along Spanish Banks Beach, just down a steep slope north of the campus looking out to English Bay, Stanley Park, and the North Shore Mountains—a spectacular view. We continued to attend dances, concerts, and movies. I played the guitar, and I even wrote her some love songs. I felt we had a desire to share our lives together, so on Tuesday April 13, 1976, I proposed marriage, and she accepted. We were engaged for a year, and then married on May 7,1977, the same month I received my Bachelor of Arts degree. Later, I was accepted to law school at UBC, which allowed us to live in family housing on campus, in a one-bedroom apartment on the second floor in the Acadia Park High-rise.

Beth decided to have children rather than continue her studies at UBC to become a teacher. While I was attending law school, we had two children, James and Jessica, all four of us sleeping in the one bedroom. I never noticed we were poor; we just didn't have any money. Our entertainment was to enjoy long, family walks on the beautiful campus.

When Beth was pregnant with James, I had my first-year mock court. I arranged with Beth to attend, so that if the mock court was not going well, I would raise my right hand as a signal to start moaning that the baby was coming, and we could escape, saying we had to rush to the hospital. Fortunately, it was not necessary to use this clever ploy.

We divided our duties at night. If James woke up crying, I would have to attend to him, but if Jessica woke up and caused a fuss, Beth would have to take care of her. Fortunately, I trained James to sleep through the night, and it was almost always Jessica who woke up crying. After I became a lawyer, we had two more children, Jennifer and Jane, who became quite the baseball players, and I coached them for many years. I also coached James in basketball and soccer. With Jessica, we prepared many excellent arguments for her classes at school, resulting in her winning the most difficult debates.

The law was a rewarding way to solve problems for clients that they could not resolve on their own. The law provided a means for people to resolve their disputes without resorting to violence, which made for a very rewarding career; however, I was not married to it. There were important priorities outside of the law, like family, God, and tennis—not necessarily in that order. I would leave a message at the office with the receptionist at times that I had gone to court, which my good clients understood to mean "the tennis court," and they could call me when the match was over.

Marriage day of Beth and Robert Kearl, May 7, 1977

Let me now take you to a most unlikely marriage, a union made in heaven, after a terrible tragedy. This story begins late one evening when Lawrence, aged twenty-five, and his buddy Phil, one year older, had a burger, fries, and a couple of beers at a pub in Langley

City. The car they were driving was owned by Phil's brother, an old, two-door, silver Toyota Corolla. Sometimes Phil would drive it, but Lawrence would drive it just about as often. It was a dark, rainy night—the kind that made it very hard to see the road. The two of them were travelling north on Glover Road, the main highway between Langley City and Fort Langley, which is about a ten-minute drive down a narrow road with one lane in each direction. The car dropped down the slope onto the flood plain that surrounds Fort Langley, where the Salmon River meanders on its way to the mighty Fraser River. Here, the car picked up speed to about seventy kilometres per hour in a posted sixty zone. There was a sharp curve to the right with a sign that signalled a reduction of speed to fifty kilometres per hour, and a bridge that spanned the Salmon River just before arriving at Fort Langley. Instead of making the turn to the right, the silver Toyota went straight off the road on the left-hand side, crashing through the barrier at the bridge, taking flight for about twenty metres and then crashing in to the ground on the north side of the Salmon River.

The two occupants of the vehicle were thrown through the windshield due to the violent nature of the collision. Phil died almost immediately at the scene. Lawrence was taken by emergency to G.F. Strong Hospital in Vancouver. I received a call from his older brother Ray to visit him there.

G.F. Strong is the largest rehabilitation hospital in British Columbia, providing expert care to patients with brain and spinal cord injuries. It shocked me when I entered the hospital room to see Lawrence lying in the bed with a cage around his head with spokes to keep it from moving, as any movement would cause further damage. He was awake, but heavily sedated; still we visited for a time. I asked him about the accident, but he had no memory of anything relating to it, either before or after it occurred. I inquired about a key piece of evidence, who was driving. He did not know.

He was unable to move his legs—paralyzed from the waist down to the end of his toes. He also had no control over his hand movements, so he could not grasp items or make other motions that would allow him to do anything. Lawrence asked me if his friend was really dead, as he was finding it hard to accept this devastating news given to him at the hospital. It was painful to confirm the tragic death of Phil. After our visit, I drove home determined to investigate the accident to determine what could be done for Lawrence.

The doctors confirmed that Lawrence was a quadriplegic, which was the result of an injury to the neck area of the spinal cord suffered in the motor vehicle accident, leaving him permanently paralyzed from the waist down. Although he could move his arms, he had no control of his hands. He remained in the hospital for many months, working hard at rehabilitation, but there was little improvement.

I was amazed at his courage and resilience. Lawrence was six-foot-two-inches tall, weighing a muscular 205 pounds. He was a pure athlete. He had played junior hockey for the Brandon Wheat Kings based in Brandon, Manitoba in the Western Hockey League. Lawrence played defence, and I could imagine him thumping any opposition player who challenged him. He was good enough to have a tryout with a National Hockey League team; I think it was the Chicago Black Hawks that released him on the final cut. As a result, he moved to Langley to start an excavation business with his brother Ray. Lawrence was single with a girlfriend named Judy, who had a joyful, enthusiastic personality.

Lawrence loved to dig home foundations with his backhoe. Langley was growing quickly, so he had lots of work. The only things he knew and loved were the physical aspects of life. He completed high school back in Manitoba, but barely. Anything to do with books was not to his liking. I met Lawrence and Ray when a customer failed to pay a bill after they completed digging a foundation. I filed a builder's lien on the land, forcing payment for the work, as the mortgage company would not advance any further funds for the construction of the house until the lien was removed. I knew this would be the case, therefore, we collected interest on the amount owing and legal costs, in addition to the amount of the lien. Ray liked the way I was able to obtain swift justice for them. I suppose this is why he called me to help his brother Lawrence.

The most critical question to be answered regarding the accident was: Who was driving? Lawrence never recovered any memory of the accident, including who was driving, and Phil was dead, so he could not tell us. There were no witnesses to identify who was driving—none at the pub where they ate, nor along the route they drove to the scene of the accident. If Lawrence was driving, the accident was his fault, so he could not recover, from his car insurance, damages for the catastrophic injuries he suffered. Of course, if Phil was driving, the accident was his fault, meaning Lawrence could make a claim against the insurance company. I hired an engineer, who was an accident reconstruction expert, to investigate who had been driving. I had been careful to preserve the evidence—that is, the car—so it could be examined by the engineer. He discovered hair follicles in the windshield, since Phil and Lawrence were both thrown through the windshield in the accident. Fortuitously, Lawrence had short, light-coloured hair, while Phil had long, dark hair. The engineer determined that the short, light-coloured hair follicles were in the windshield on the passenger side, while the long, dark hair was found in the windshield on the driver's side. The engineer provided his expert opinion that Phil was the driver, and Lawrence was the passenger.

The next issue was whether the damages should be reduced for contributory negligence, because Lawrence was not wearing a seat belt. It was obvious neither of them were wearing a seat belt, as they were both thrown through the windshield. I requested an expert report from the same engineer on whether the injuries would have been less severe if Lawrence had been wearing a seat belt. The engineer concluded that since the car was totally crushed, with the roof entirely collapsed upon the driver and passenger seats, Lawrence would have suffered the same devastating injuries, even if he had been wearing a seat belt and remained in the passenger seat.

Armed with the engineer's expert report, I was ready for trial. In addition, I had calculations of non-pecuniary damages, meaning pain and suffering and loss of enjoyment of life, past wage loss, cost of past and future care, and by far the largest loss, future income, which consisted of the amount Lawrence would have earned over his working lifetime, amounting to a claim of a few million dollars. I knew we could only recover an amount over one million dollars as that was the limit on the insurance, and it was of no use to proceed any further against any of Phil's assets, as he had none. However, to prepare for trial, it was necessary to have an accountant prepare an expert report on the future wage loss, brought into present-day value dollars, as the onus is always on the plaintiff to prove the loss. At that point, it was assumed that Lawrence would never work again, as he had no training, aptitude for, nor experience with non-physical work.

Shortly before the trial, the insurance company concluded we would win, so they decided to avoid the extra legal costs of a trial, and paid out the full amount of the third-party liability insurance on the car—over a million dollars. It was a complete victory, and, at that time, a huge win for Lawrence.

With some of the insurance money from the settlement, we researched vans that could be operated by a quadriplegic. Lawrence bought the best wheelchair-accessible van at the time. It was back entry with a lift that would raise Lawrence in his wheelchair into the van. He would then roll forward beside the driver's seat and lift himself in behind the steering wheel. He had hand controls adapted to his capabilities. All he had to do was pull back to accelerate and push the control forward to brake.

Lawrence took off to visit the giant redwoods of California, on his first great adventure alone since the accident. He returned with a gift for me, a chainsaw carving of a grizzly bear made of redwood. The carving remains a cherished keepsake, standing in a prized position beside my fireplace in the living room.

The next time I saw Lawrence, after his return from California, he picked me up from the office to watch him dig a foundation with his treasured backhoe, which was quite a surprise as it was assumed he would never work again. Yet he had discovered a lift that would raise him into the seat of his backhoe. He was happy as a clam at high tide, because now he was back on the job. It was an amazing miracle I had thought would never be possible when I first saw him in that hospital bed shortly after the accident. Over the following years, every time I saw Lawrence driving through Fort Langley, he would stop, and we would have a great chat. Lawrence was never defeated. He triumphed.

A new miracle eventually took place in his life. Judy, his girlfriend, who stood beside him all through the hard times, accepted his proposal of marriage. It was a great day for Lawrence, having faced fear, anxiety, and depression. Yet he had risen up and was a man on top of his game again.

The doctors said that due to the fact Lawrence was paralyzed from the waist down, he could never have biological children. Nonetheless, defying all odds, a few years later, Judy was pregnant, which resulted in the miracle birth of a healthy baby girl. It was an unlikely marriage and an improbable birth of a baby girl; nevertheless, it all happened. I can say, without a doubt, theirs was a union made in heaven. I was happy that Lawrence was able to experience the same joy of being a husband and father as I did. His daughter was about the same age as our youngest, Jane.

Nineteen years later, when their baby girl was an adult, I acted on her behalf in a personal injury claim arising out of a motor vehicle accident. The injury was not terribly serious, so it was settled about a year after the accident. I was now acting on behalf of the next generation. Time was passing me by, but I didn't notice, since I thought I was running just as fast on the tennis court. But, perhaps I have a flawed memory of my running speed.

CHAPTER SEVEN

The Supreme Court of Canada

Lying in bed, staring at the ceiling in a futile attempt to fall asleep, Ed Easingwood began to count imaginary sheep jumping one by one over a hedge. However, that didn't work, so his thoughts instead turned to the accident he had a number of years ago when he slammed into a car that turned left in front of him while he was riding his motorcycle. The pain caused by the damage to his leg muscles and bones never ceased; even though occasionally it seemed to diminish to a mild dull throb, it would always return in a wave of sharp, stabbing agony.

Ed was a forty-six-year-old family-practice physician. He had been out of shape until he started a regular and reasonable aerobic exercise program, leaving his couch potato days behind by walking White Rock's promenade running the entire length of the beach, as well as the famous pier, the longest in Canada, extending 470 metres out over the warm, shallow waters of Semiahmoo Bay. White Rock is named for a large, white boulder on its beach near the promenade, a glacial erratic that migrated south during the last glaciation. The 486-ton granite boulder was kept white in the past by shellfish-eating seabirds, whose guano covered the rock. However, today it is kept white through monthly applications of white paint.

White Rock gained a reputation for being a retirement centre, as it features the lowest rainfall accumulations in the Vancouver region, while benefiting from the warming influence of the Pacific Ocean in winter. Ed lived in one of the many small, cliffside dwellings with a great view of the ocean. The medical office in which he worked was located nearby in a new development in the business centre of the city.

His mind wandered back even further to when he developed an addiction to opiate medications while treating a peptic ulcer. At the time, Ed completed a residential treatment program, overcoming his addiction, and then returned to his medical practice. However, the pain in his leg led to a dependency on both morphine and Demerol. He was placed on a program of gradual withdrawal from these drugs, after which he was able to return to work. Demerol is known as an opioid analgesic and is similar to morphine, as it works in the brain to change how the body feels and responds to pain. The medication is given by injection into a vein or into a muscle or under the skin. The injection site used by Ed was in the groin area so the injury to the skin would not be detected.

Ed rolled over to his wife, nudging her until she woke up, to tell her that he couldn't sleep and was going to go for a drive in an attempt to relieve the pain in his leg. He drove to the office. When his wife woke up in the morning, she had a terrible feeling that something had gone wrong. Ed did not answer his cell phone.

She called the office, but there was no answer, so she decided to drive there. It was a terrible shock to her when she found Ed in his office, sprawled out on the floor, with his broken glasses beside him and a bloody tissue in his right hand. He was dressed in street clothes with his jeans partially pulled down. She fell to the floor beside him, overcome with fear and grief. She called 9-1-1. The police and an ambulance attended within minutes.

It was a terrible tragedy for my partner, Hank Easingwood, as this was his brother. When I was asked to get involved in a legal case involving the insurance, I felt an extra degree of pressure to succeed. It was an all-consuming type of case.

The coroner found that Dr. Edward Joseph Easingwood died from an overdose caused by an intravenous injection of Demerol. The coroner noted that the level of Demerol found in his blood was 2.4 mg, which was at the low end of the range for lethal doses.

Ed's wife was the beneficiary of a life insurance policy with double indemnity for accidental death. There was an exclusion denying recovery in the case of suicide. The coroner noted in her report that Ed "had spoken to friends in the days preceding his death and sounded enthusiastic and was planning for the future." She also noted that he admitted to his physician that he was still taking Demerol for management of the pain caused by his orthopedic injury.

Based on these facts, American International Assurance Life Co. was convinced that Ed did not commit suicide and paid out the life insurance portion of the policy in the amount of $250,000. The company denied coverage under the "Accidental Death Benefit Provision," maintaining the position that the death was not effected through "accidental means." They argued that Dr. Easingwood's self-injection of that particular dosage of Demerol was a deliberate act, and that his death was a consequence that he must have foreseen as possible.

I researched cases throughout the common law world—meaning England, Scotland, Canada, Australia, New Zealand, South African, and the United States—on the distinction between "accidental means" and "accidental result." It seemed to me that such a distinction ought not to be recognized by the law, as most accidents are preceded by intentional acts. In one case in Scotland, an insured started his car on the ferry, put the car in gear, pressed on the gas pedal, and drove off the deck, all intentional acts, in the erroneous belief that the ferry had docked. His car plunged into the ocean, causing him to drown. The reasonable expectation of the insured and the ordinary person would unhesitatingly classify this as an accidental death. The court in Scotland held it was an accident.

Another example would be a person who intentionally drinks a lethal substance believing it to be water. The ordinary person would call this an accident. It seemed to me that the insurance company had invented a distinction that did not make sense, using the words "accidental means" just to avoid paying the additional amount for accidental death, even though the insured had paid the premium for accidental death. It was not just.

In my research, I found two cases in the Ontario Court of Appeal that in my opinion applied to my case. The first involved a dentist who regularly applied laughing gas to himself for enjoyment. For some unknown reason, he held the mask over his face too long, which caused an overdose of nitrous oxide, resulting in his death; yet the court held this was an accident. I felt my case was stronger than this case, as Dr. Easingwood was injecting Demerol for the legitimate purpose of relieving pain, not for enjoyment. The second case involved a patient taking pills for a medical condition as prescribed by his doctor. He had successfully taken the correct number of pills for many months, yet for some unknown reason, he took a few too many pills on one occasion, resulting in his death; yet the court held this was an accident. I felt confident the Supreme Court of Canada would agree with this line of reasoning. In these cases, accidental death means an unintentional or unexpected death, or as stated in the cases, "an unlooked-for mishap or an untoward event which is not expected or designed."

In another case, the insured failed to notice an oncoming train, while crossing a railway track to get from one part of his farm to another. This was held to be an accident. In an additional case, the insured was held to have died accidentally when he mistakenly inhaled more chloroform than he expected during a procedure that he used regularly to relieve headache and insomnia.

However, the Court of Appeal in Alberta and Manitoba recognized "accidental means" in a policy of accidental death insurance to restrict recovery. In several instances, a number of people insured for accidental death drank such a large quantity of alcohol so rapidly that it caused their death. The court held that these deaths were not caused by an accident, since the alcohol was consumed intentionally; therefore, they did not die from "accidental means." I did not think the Supreme Court of Canada would agree with this reasoning.

I also considered an important line of cases that possibly posed a problem, originating in the courts in England, that involved individuals who would "court the risk" of death. In these cases, the courts decided that the deaths did not result from an accident. For example, in the case of "Candler," the insured balanced himself on the balustrade of the patio on the thirteenth-floor hotel suite, carrying out many precarious positions until he lost his balance and plummeted to his death. These types of cases involve people who engage in activities that carry an inordinate risk of death, like the player of Russian roulette, or the young man who deliberately lies down along the centre line of the highway with traffic approaching. All of these fact patterns were actual cases, but in my opinion, these cases were distinguishable from my case, as Dr.

Easingwood did not act with such reckless abandon in the face of possible death.

In light of my extensive research, it was my opinion that to win we would need to go all the way to the Supreme Court of Canada. I told Dorothy Martin, the widow and beneficiary named in the insurance policy, that this battle could take five to nine years, so we should make a reasonable offer to the insurance company to settle the claim. We made a very low offer of around $100,000 to settle, which the insurance company rejected. They refused to make any counter offer, and the die was cast.

I went to trial to seek justice. I lost. The trial judge in the Supreme Court of British Columbia held the erroneous view that Dr. Easingwood's experience as a drug-user and his knowledge as a medical practitioner made him aware of the risks posed by injecting Demerol; therefore, Dr. Easingwood's death was not effected through accidental means. In my view, Dr. Easingwood's experience and knowledge, having used Demerol successfully for many years, meant just the opposite—that he accidentally injected a little too much on this one occasion, an accident resulting in his death.

I appealed to the British Columbia Court of Appeal. Normally three judges sit on an appeal, but I requested five to enable the court to overturn any authority in British Columbia that recognized the distinction between accidental means and accidental result. I was fortunate to have Madame Justice Huddart and Madame Justice Saunders on the appeal, as I could see by their comments that they understood my argument immediately, and then I believe they convinced the other three judges. Madame Justice Huddart rendered the unanimous decision of the court, agreeing with me that an unintentional overdose would be regarded as an accident by the ordinary person, in all of the circumstances surrounding Dr. Easingwood's death. We won the appeal.

The insurance company sought leave to appeal to the Supreme Court of Canada, which is not an appeal by right; instead, leave must be granted by this court. I filed my material opposing leave to appeal, but I knew the Supreme Court would hear the case, because the distinction between accidental means and accidental result was recognized in the Manitoba Court of Appeal and the Alberta Court of Appeal, but rejected in the Court of Appeal in Ontario, Nova Scotia, and now British Columbia. This meant the case had national importance, and the Supreme Court of Canada needed to determine the law for the entire country. Justice requires that the law be the same for all of Canada. Leave to appeal was granted.

The factums, containing the facts, the law, and the arguments, were all filed well in advance of the hearing. All of the cases and the materials are studied thoroughly by each judge, and they each have a clerk to perform whatever research the judge deems necessary in preparation for the hearing. The Supreme Court of Canada is the court of last resort. The bench has nine justices. Usually on a civil case, like this one, five justices would be appointed to hear the appeal, but due to the importance of this case, that is, to determine the law for all of Canada on a point of law never decided by the Supreme Court of Canada before, all nine justices were appointed to sit on the case.

The Chief Justice of Canada at that time was Beverley McLachlin, who was born and raised in Pincher Creek, a little town in Southern Alberta. In her early years, she lived on a ranch where, for part of the time, she did not have running water or electricity. The story of how this young girl rose from the humble beginnings of her small hometown is truly inspiring. She qualified for, attended and completed law school in Edmonton, practiced law there, and then moved to Vancouver where she practiced law and later taught law at the UBC. From there, she was appointed as a judge of the County Court of Vancouver, the Supreme Court of British Columbia, the Court of Appeal, and ultimately, to the Supreme Court of Canada. I had appeared in front of her in the courts in British Columbia. She was also a professor at UBC, when I was a student there. I was always impressed by her kindness, but also by her firm grasp of the law.

The Supreme Court of Canada building is a massive, granite building situated just west of the Parliament Buildings in Ottawa, on a bluff high above the Ottawa River, and set back from busy Wellington Street by an expanse of lawn. The setting for the building provides a dignified venue worthy of the country's highest tribunal. The day finally arrived for the hearing. I had flown from Vancouver to Ottawa, along with an associate from the Fort office, David Critchley, and we were staying at a hotel close enough that we could walk to the courthouse. I passed the statue of former Prime Minister Louis St-Laurent, standing on the lawn in front of the building. As I walked up the steps I noticed two tall statues: Veritas (Truth) to the west, and Ivstitia (Justice) to the east. Two massive bronze doors stood in front of me, giving access to the impressive grand entrance hall with walls and floor of marble.

I walked up one of the two marble stairways leading from the grand entrance hall to the massive, carved wooden doors of the main courtroom, which is the exclusive venue for the Supreme Court of Canada. The doors were still locked. It was nine o'clock in the morning. I was an hour early. I was nervous, so I headed downstairs to find the barristers' room to change into my robes. There, I found the lawyers for the insurance company gathered. As we were changing into our white shirts with wing collars, tabs, vests, dress pants, and robes, I thought I would see whether these lawyers from a big international law firm in Toronto had a sense of humour.

I started out, "I have been in the Provincial Court of British Columbia," motioning my hands down low; "I have been in the Supreme Court of British Columbia," motioning my hands a little higher; "and I have been in the Court of Appeal of British Columbia," raising my hands even higher. "And now the Supreme Court of Canada." I raised my hands high in the air above my head, and my eyes stared up at the ceiling. "But I have been in the highest court…." I paused and waited while they thought about what kind of court I could be talking about, since there is no court higher than the Supreme Court of Canada. Maybe they thought about some court hearing with God passing out judgment or something else religious…until I finally spoke emphatically, "The Tennis Court!" They all laughed, and this is how I discovered that even lawyers from Toronto have a sense of humour.

After getting dressed in my robes, I returned to the main courtroom, entered through the large wooden doors, and noticed translators and television cameras on both sides. The hearing would be translated into French, as we spoke, and televised to show on a late night TV channel for lawyers who could not fall asleep. The main courtroom is large, measuring twelve metres by sixteen, with black walnut walls and six tall windows open to the naturally lit interior courtyard on the one side. Along these windows were desks, where the law clerks who had done legal research for each of the justices sat. I jokingly asked them if I was going to win, as I knew they were not allowed to say anything. They just smiled.

At the front of the courtroom were two large wooden doors through which the Supreme Court justices would enter and then sit upon nine large, red-cushioned chairs, behind a beautifully carved wooden bench extending across the front of the courtroom. In the centre of the room was a lectern, where counsel would stand to speak to the court. It was a unique lectern, as around the outer edge were nine little red lights marked with the names of the justices below each one, in the order of where they sat. When a justice posed a question, each would push a button that illuminated their light, allowing counsel to identify, by name, to whom to respond. The judges of the Supreme Court of Canada were addressed as

"Justice," not "My Lord" or "My Lady," as required in the higher courts in British Columbia.

Finally, ten o'clock arrived, and the clerk called out, "The Supreme Court of Canada, La Cour Supreme du Canada." We all stood, and the nine justices entered the courtroom. The chief justice sat in the middle, with the senior justices next to her, fanning out to the junior justices seated in the outside seats. The lawyers introduced themselves, and then the lawyers for the insurance company commenced with their appeal. The justices had many pointed questions, which seemed to suggest that they were leaning my way. I was the little guy, from the small village of Fort Langley, facing the lawyers from a large international law firm in the big city of Toronto. If ever there was a case that reminded me more of David vs. Goliath, this was it! However, I knew where the chief justice was from: a small town even smaller than the little village of Fort Langley. This brought me a fair amount of comfort.

Our presentation was brief as we only had one hour to reply. I felt that the court, especially the chief justice, was on our side, and that she would bring the rest of the court around to her point of view. We anticipated a very unique question, taken from a decision of US Supreme Court Justice Cardozo, in a dissenting opinion, stating: "The attempted distinction between accidental results and accidental means will plunge this branch of the law into a Serbonian Bog." One of the justices asked, "What is a Serbonian Bog?" The answer: "It is a little known reference, to an obscure passage in Milton's *Paradise Lost,* to that "Serbonian bog…Where armies whole have sunk," and relates to Lake Serbonis in Egypt, as described by Herodotus. Because sand blew onto it, the Serbonian Bog had a deceptive appearance of being solid land, but it was a bog. The term metaphorically applies to any situation in which extrication is difficult. Apparently, the bog has dried up now, which is what I challenged the court to do in this area of the law by eliminating the distinction between accidental means and accidental result.

The court reserved judgement as expected. Several months later, I received the written reasons for judgment. We won! The appeal was dismissed in an unanimous judgement of the court written by the Chief Justice Beverly McLachlin. She wrote:

"The first set of facts concerns the circumstances in which Dr. Easingwood's body was found. The body was found in a dishevelled state inappropriate for someone who anticipates death as a potential result of his actions. He was lying prone in his office with his glasses broken on the floor beside him, with his jeans partially pulled down, revealing the site where he had injected the Demerol. These facts point strongly to the conclusion that Dr. Easingwood did not expect to die; indeed they suggest that he did not so much as turn his mind to the possibility that death would result from his actions. They suggest, instead, that he miscalculated how much his body could tolerate."

The Chief Justice continued by summarizing Dr. Easingwood's conduct with his friends in the days preceding his death, which *"does not support the conclusion that Dr. Easingwood expected to die,"* since he spoke with them enthusiastically about his plans for the future.

Finally, she concluded: *"These two sets of facts, combined with the fact the dosage of Demerol was at the low end of the scale, suggest that Dr. Easingwood was simply attempting to ease the pain in his leg and perhaps also to satisfy his addiction to painkillers, and that he would not have willingly taken on the risk of administering a potentially lethal dose."*

There was a great celebration with Hank and the widow, Dorothy Martin, as Dorothy recovered the amount of $250,000 for accidental death, and in addition, interest on that amount, plus legal costs. It was seven years from the death of Ed to the final judgment in the Supreme Court of Canada, a lengthy legal battle, therefore, the amount of interest was substantial. The legal costs were considerable as well, as they included not only costs in the Supreme Court of Canada, but also legal costs in all the courts below. This precedent cost the insurance company far more, as many other claims were waiting for the outcome of this appeal. It established an important precedent, binding in Canada, and persuasive throughout the common law world. Ultimately, it cost the insurance company tens, maybe even hundreds of millions of dollars. The insurance company made a monumental mistake when it could have settled with us from the outset for $100,000.

I felt satisfied and happy as I thought about how the law exists to regulate disputes. Hopefully, it will provide justice for all; it certainly did for Dorothy Martin, widow of Dr. Easingwood.

The case was reported widely in the newspapers with the headline, "Lawyer wins landmark ruling. Robert Kearl's journey to Canada's top court ended with a ruling that a life insurance company must pay $250,000 to the wife of a White Rock doctor." It was front page news with a photo of me in my court robes. *The Lawyers Weekly*, which is a paper sent to every lawyer across the country, read, "Supreme Court ruling seen as expanding insurance coverage in cases of accidental death." *The Lawyers Weekly* sent a photographer to take a photo of me in front of the historic Fort Langley Community Hall, constructed by volunteers in 1931 and recognized for its landmark status. The photo and the article took up the complete front page. There are very few lawyers in Canada who ever appear in the Supreme Court of Canada, let alone have all nine justices appointed to hear their case, and then triumph with an unanimous judgment written by the Chief Justice of Canada.

To put this victory in perspective, so my two brothers can understand, this win is to a lawyer what it would be like scoring the winning goal in overtime in the seventh game of the Stanley Cup final.

Many years later, shortly before my retirement, an articling student at the law firm approached me, with what I could see was a certain degree of awe, as she asked, "Is it true that you won the Dorothy Martin case? It is an important case that we studied in law school. It is studied in every law school across the country on the issue of what is an accident."

I humbly answered, "Yes, it was me."

CHAPTER EIGHT

The Rhyme of the Ancient Farmer

Superstition is a powerful social phenomena, especially when transferred generation after generation through odd behaviours and old wives' tales. A few favourites I have heard over the years are: don't whistle inside or it will cause bad luck; never return straight home after a wake or a bad spirit will follow you to your house; itchy hands mean you will soon lose money; knitting outside can prolong winter; and (my personal favourite) pregnant mothers who crave fish but do not satisfy the craving will give birth to a child with a fish head! While people may have fun reciting such strange folklore, most recognize that there is very little logic or truth in these behaviours or warnings, and yet, perhaps motivated by that nagging "what if?" in the back of their brains, they choose to follow them anyways. If it doesn't hurt anyone, why not? What if there is some magical force in the world upon which these stories are based? What if, by ignoring the legends of old wives, old fishers, or old farmers, one inadvertently brings disaster upon oneself? On the other hand, what if fully investing in a superstition or magical belief has the potential to make a misfortune much much worse? This was the case with one of my clients – an ancient farmer.

Out of the blue, on an unremarkable cloudy day, an ancient farmer with a weathered face and glittering blue eyes tromped into my office, each "clunk" and "clonk" of his heavy boots marked by crusted mud. He swung the door open wide and stopped me in my work, demanding my attention immediately. Clutched in his weathered hand while stroking his long grey beard, he held aloft a tattered, sodden piece of paper so soiled it was only with extreme difficulty that I was able to identify it as a court document. It read, "Notice of Hearing." Apparently, the old man was due in court for some such matter. Upon gently handling the document and reading further, to my shock and dismay, I discovered that, not only was he due in in the Supreme Court of British Columbia in New Westminster, but he was to appear later that very morning for an order absolute of foreclosure! If he did not appear, the bank would own his farm. No longer would the ancient and peculiar looking farmer, standing across from me with clay jammed under his fingernails and a dubious expression darkening his brow, be the owner.

The ancient farmer continued to tell his tale as he carried another shredded and muddy set of papers, which he said were delivered to him over six months ago from the bank. Below the barn, below the hill, below the Fraser River, the ancient man dug a hole deep and dark. In the hole he buried the documents from the bank and placed a charm upon the loose dirt believing he would not have to pay the mortgage if his conjuring should work. I could read from the earlier documents shredded and mud-covered, it was the "Petition of Foreclosure" which would give the farmer six months to sell the property.

I asked him what he thought his farm was worth. It was a figure well above the amount owed to the bank so I dropped everything to drive to the courthouse. When they called his case, I explained to the judge what the ancient farmer, in his desperation and superstition, had done. Given the potential value of the farm and the extremely eccentric nature of the old farmer, the judge exercised his discretion to grant further time for the farmer to sell the property, pay the bank and keep the balance of the funds.

I obtained the old farmer's instructions to list the farm property for sale, the real estate agent found a buyer, the bank was paid, and a significant surplus was now available to the ancient man. I was so happy to have "saved the day," so-to-speak. I had dropped everything to help someone who could not face the cold hard facts – who had literally buried their problems in the earth. I felt deep satisfaction knowing that if I had not helped him, the bank would have taken ownership of the farm and the farmer would have received nothing.

I sat in my office with a cheque in a significant amount payable to the farmer in my hand, knowing I had done a good job. The farmer arrived at my office, walked down the hall in a cloud of dust, mud sticking to everything he touched. He stood before me, his glittering eyes now filled with malice, as he abruptly snatched the money out of my hand without even a thank you. The ancient farmer then turned on his heel, marched down the hall and slammed the door shut, almost knocking it off its hinges. Alarmed by the tumult, the usual merry din of administrative assistants fell silent as the farmer flew by, his beard and long jacket flowing in a wind of his own making. And just like that, he was gone.

I cannot explain the bizarre behaviour of the ancient farmer. He clearly did not want anyone to force him to face the facts and pay his dues. At many points in our lives we refuse to see what is directly in front of us, to our own detriment. The people around us and those who love us point to the dangers of our actions, to the harm we will cause to ourselves, but we refuse to see, and instead bury our heads in the sand. The ancient farmer was a classic case of this problem. As the saying goes, "Sometimes we bite the hand that feeds us."

CHAPTER NINE

The Jewish Russian Tenor

The historic Bolshoi Theatre is the home of the leading theatre company for ballet and opera in Russia. The original group was organized in Moscow in the mid-1770s. The company was kept intact during the Russian Revolution of 1917, both world wars, and the dissolution of the Soviet Union in 1990–91.

Grigory Abrams was a tenor who sang opera at the Bolshoi Theatre during the height of the Cold War in the 1960s. The Cold War was a period of tension between the Soviet Union and the United States and their respective allies, the Eastern Bloc and the Western Bloc, after World War II. It spanned the period from 1947 until the dissolution of the Soviet Union in 1991. The term "cold" is used because there was no large-scale fighting directly between the two superpowers. The conflict was based around the struggle for global dominance between the liberal democracies of the West and communism in the East.

Grigory had a free spirit. He hated communism with a deep rage that burned within him. He longed for the opportunity to escape to freedom in the West. From an early age he studied English, Italian and French, and had become quite fluent in them. By the time he was twenty years old, Grigory was one of the leading tenors in Russian opera and began to travel the world with the Bolshoi Opera Company. However, whenever they travelled to the West, the KGB, the secret police force of the Soviet Union, monitored his every movement. Any false move would mean a trip to the Gulag, forced labour camps in Siberia. He had read a smuggled copy of Aleksandr Solzhenitsyn's book *Gulag Archipelago,* about his incarceration for eight long years of extreme penal labour. He did not want to experience a system where people were worked to death, hence he had to bide his time while he watched for an opportunity to escape.

The Russian Empire had a long history of anti-Jewish pogroms, violent riots aimed at the massacre or expulsion of Jews. The 1917 Russian Revolution overthrew the Russian Empire, however, the previous legacy of antisemitism continued in the Soviet state. Grigory detested the treatment he received simply because he was a Jew. Karl Marx, who wrote *The Communist Manifesto*, was a Jew. Grigory wondered why the Soviet state would persecute him, when a Jew formed the ideas that led to the Russian Revolution and the establishment of communism.

Grigory was better off than most Jews in the Soviet Union because of his talent as an opera singer, but there remained constant discrimination against him. He was given a smaller apartment in Moscow, only 540 square feet—much smaller than the other members of his opera company. His food allowance was also less generous. His talent had to be markedly above his peers, or they would be given the choice parts in the opera. The unjust and prejudicial treatment he received on the grounds of his ethnicity added to his deep desire to escape the Soviet Union. He was considered Jewish because his mother and father were Jewish; it was a matter of ancestry.

His father and mother died in a car crash when Grigory was sixteen years old. He had lived on his own since then, as he was an only child. Because Grigory never married, nor had any children, he had not developed any close family ties. This turned to his advantage when fleeing the country, as the communists would not be able to punish family members left behind. It was just a question of time before an opportunity would present itself for him to get out.

That opportunity finally came when the company left for Rome to perform *La Traviata* by Verdi at the Teatro dell'Opera di Roma. "La Traviata" means "the one who goes astray," and this is what Grigory sought to achieve. He was playing the understudy to the lead character, Alfredo Germont, who was involved in a tragic love story with the courtesan, Violetta. He would take the risk of slipping out the side door, then catch a cab to the US Embassy in Rome. He had planned the escape many times in his mind. He knew where the taxis waited outside the theatre and exactly how far it was to the US Embassy. The opportunity presented itself; when the side door was clear, Grigory fled, catching a cab for a six-minute (2.3 kilometre) ride from the theatre to the Embassy of the United States of America to Italy.

At the US Embassy, Grigory was accepted as an asylum seeker, fleeing from the Soviet Union. The embassy made plans for his escape to New York City, which was a dream come true for Grigory. He had studied where Jewish people had settled throughout the world, and he knew many had settled in New York since the seventeenth century, and had grown from a population of 80,000 in 1880 to 1.6 million in 1920, making it the largest Jewish city in the world. The US officials in Rome arranged for Grigory to fly with the next military plane leaving for LaGuardia Airport in New York City. Grigory was so ecstatic when the plane touched down in the land of the free that as soon as he got off the plane, he knelt down to kiss the ground and pray, giving thanks to the one true God for his safe arrival.

The US officials had arranged for Grigory to meet the leaders of the Central Synagogue, a thriving congregation in Midtown Manhattan, serving 2,600 families—one of the largest Jewish congregations in North America and the oldest synagogue in New York City. Grigory had trained in the Soviet Union as a cantor, as well as being trained for the opera. In Judaism, a cantor is a trained vocalist and member of the clergy who leads the congregation in song and prayer and teaches music to both children and adults. The Central Synagogue was delighted to offer such a distinguished tenor as Grigory a position of cantor for a yearly salary of $62,000.

Grigory also went to the Metropolitan Opera House located on Broadway at Lincoln Square on the Upper West Side of Manhattan. He thought he would audition to join the opera company, but he never did. Enthusiasm for the opera had waned in his life. He was content to be a cantor.

In the beginning, Grigory thought Midtown Manhattan was one of the best places to live, with lots of restaurants, coffee shops, and parks. Manhattan is the most densely populated district in New York, which began to create a great deal of anxiety for Grigory. He started to feel hemmed in by all the people and buildings. Even more significant, after two years working as a cantor in the Synagogue, Grigory felt empty. He experienced a crisis of faith. He began to doubt Judaism, a monotheistic religion developed among the ancient Hebrews, characterized by a belief in one God who revealed himself to Abraham, Moses, and the Hebrew prophets. Repeatedly in the synagogue he sat through the rabbi reading from the Torah, the five books of Moses, which only caused him to doubt even further. He decided he was "just Jewish" but non-religious.

At that time, a Jewish friend came for a visit. He had started a business selling frozen meat door to door in Western Canada. It was a very successful business, and he wanted Grigory to join him. After studying the financial statements as well as the offer to participate in the company, Grigory decided to move to Winnipeg, Manitoba to help manage the fleet of refrigerated trucks and employees that sold the frozen meat right across Manitoba, Saskatchewan, and Alberta. He felt that Western Canada would give him the freedom he needed, with its abundance of wide open spaces.

After two years travelling to every town and city in the Canadian Prairies, Grigory decided he would start his own business doing the same thing in British Columbia. He had an amiable parting with his partner, and then decided to live in Langley, as this would be a central location in the Lower Mainland, located in the southwestern corner of British Columbia and encompassing Vancouver and its surrounding area. Business was booming. Grigory was more successful than he ever dreamed. He had a full fleet of refrigerated trucks and salespeople to market the frozen meat products across British Columbia. Unfortunately, Grigory was injured in a car accident.

It happened at an intersection. Grigory was proceeding through a green light in his BMW, when he was broadsided on the driver's side door by a pickup truck accelerating through a red light. His head was thrown toward the centre of the car, then whiplashed back, smashing against the driver's door window. He was knocked unconscious for an undetermined period of time. The last thing he remembered before the crash was driving down the street toward the intersection, while the next thing he could recall was being placed in an ambulance.

The main problem for the next few months was the extreme pain in his back, neck, and shoulders. He suffered from severe headaches, dizziness and blurred vision, but any symptoms regarding a possible head injury were overshadowed by the excruciating pain in his neck and back.

A year after the accident is when the insurance adjuster made an offer of $40,000 to settle his case. This is when I met Grigory for the first time. He came to see me to get legal advice regarding what to do about the offer. I asked, "Have you fully recovered?"

He replied, "No."

I told him not to settle because some of his symptoms really worried me—not just the dull pain in his neck and back, but also headaches, memory problems, and disorientation. He said the insurance adjuster told him that he had been to his superior and that $40,000 was a generous offer—the best offer the insurance company would ever make. The insurance adjuster added that if he went to see a lawyer, he would get less because the lawyer would just take all his money. I assured him that I would not charge for the initial consultation, nor would I be taking any part of the offer of $40,000. He started to listen. I gave him advice based on my extensive repertoire of legal experience representing victims of mild traumatic brain injuries. Though he was clearly confused and had not yet received diagnosis of his full injuries, I easily recognized his symptoms: a period of loss of consciousness, loss of memory for events immediately before and after the accident, loss of short-term memory, and an alteration in his mental ability to organize and process thoughts and ideas in his mind starting from the time of the accident and continuing to the present; in place of his previous sharp mind, was a feeling of disorientation and confusion.

At this point, we covered his background from his time as a Jewish, Russian tenor, to his escape in Rome, his singing as a cantor in New York, his crisis of faith, and finally his frozen meat business, first in the Prairie Provinces and now in British Columbia. Grigory Abrams was one of the most unique people I had ever met, with a most intriguing background. I found his story fascinating.

I told Grigory that he had overcome persecution, risked his life to escape communist Russia, lived through a faith crisis, and moved to yet another country and learned its customs. I went on to say that after he had displayed such courage and adaptability, would he now allow himself to be taken advantage of and bullied by an insurance company? I looked him in the eye and said: "If you can stand up to the KGB, surely you can stand up to the pencil-pushing suits!"

He decided to retain me to act on his behalf. I gathered his clinical records from his family doctor, orthopaedic specialist, physiotherapists, massage therapists, and chiropractor. I sent him to a neuropsychologist who specialized in understanding the relationship between the physical brain and behaviour. The brain is complex. Disorders within the brain and nervous system can alter behaviour and cognitive function. Grigory was experiencing difficulty managing his business, which eventually led to a complete shutdown. He could not operate the way he used to, since he felt disoriented and confused and suffered from short-term memory loss. As a result, he was never able to start up his business again. I obtained the expert opinion of a neuropsychologist that the failure of his business was due to mild traumatic brain injury caused by the motor vehicle accident.

Unsurprisingly, the insurance company did not agree. They hired specialists that denied any brain injury. To the insurance company, this was just another case of a moderate whiplash injury to the neck and back, which meant they denied any damages caused by the loss of his business.

I had started a legal action, arranging examination for discovery dates and a trial date. The insurance company elected to have a jury, so we were set with a three-week jury trial. Juries in British Columbia are notoriously unpredictable, therefore, the insurance company elected a jury to put further pressure on Grigory to settle. An examination for discovery is an important part of almost every civil lawsuit. It is not a trial, but rather a pre-trial process at which lawyers for each of the parties question the other party, under oath, about the matters involved in the lawsuit. A court reporter records all the questions and answers, after which a transcript may be ordered and used as evidence at the trial. Grigory did very well at the discovery.

We decided to hold a mediation a week before the three-week jury trial, with a mutually selected mediator, who was impartial and neutral, to assist in the negotiation of our differences. After discussions were held across the table, the parties involved retreated to get further instructions from their clients. The mediator went back and forth between the two in an attempt to keep the negotiations on track. Offers and counter offers flew back and forth. At the end of a long day, which extended into the evening, we reached a settlement. The insurance company offered $800,000 plus legal costs; we accepted. Remember, the insurance company promised that they would never offer more than $40,000 as it was a generous offer. It was a two-year battle, but well worth the effort to achieve such a favourable outcome.

Grigory Abrams was happy. He expressed his appreciation openly with big Jewish Russian Tenor bear hugs. I don't know how tenors hug, but I know the bear is a symbol of Russia, and Jewish Russian bear hugs are warm, tight, and filled with enthusiasm.

I had never met a Jewish Russian Tenor before, which left this experience indelibly impressed upon my memory. I shall never forget Grigory Abrams, nor his unique personality and background.

CHAPTER TEN

Was It Murder?

Every night, before I can fall asleep, I set my alarm clock to ensure I get up on time. Even though I always wake up half an hour before the alarm, then turn it off, just knowing it is there gives me a sense of security. I can be sure that if my natural system fails, I have a backup. This assurance is soothing, as there is always pressure to be at the next scheduled appointment on time. Where did I have to be today? My examination for discovery of the defendant was booked for 10:00 a.m. in Powell River.

I slipped out of bed at 6:00 a.m., so I wouldn't wake up my wife, Beth, and then showered while whispering the songs I usually sing with great gusto. After the shower, I shaved, quietly chanting my favourite couplet whenever I shower and shave: "A shower of power and a shave of the brave. A shower of power and a shave of the brave."

I put on my grey business suit with my Louis Vuitton, Parisian blue tie as this is what I call my "power outfit," which I wear to attempt to intimidate witnesses to tell the truth during my cross examination. I looked at Beth sleeping deeply, gave her a kiss and said, "Love you, see you soon." I knew she was asleep and couldn't hear me, but later when she wakes up I can remind her of this moment—that I did tell her I love her. She seems to think I don't say it very often, but then how does she know, since she is usually asleep when I tell her?

I walked across the hall to watch my oldest daughter, Jessica, as she slept. She looked so beautiful. I didn't have much time, so I ambled over to the other bedroom upstairs, where Jenny and Jane were sleeping. Jenny was so cute with stains from the blueberry pancakes she had eaten the previous night still on her lips and cheeks. Jane looked so peaceful, a far cry from the climbing, running, and jumping activities of the day.

Downstairs, on the main floor, I got a drink of water in the kitchen and then looked in on our oldest child, James, who was no doubt dreaming of playing basketball in the NBA like Michael Jordan. Family is the most important reason I do the things I do. Love of family provides purpose to my life. Rather than a quest for pleasure or power, life is more a search for meaning. Happiness, then, is the natural by-product.

Time glides by so quickly that today our four children are grown, married, and have children of their own. It is a difficult transition from having a home filled with the enthusiasm of children to being empty nesters. However, just in time, grandchildren come along to bring a renewed freshness to life. Beth and I have sixteen grandchildren. One of our grandchildren passed away shortly after birth, but we always count him. I am like the "little cottage girl" in the poem, "We Are Seven" by William Wordsworth, who insists, even though two of her siblings lie in the churchyard, that: "We are seven!"

I also love to help people resolve their problems and obtain justice by the proper application of the law. This gives me a reason to get up every morning; it is very rewarding. I find meaning for my life as I advocate for others in my legal career.

We live in a beautiful community called Walnut Grove in northwest Langley. Behind our home is a ravine with many old-growth red cedar trees, maples, alders, western hemlocks, and oaks. Western red cedars are the longest-living trees in the coastal rainforest; many of them are over 1,500 years old and going strong. We have one particular red cedar that is probably over five hundred years old, which we call "Mother Nature." Leaning against "Mother Nature" we used to look up at six cedar trees that had sprung out of one giant red cedar stump. These trees were twisted around in a manner that resembled a great woolly mammoth, so we called them the "Elephant Tree." Recently, the trunks from the six trees crashed to the ground—due to the ever-present force of gravity—and now cross a small stream, called West Mundy Creek, to form a bridge. Now we call it the "Elephant Bridge."

In addition to finding meaning in my life from love of family and significant work, I experience pure joy in nature. Just a few feet from my back door, I walk into the ravine behind my house, where I enter a new world filled with the spirit of Mother Nature. My favourite romantic poet, Wordsworth, describes how I feel in his poem, "My Heart Leaps Up." He expresses how he experiences joy when he beholds a rainbow in the sky. He says it was this way as a young child and is still the same as an adult, and he declares it will be the same when he grows old; otherwise, he would rather die. I echo his feelings.

West Mundy Creek is a small stream, but in the fall while I was raking huge maple leaves in our backyard, I heard the water rustle in an unusual way. I went down to investigate and discovered large salmon spawning in the gravel bed. It is amazing that these salmon could find their way home. They had been born in that exact spot, swam down the creek around five kilometres until they reached the Fraser River (with some of the largest salmon runs in the world), and then swam approximately fifty kilometres to the ocean. There, they remained for about four years, only to return to the same spot to spawn. I would call the life cycle of the salmon one of Mother Nature's miracles.

Let me get back to the discovery in Powell River. It was a lovely spring morning in March as I drove up Walnut Grove Drive, which is an ideal showcase for the beloved cherry trees bursting with pink and white blossoms. *This is another reason why I live here*, I thought. Since rush hour starts early, the traffic was just starting to get heavy as I made my way to the airport in Vancouver for my flight to Powell River.

Powell River is located on the northern Sunshine Coast of BC, next to the Salish Sea, which is part of the larger Georgia Strait between Vancouver Island and the mainland. A deep inlet separates Powell River from the rest of the British Columbia mainland, resulting in the area having a rare, unspoiled, natural beauty. Travelling by car, it is about five hours north from Vancouver. However, it is not connected to the Provincial Highway network and requires a couple of ferry rides: Horseshoe Bay to Langdale and Earl's Cove to Saltery Bay. This makes it a great way to travel if you have lots of time, but I didn't, so I decided to fly.

Getting to Powell River is a thirty-five minute flight aboard a small propeller airplane with spectacular views of the rugged coastline, deep inlets, islands, and bays. I marvelled at the unparalleled beauty I viewed that sunny morning. Approaching Powell River, we flew along Texada Island, where the accident that was the reason for my journey had occurred.

Nine months earlier, Lucas, a young father, came to my office in Fort Langley with his two small children. He explained that his wife, Olivia, had deserted him and the children for several months, during which time they had no contact. He had no idea where she went, which left him living in fear that she had come to some dire end. Finally, the police came to his home one night to inform him they had discovered Olivia's badly decomposed body in a Texada Island bog.

Olivia's identity had been determined by her dental records. When her death was reported in the local newspapers, a man named Parker came forward—remembering for the first time—that he had a passenger on his motorcycle when he drove off the road into the bog on Texada Island. He reported to the police that he had no recollection of the incident until he read about it in the paper months later, which explained why he didn't report the accident earlier. He claimed the newspaper article triggered the return of his memory.

The police report explained that Harper met Olivia for the first time in a bar at Gillies Bay, where they had some drinks together. Harper invited Olivia to come to his home, about twenty-five kilometres away, which he said she agreed to do. He drove a Ducati motorcycle, and Olivia hopped on the back. Harper said he woke up in a large swamp about two kilometres down the road, with no recollection of how he got there. He walked back to the bar where he stayed for the night. The next day, he returned for his motorcycle, pulling it out of the marsh, but claimed to not remember that he had had a passenger. Harper insisted the amnesia caused a loss of memory of the facts and experiences of that night. The police were suspicious, but did not charge him with any offence.

I was acting on behalf of the children, seeking damages for the loss of love and guidance of their mother. The lawsuit named Harper as the defendant. The insurance company lawyer would be there representing Harper, while I cross-examined him in the court reporter's office. Harper was put under oath to tell the truth, the whole truth, and nothing but the truth. He even swore on the

Bible. As I questioned him about how he could possibly forget about a passenger on the back of his motorcycle, even when he returned to the scene of the accident to pull his motorcycle out of the swamp the next day, I could tell that Harper lied like other people breathe.

I questioned him, "How many motorcycle helmets did you have the evening of the accident?"

Answer: "Just one, my helmet."

Question: "Who was wearing the helmet when you left the bar on your motorcycle?"

Answer: "Olivia."

Question: "Did you secure the helmet strap under her chin?"

Answer: "Yes."

Question: "When you returned the next day to retrieve your motorcycle, did you retrieve your helmet as well?"

Answer: "Yes."

Question: "How could you retrieve your helmet when it was secured to Olivia's head without remembering Olivia was your passenger?"

Answer: Silence…

It would take a long time to recount the many mendacities told by Harper, who was under oath to tell the truth that day, but suffice it to say, everyone there—me, his lawyer, and the court reporter—knew he was a liar of the highest order. The only question left in my mind was: "Was it murder?"

This was a rare case where I found the insurance company lawyer sympathetic to my clients, the young children of Lucas and Olivia. He recommended to the insurance company to pay the maximum amount ($25,000 each) for loss of love and guidance of a mother, even though she may have been a less than good mother. The money was paid to the public trustee to be held until the children turned nineteen years of age, at which time that amount plus interest would be paid to each child.

The happy elements of my life described earlier in this story seemed disconnected from this possible case of murder. However, I couldn't help but think at the time, and even today, about what my life would have been like if my family was visited by tragedy and loss. It was the juxtaposition of these two images when seen close together with contrasting effect that touched me deeply to appreciate and not take for granted what I have.

I never learned much about Olivia, other than that she accepted a ride on the back of a motorcycle with a stranger and ended up dead in a bog. Was it a common occurrence for her to go out to bars and go home with strangers? Maybe it was a unique event, and the only time she displayed what appears to be such poor judgment. Was she a bad mother? Was she negligent? In any event, surely, she did not deserve her untimely death. Did she abandon her family and then die, or did she die, which was the only reason it appeared she had abandoned her family?

A bog is a freshwater wetland of soft, spongy ground consisting mainly of partially decayed plant matter called peat. Bogs have a strong, earthy smell, and the water is dark brown and black. The thick darkness of the water makes it impenetrable by the naked eye, obscuring everything below the surface from sight. It is impossible to see the bottom of a bog. With so many unanswered questions, perhaps the truth is found at the bottom of the bog. This is where they found Olivia.

CHAPTER ELEVEN

Odds and Ends

The law is a delicate balance between the truth and the facts, but also between justice and mercy. At the heart of all legal proceedings are human beings – flawed and funny – dim-witted or shrewd – all with families and jobs and opinions as complicated and varied as the voices of Old Man Coyote – all yelping and shouting and howling and laughing at the same time. Sometimes I feel as perplexed as Peter Rabbit, ears stuck straight up, straining to make sense of the melee of sounds. In this chapter, I present to you an even smaller collection of short, sometimes sweet but always "noisy" stories of the madding crowd. They may not merit their own chapters but they are memorable to me and have provided great material for a clever anecdote over the years.

In the first three condensed stories, I invite you, the reader, to prick up your ears to the many voices you hear and consider how you might solve their problems. Perhaps your powers of discernment can outmatch those of Peter Rabbit.

The pithy passages that follow involve Star Trek, marijuana, barn dances, and kickboxing, further illustrating the multidimensional nature of humanity from the playful and passionate to the farcical and ferocious.

Three Women and One Man

There were three women claiming the estate of one man. The bulk of the estate was a home with a value of one million dollars.

Woman #1 had been married to the man for forty-two years. There were no children from the marriage. The couple retained a lawyer to draft their wills during the marriage, giving everything to each other. The marriage ended in divorce, at which time woman #1 received one half of the family assets.

Woman #2 had commenced a common-law relationship with the man after his divorce, which lasted for six years. They maintained their own homes and separate bank accounts.

At the end of the six-year common-law relationship with woman #2, the man commenced a relationship with woman #3. The man was eighty-two years old at this time and in poor health with rapidly diminishing mental capacity. They maintained their separate homes and bank accounts. After one year, the man required constant care due to his poor health, which woman #3 provided in his home. The man wound up in the hospital. While in critical care due to rapidly advancing cancer, the man proposed marriage to woman #3, which she accepted.

A justice of the peace attended at the hospital for the marriage. She determined that despite his reduced mental capacity, the man did understand what a marriage was. At this point in time, the man and woman #3 had been together for one and a half years. Woman #3 brought two of her friends to witness the wedding. No one else attended. The wedding ceremony was completed.

At no time did the man ever give instructions to his lawyer to draw up a new will after the will giving everything to woman #1.

The man died two weeks after the marriage to woman #3.

At that time, the law provided that a valid marriage revoked any prior wills. (The law has been changed since then, and this is no longer the case.)

Woman #1 had an expert report that the man did not have mental capacity at the time of the marriage to woman #3 to understand what he was doing. The law is clear that there is a very low level of competence necessary to understand that one is getting married. The two witnesses and the justice of the peace had conversations with the man just before the wedding and said he understood he was getting married.

How would you divide the estate between these three women? Please write down the percentage of the estate you would give to each of these women before you proceed any further.

Woman #1 relied on the length of the marriage, forty-two years, and the fact the only will provided that she would inherit the entire estate. She argued the marriage to woman #3 was not valid, as the man did not have the mental capacity to marry. Therefore, she should inherit the entire estate.

Woman #2 relied on the law that a common-law relationship lasting at least two years is considered in law to effectively have the same legal consequences as a legal marriage—and this common-law relationship lasted six years. In addition, she also argued the man did not have the mental capacity to marry, so the estate should be divided equally between her and woman #1.

Woman #3 relied on the law that a valid marriage revoked any prior will, thus it was clear she should inherit the entire estate.

In the end, at a mediation, it was agreed that woman #1 would receive 35% of the estate, woman #2 should receive 5% of the estate, and woman #3 should receive the balance of 60% of the estate. I was acting for woman #3.

A Charity, Three Children, and a Second Wife

Larry married and had three children. After thirty years of marriage, his wife died in a car accident, leaving everything to him. During the marriage, Larry had a will giving everything to his wife, with a gift over to his children equally if his wife predeceased him.

After his wife died, Larry became a daily volunteer at a food kitchen that was funded by the Catholic Church. The food kitchen fed 150 to 200 homeless people who lived on the streets of Langley. Larry felt the food kitchen was very important. He had his lawyer draw up a new will, giving his entire estate to the Catholic Church to be used in the food kitchen. His lawyer advised him of the rights of his children to challenge the will if they felt it did not adequately provide for them, but Larry decided to do it anyway.

The bulk of his estate consisted of his townhouse worth $350,000.

Larry met a woman at the food kitchen. They formed a common-law union and lived together in his townhouse for twelve years until he died. Larry never changed his will; therefore, his will provided that the Catholic Church would inherit his entire estate.

Larry's children commenced a legal action to vary the will, as did his common-law wife.

How would you divide up the estate? Please write down the percentage of the estate you would give to the charity, the three children, and the common-law wife before you proceed any further.

Case law establishes that a husband owes his highest moral duty to his wife, and this includes a common-law wife, and then a lesser moral duty to his children, and finally, an even lower moral duty to a charity. However, the wishes of the testator (the individual who has written a last will and testament) are not to be ignored.

At a mediation, we agreed on 20% to the charity, 30% to the children, and 50% to the second wife. I was acting for the second wife.

Saul, the Police, and the Press

Saul was forty-five years old with a wife and three children: a boy aged fifteen and two girls aged thirteen and ten. With his wife and children, he lived on a large acreage in a rural part of the Fraser Valley, about a two-hour drive east from Vancouver. He was a businessman selling all types of insurance. Sometimes he travelled throughout the Fraser Valley, but often he worked from his home. He was six foot tall, muscular, and weighed 195 pounds. He was a determined individual who believed in his rights and freedoms. He was an excellent husband and father.

His fifteen-year-old son suddenly became rebellious. Saul and his wife thought it was due to their son's relationship with a neighbour of the same age who convinced him to smoke marijuana and watch violent movies. As a precaution and protection, they ordered their son to end all association with the neighbour boy. One night, their son did not come home. Saul and his wife searched in the forest, but could not find him.

The following morning, they discovered their son had slept in the neighbour's trailer along with the neighbour boy he was not allowed to see. Saul went to retrieve his son, but his neighbours, who were offended when they learned he no longer allowed his son to associate with their son, told him to stay off their property. Saul went to the property line and yelled angrily at his son to come home.

When his son appeared, Saul grabbed his jacket by the collar to drag him home. His son pulled free, so he grabbed him by the jacket again, even harder. This caused the neighbour's wife to phone the police and report that the son was being assaulted by his father. She also said Saul had a gun. Ten minutes later, she phoned the police again and retracted her claim about the firearm. She told Saul she had phoned the police and to leave his son alone. Saul dragged him home.

When Saul entered the house, still holding a firm grip on his son, he told his wife about everything that had happened. His wife immediately phoned the police and told them her husband did not assault their son, and everything was fine now as their son was at home. The police asked if her husband had a gun. She responded that he did not. She said they did not have any guns in the house.

The police searched for any record concerning Saul. They discovered that he had never been in trouble with the law in any way before, and they had never been called to his home. There was no record that he had a gun.

Saul had three German shepherds. The police phoned him and told him to secure the dogs, then walk out the front door with his hands in the air. Minutes later he complied while his wife and their three children looked on. Seven officers stood around the yard with their firearms drawn. Some of them shouted for Saul to keep his hands up, while others demanded he drop to the ground. Saul had no idea what to do.

At this point, three officers charged Saul from behind. They knocked him to the ground, pepper-sprayed him, and then put him in a chokehold while they cuffed him behind his back. While Saul was being subdued, other officers entered his home and conducted an extensive search for firearms. They came away empty-handed.

Saul's wife and children were crying as they watched this nightmare unfold.

Saul was informed he was under arrest for assaulting his son, and he was taken to the police station. His son protested, but the officers did not slow down long enough to listen to him or take his statement. He was denying that his father had assaulted him.

Saul ended up behind bars for fifty hours. They said they would not let him out because of the violent nature of his arrest. He was finally released on the condition that he not be alone in the same room with his son.

A few days later, I appeared on his behalf to convince a judge to drop all release conditions, except the standard "be of good behaviour." About a month later, in reviewing the evidence with Crown counsel, it was clear there was no evidence to proceed with the charge, therefore, I obtained a stay of proceedings on the assault charge, which was the only charge against Saul.

Saul was still in disbelief as his only crime was to grab his son by his jacket to bring him home. Over and over in his mind the words repeated: "This can't be happening—I've done nothing wrong."

To make matters worse, the local newspapers portrayed him as a child-beater, and even though he was cleared of any wrongdoing, authorities did not apologize. The stay did nothing to restore Saul's reputation in the community. Despite the assurance of the staff sergeant that police would not discuss the case with the media, the local newspapers reported that Saul had allegedly beaten up his son. A police spokesperson was quoted in the newspaper as saying it was "part of an ongoing problem."

The police reported to the newspaper that "officers acted appropriately and on reasonable grounds at the scene of Saul's arrest. We can't discuss the matter in its entirety, given that he has filed a civil suit against us. One would hope that Saul would allow the legal process to occur and not make comments to the press."

Saul had no intention of keeping quiet. He reported to the press that he lost business because of the false allegations they had published, and that his children were getting heckled by other kids in school. He added that when his son read the newspaper articles, "He looked at me in tears and said, 'We'll sue them.'"

I commenced a civil lawsuit against the police and against the two local newspapers. The defence of the newspapers was that they just repeated what the police told them. However, the newspapers did not contact Saul or his family to obtain his side of the story before repeating the falsehoods told about him by the police.

The police maintained they acted reasonably at all times.

Do you think Saul should succeed in his legal action against the police? If so, what amount would you award as damages?

Do you think Saul should succeed in his legal action against the press? If so, what amount would you award as damages?

Unfortunately, in the end, the plaintiff, exhausted by the mental effort of moving forward with his legal action, gave up. The case never made it to trial. I've always thought we would have recovered approximately one-hundred thousand dollars from the police and two-hundred thousand dollars from the press if we had persevered. Sadly, we will never know.

Crown Counsel Had a Good Laugh

During the first few years of my legal practice, I appeared in every Provincial Court in the Lower Mainland, from Vancouver to Chilliwack, defending criminal cases. At that time, there was a Provincial Court in Langley and White Rock, but these two courtrooms closed years ago. In Provincial Court, it is not necessary to wear a gown like in Supreme Court. It is appropriate to wear a dark suit.

I remember vividly my first appearance in Provincial Court in Burnaby. The courtroom was very odd—unlike any I had seen before. There were no windows to let in natural light except a skylight directly above the bench where the judge sat. The walls were dark, and the courtroom was gloomy with poor lighting. The bench where the judge sat was extraordinarily high.

I was standing beside Crown counsel when the judge entered the courtroom, climbed up the stairs to the high bench, and sat down. At that exact moment, sunshine burst down upon the judge from the overhead skylight. It was as if a shaft of light had come from the heavens, falling upon the judge dressed in black.

I leaned over to Crown counsel and whispered in his ear: "Beam me up, Scotty." He burst out laughing, incurring a critical scowl from the judge high up on the bench obscured in bright light.

Just in case you are too young to have viewed the science fiction television series *Star Trek*, "Beam me up, Scotty," is a catchphrase that made its way into popular culture and originates from the command Captain Kirk gives his chief engineer Montgomery Scott ("Scotty") when he needs to be transported back to the Starship *Enterprise*.

Federal Prosecutions

During the Jean Chrétien and Brian Mulroney era in politics, from 1984 to 2003, whenever Chrétien, "the little guy from Shawinigan," won the election, federal prosecutions were farmed out to Liberal lawyers. Of course, when Mulroney won, Conservative lawyers were awarded the contract.

My partner, John Cherrington, worked in the Conservative Party for many years, forming many friendships with the powers that be in Ottawa. In particular, he worked closely with John Crosbie who was made Justice Minister in the new Mulroney Government. Crosbie sent Cherrington, Easingwood & Kearl an official letter with a copy sent to the courthouse in Langley and Surrey that we would now do all the federal prosecutions in Langley and divide the prosecutions in Surrey with a second Conservative law firm.

I remember the day we walked into the courthouse in Langley to take over. It was hilarious. The in-basket for all future work changed its name from the Liberal lawyers to our law firm. We carried out what some would call "a courtroom coup." We hired two lawyers to do the federal work as the hourly rate of remuneration was very low, but there was a large volume as it involved illegal drug prosecutions.

I only did a few federal drug prosecutions when the lawyers we hired were both sick. One case involved a fellow with a lot of marijuana in his home. Due to this large amount of the drug, we charged the individual with possession for the purpose of trafficking, which would result in a $1,500 fine. His lawyer phoned me to say he needed that much marijuana because he cooked it in his brownies. I checked with the police in the drug squad who confirmed he had brownies filled with marijuana when they made the seizure.

At that time, simple possession of marijuana was illegal. I confirmed with the lawyer that we would take a guilty plea to simple possession, then withdraw the charge of possession for the purpose of trafficking. When the accused showed up in court, he looked so disoriented that the judge would not take his plea as he thought the guy didn't understand what he was doing. A conviction for simple possession of a small amount of marijuana at the time would usually result in a $50 fine. Yet this minor conviction would result in the more serious consequence of being barred from crossing the border into the United States, where they took minor drug convictions much more seriously than in Canada.

We stood the matter down. I spoke with the accused, with the permission of his lawyer, who was present. I determined that his mind was fried by eating too much marijuana over a long period of time. He had no clue what was going on. It was clear the grey matter in his brain was no longer functioning so how could we determine guilt or innocence. I stayed the charge, as it would only be harmful to the individual and the justice system for the case to continue.

My second prosecution involved a man named Dale. Dale was so stupid that he had left six grams of marijuana in a bag in a garbage can in a washroom in the Langley Provincial Courthouse one Friday morning. Attached to the bag was a note indicating money was to be left in the bag. The note was linked to Dale, who was arrested on a charge of possession for the purpose of trafficking.

Idiot Dale pleaded guilty. Dale had a lengthy criminal record. The judge was not amused by a drug deal at the courthouse, so he sentenced him to nine months in jail! The judge commented on the stupidity of the incident and made a remark about Dale's audacity. I had only asked for the usual sentence, a fine of $1,500 and one day in jail. The defence lawyer was astounded. So was I. We had never seen anyone go to jail for nine months for this type of offence. The sentence was overruled on appeal, and my suggestion of a $1,500 fine with one day in jail replaced the nine-month sentence.

My third case involved a serious drug prosecution. Unfortunately, the lawyer we hired to do the drug trials was sick. We didn't have another lawyer available, so I had to go. The case involved a gang bringing cocaine into British Columbia from El Salvador. When one of the members of the gang was caught with the drugs, he decided to make a deal to become an informer and snitch on the other members of the gang. The RCMP had the stool-pigeon hidden somewhere in the province, but no one knew where. They would whisk him in to the Supreme Courthouse in New Westminster only when he was about to give his evidence.

The courtroom was secured, as anyone entering had to pass through metal detectors, and in addition, members of the RCMP were strategically positioned. These drug dealers looked just like what you see in the movies, with violently ugly tattoos all over their arms and faces and many body piercings—and not just from the ears and nose. These were drug dealers who had no respect for life. They would kill anyone at the drop of a hat. When they brought the squealer in, I made sure I stayed far away from the witness box, close to the side wall, as I conducted the examination-in-chief where I questioned the witness so they could give a clear account of what took place. I made sure to never get between the witness and the gallery, so I would not be in the line of fire.

They all got seven to ten years in jail. I never want to see guys that ugly ever again.

Barn Dance

The survival of a country barn dance planned for the weekend was hanging in the balance as I battled with lawyers for the Township of Langley in BC Supreme Court over whether or not the event could take place. More than 2,500 people had purchased tickets for the great hoedown with three famous country bands ready to go. The organizers had spent $20,000 by the time Langley went to court to obtain an injunction in an attempt to put an end to the event.

The organizers were quoted in the local papers saying: "It's a great community event, and it's being completely squashed by Langley Township."

The main issue was safety. "The building was designed for agricultural, and it's being used for non-agricultural use," the lawyer for the Township explained just before the hearing commenced in court. The lawyers proceeded to clarify that "the Township did not approve the event because the organizers have not met requirements regarding zoning, building codes, and safety and fire issues."

I was described as a Fort Langley lawyer and quoted as saying: "My clients have come face to face with massive bureaucracy." I expounded further, "A barn dance doesn't breach agricultural zoning, there's parking in the field, and it's a one-time charitable event that doesn't require a business licence. All proceeds from the event will go to Basics for Babies. Does the Township not care about babies?"

But there was no negotiating with City Hall. After learning a fire inspector wouldn't pass the huge barn and stables for the event, the organizers met with Township staff and were told the Township felt the event was unsafe.

In court, I argued the barn could be emptied in two minutes as there were three large doors. In addition, the organizers had insurance and a liquor licence for the event. There would be security on site, and there was emergency lighting. "And if there is no barn dance, there is no money for the babies," I contended.

Sympathy was on my side, but you know what they say: "You can't fight City Hall," meaning it is foolish to fight a battle you can't win against the faceless, nameless, and soulless white shirts called bureaucrats. The BC Supreme Court judge backed the Township of Langley. My client was quoted in the newspapers saying, "I've basically lost my confidence in municipal bureaucracy."

The reporters gave me the final word: "It's a big shame: no barn dance, no money for charity and the children, and in addition, the loss of a good, foot-stomping hoedown, which would have been fun for everyone."

Kickboxing

Kickboxing in North America is a blend of boxing and karate. It strictly prohibits strikes with anything but the hands and feet. Attacking an opponent's groin, legs, or back is off-limits.

I learned these facts as I prepared to attend a match, ring side, with my wife at a large venue for thousands of kickboxing fans in Vancouver. My client was the Kickboxing Champion of the World. His sponsor was afraid a competitor claiming to be the kickboxing champion of the world was in the process of obtaining an injunction to stop the championship match. I was given two coveted ring side seats, so that if an order of the court was served at the event, I could determine, in my legal opinion, whether the event could proceed.

The kickboxing ring was just like any boxing ring with a square, raised platform and a post at each corner. Four ropes were attached to the posts and pulled parallel under tension to form the boundary for the fight.

There were three preliminary fights before the main bout. It was brutal. I regretted being there, let alone bringing my wife to such a violent event. What was I thinking? There were only three rounds to each fight, but it never lasted that long. One of the combatants would be kicked in the head, knocked out, and then dragged out of the ring on a stretcher, blood gushing from his nose and mouth, before the end of the second round.

I still remember the smell. There is no doubt that stink is a weapon. I don't think they washed their shorts before the fight, and they must have trained in them too. The stench was overwhelming, as some of the fighters defecated in their shorts during the match.

The sound was just as overwhelming. I would describe the noise of the impact between the fist and jaw or the foot and gut as crack, wack, and thump, while the sounds of the voices in the ring were like the growling of a pack of wolves on the hunt. After the landing of blows, we heard sounds like the whine and murmur of an injured animal caught in a leg-hold trap.

There were people hyping up the crowd into a furious frenzy. Thousands of people in the stands were in a tumult and uproar. The best words to describe the atmosphere of the crowd was grotesquely brutal, like when the Christians were thrown to the lions in the Coliseum in Rome.

It definitely was a sad, sad sight—so sad that a compassionate person would scream with anguish amid all the shouting. Even the T-shirts were graphic, with words printed on them like "Built For Violence," or "Heathen By Nature."

Body fluids flew by us on the front row—blood and saliva, splashing and splattering on the fans behind us. I could see them wince as they unexpectedly touched and tasted some of the fallout of each brawl.

The whole scene caused a loss of my sense of balance, and I seemed unable to understand where my head and body were in space. Thankfully, the pathetic panorama before us was almost over.

The championship match involved five rounds. The competitors were more cautious, just feeling each other out, until the final round. At that point, my client performed a powerful back kick into the stomach of his opponent. The poor guy never got up. I am sure he was transported directly to the hospital, never to fight again.

The referee lifted my client's right arm high into the air, declaring him to be the Kickboxing Champion of the World. An injunction to stop the proceedings was never delivered, but my wife and I were clearly of the opinion that it would not take an injunction to stop us from ever attending a kickboxing fight again.

CHAPTER TWELVE:

Was the Gift Perfected?

Ivan and Olga Ivanov lived in Minsk, the capital and largest city of Belarus. The region was annexed by the Russian Empire in 1793; subsequently, it formed part of the Soviet Union after the Russian Revolution. (In 1991, during the dissolution of the Soviet Union, Belarus declared independence. By that time, Olga and Ivan were no longer living there, but they enthusiastically applauded the breakup of the Soviet Union from their Fraser Valley home in British Columbia, where they had fled many years earlier)

Belarus means "White Russia," a name derived from the fact this is the one part of Russia that was never settled by the Mongols in 1240. Therefore, "white" refers to the "purity" of the people who never intermarried with the Mongol Hordes.

Olga and Ivan loved Belarus' natural beauty, with its many lakes, virgin forests, and variety of rare plant species. However, there were few opportunities to work their way to prosperity. Economic growth was anemic due to the inefficient, state-run industries imposed by the Soviet-era economy.

Olga hated to leave Minsk, as each week she attended the Church of St. Mary Magdalene, a Russian Orthodox Church. She placed her faith in God, while her husband relied more on hard work. He insisted they had to escape to Canada in order to build a family that could enjoy the fruits of their labours. Ivan was ambitious. His greatest desire was to own a home and build a business that would provide prosperity to his family for generations.

Ivan loved the forests of Belarus, which was the reason he was drawn to the temperate rainforest of British Columbia, with its magnificent mountains, lakes, and rivers. It was the perfect home. He researched the prospects available in this free and growing land of opportunity and convinced Olga it should be the place to start their family. In addition, he was able to demonstrate to her it was the place that God wanted them to flee to, and she could choose which church they would attend: the Saint Nicholas Russian Orthodox Church, the Holy Resurrection Russian Orthodox Sobor, or the Russian Orthodox Holy Trinity Church, all located in Vancouver.

Olga was finally ready. They had been preparing for many years, sewing all their savings into their clothes. They crossed the border into Poland in the late 1950s, and then made their way to Germany. From there, they obtained permission to immigrate to Canada.

Ivan and Olga arrived in the Fraser Valley with next to nothing. Ivan immediately started a concrete business, mixing concrete by hand. All he needed was gravel and sand, cement powder, a shovel, water, and his muscles. In no time, he could afford a portable concrete mixer and then concrete-mixing trucks. Eventually, he built a large industrial concrete mixer. The business was growing rapidly as there was a great deal of growth in the Valley. The family was also growing, as Ivan and Olga had two sons, Alex and Pavel, and a daughter, Anastasia.

The boys worked long, hard hours of manual labour with their father, before and after school, building up the business. When they graduated from high school, they worked full time with their father. The concrete industry continued to expand until they owned one of the most successful concrete companies in British Columbia. Ivan had achieved his dream of owning a business that would provide prosperity to his children and his grandchildren and continue on for generations. As part of his plan to ensure his family's success, he transferred an equal number of shares in the company to each of his sons. Now Ivan and his sons, Alex and Pavel, were equal shareholders and equal owners of the concrete business.

In addition, Olga and Ivan owned their own lovely home on a picturesque acreage. It was everything Olga ever wanted. She felt that God had blessed her and her family. She was grateful. She expressed her gratitude every night in her prayers and every week when she and Ivan went to church.

Time passed by quickly as Ivan continued to work incredibly hard. Ivan was getting older, and as he aged, he worried about providing equal benefits to his daughter, Anastasia. Therefore, he instructed his lawyer to transfer an equal number of shares in the concrete company to her. When he informed his sons of his idea, they disagreed with transferring any shares to their sister, since they felt they had done all the work with their father to build up the business. By now, they had children of their own, and eventually they wanted to pass the business on to them. Three months passed since their conversation, but Ivan did not go into the lawyer's office to sign the transfer papers. Then unexpectedly and suddenly, Ivan had a heart attack and died.

Anastasia commenced a lawsuit against her brothers, seeking a declaration that the share transfer be perfected by the Supreme Court. She was represented by a large law firm in Vancouver, with a senior lawyer who was renowned for his formidable cross-examination skills. The junior lawyer who graduated in the same class as I did at UBC, had an arrogant personality. The sole issue in this case was whether the father intended to perfect the gift to his daughter, despite his sons' objections, but only failed to do so because of his untimely death.

I acted for Pavel, the younger son. An elderly lawyer from the valley acted for Alex, the older brother. Whenever I met with this elderly lawyer to plan our strategy, he was in his office playing poker, drinking Johnnie Walker Blue Label Whiskey, and smoking big cigars. I didn't mind the poker or the whiskey, but the cigar smoke made me sick, so I gave up trying to coordinate our defence. I would just go it alone.

The first witness at the trial was Anastasia. I had carefully prepared a cross-examination, but I knew it would be difficult as she was a smart lady. Usually it takes about three hours of preparation for every hour of cross-examination, but I decided to keep my examination short—hopefully to only half an hour. I had an unusual strategy in mind.

There are two cardinal rules all lawyers know they should not violate during cross-examination:
1. Ask a question to which they do not know the answer, and
2. Ask questions that allow the witness to repeat their evidence, which only serves to cement it in the mind of the judge.

My unusual strategy was to break cardinal rule number 2.

For about half an hour, I asked a series of questions that allowed Anastasia to repeat the evidence she had given during the questions posed by her own lawyer. Sitting beside me on my left was the arrogant junior lawyer, whom I could hear scoffing at my seemingly inept cross-examination. The senior lawyer was quiet. No doubt he had experienced many wins and many losses, leaving him humbler. I continued with easy statements about the character of her father, to which she readily agreed. Finally, I asked, "So your father was the type of person, that if he decided to do something, he would do it?"

She answered, "Yes." I sat down.

The junior lawyer was now red-faced as he realized where I had just led the witness. It was to the very central point of the litigation. If the father intended to perfect the gift, he would have done so. The fact that he had not gone to the lawyer's office to sign the papers to transfer the shares was evidence that he did not intend to give Anastasia the shares in the face of his sons' objections.

After all the evidence and legal arguments of a ten-day trial, the judge decided the case on that very point—since the father was the type of person who acted on his intentions without delay, and he did not perfect the gift in over three months, he clearly did not intend to do so. It was a win for the sons. The gift was not perfected. The sons now owned the company.

Usually any family company begins to decline with the third generation, as they are raised in a life of ease and no longer see the need for hard work. However, in this case, the third generation has carried on with the vision of their grandfather, Ivan, and even expanded it. They have invested in the latest technology, worked hard to increase productivity, and the company is more successful than ever. Whenever I talk with the grandchildren, they speak with awe in regard to their grandfather who came to British Columbia with nothing, and then accomplished everything through hard work. I think it is his example and spirit that keep them on the right track.

A number of years later, Olga transferred land to Anastasia to ensure that she received equal treatment. Anastasia was anxious to be treated equally, and in the end, she was.

CHAPTER THIRTEEN

A Modern Legal Don Quixote

During the first few years of my legal practice, I acted on a small number of family law cases. For instance, I completed a custody trial in Supreme Court in the New Westminster courthouse. In those days, there was a significant bias in favour of the mother, especially if the child was very young. In those circumstances, it would be necessary for a father to show that his wife was an unfit mother in order for him to gain custody. This was a heavy onus to overcome. I was acting for the mother seeking custody of a baby girl. My client was an excellent mother. Winning this case would be as easy as falling off a log, and it was. Today, with so much emphasis on equality, it would not be so easy. The courts now treat men equally with women.

The interesting aftermath of my only custody trial is that twenty years later I acted for that baby girl in a personal injury claim when she was injured in a motor vehicle accident. It was perplexing to think about how time had passed by so quickly. The baby girl was now an adult, and her mother would soon be a grandma.

In those early days of my career, we had to attend court to obtain uncontested divorces. Once a month I would appear in court to obtain four or five of them. (Now they are done by desk order, so there is no need to appear in court). We would have to ask three questions of the person seeking the divorce: 1. Has there been any collusion? 2. Has there been any connivance? and 3. Has there been a condonation? I would explain what these questions meant to my clients, but it was often difficult for them to remember, so I would tell them to just say "no" to the three questions with the three big words beginning with "c."

I have a vivid recollection of one of these divorces as I represented a man named Jekyll, and we happened to appear in front of Mr. Justice Hyde, who was well known for his sense of humour. He leaned over the bench toward me and said: "Mr. Kearl, is this the strange case of Dr. Jekyll and Mr. Hyde?" Everyone in the courtroom burst out laughing, including the judge.

I did act on behalf of a car dealer whose wife was an emergency room nurse. The marriage lasted about fifteen years, and they did not have any children. They kept separate bank accounts. The only issue was if the car dealership would be divided equally. It was acquired during the marriage, which meant it certainly was a family asset.

I argued that since the husband had supported his wife to train as a nurse, and he would not be receiving any monetary value for the support he provided for her career, then the wife should not receive an equal amount for the car dealership, which he had built up on his own. The lawyer for the wife was an experienced family law specialist. I rarely did family law. I was fortunate to obtain a 70/30 distribution. The 30% of the car dealership going to the wife was valued at $330,000, which was quite the sum back then.

Even though I had taken on very few family law cases, I had positive results. The next case is the reason I never acted on a family law case again.

A young lady came into my office on a Friday morning. She told me that her husband had chopped down the door to their apartment with an axe and left the axe under her mattress. Fortunately, she was not home at the time. Her voice was thick with fear, and she was shaking like a leaf. She was in a complete state of panic. Luckily, they did not have any children. She described the argument they had the day before, which resulted in her husband leaving. It was violent.

Violence in this relationship was not an isolated event. The young lady disclosed a history of violent behaviour on the part of her husband. However, the ferocity had never been raised to this level before. She was terrified that her life was in danger.

I dropped everything. I drafted the necessary affidavit and other legal papers necessary to obtain a restraining order. I rushed to the courthouse in New Westminster on Friday afternoon to obtain the order. I provided a certified copy of the order to the police. I felt like Don Quixote, chivalrous and an idealist, but as it turned out, I was unrealistic.

A few weeks later, when I hadn't heard from the young lady, I called her to explain what we needed to do to proceed with the divorce. To my absolute surprise and horror, she instructed me not to proceed with the divorce as she was back together with her husband. I was incredulous. Why would she return to him?

I was an inexperienced lawyer. I didn't know anything about battered wife syndrome. We didn't really know much about it back then. Later, I learned it is considered a category of post-traumatic stress disorder where the woman develops a learned helplessness that causes her to believe she deserves the abuse and can't get away from it. The young lady fit the cycle of abuse. She described how her husband engaged in behaviours that created tension in the relationship. He would then explode, committing physical and emotional abuse. Lastly, he would try to fix his wrongdoing and apologize with flowers.

At the time, I did not feel I had failed the poor woman, but I thought she had failed me. How could she go back after everything I had done for her? I quickly determined the raw emotions and volatility involved in family law would be more than I could handle. It would take too much of a mental toll on me. It was too emotionally taxing.

I hope the poor woman finally received counselling from an experienced therapist in this area. Perhaps she has overcome the denial, guilt, and belief that she caused the abuse. With the right help, she will understand that she didn't deserve the abuse and realize that her husband has an abusive personality. I imagine she came to recognize that her husband was responsible, leading her to escape the relationship. I don't know, because I never saw her again.

CHAPTER FOURTEEN

The End of the Road

The largest case I handled in my career, from a strictly monetary point of view, was a construction matter for one of the largest road builders in British Columbia that involved $55 million. John, the owner of the company, placed a bid with the Provincial Government for a road maintenance contract on Vancouver Island. One of his competitors, who had bid on the project, alleged a conflict in the bidding process that would disqualify John's company and give the contract to the competitor.

It was a spurious allegation, but the competitor brought an application to the Supreme Court in Vancouver to disqualify John's winning bid. I had to delay our annual family holiday to visit Mom and Dad as well as my two brothers in Calgary to argue the case. I learned of the win as I was skimming down the water slides at our hotel in Salmon Arm with my wife and our four kids. We were having a wonderful time, and this happy news added greatly to the boundless energy we felt gliding down the slides.

Perhaps this explains why John retained me to act on his behalf involving a dispute with the Federal Government. The claim was for extra expenses amounting to slightly over one million dollars in connection with certain road works on Haida Gwaii, formerly the Queen Charlotte Islands. Since the contract was with the Federal Government, we proceeded against Her Majesty the Queen, in the Federal Court of Canada—Trial Division in Vancouver.

The Federal Court's jurisdiction includes Aboriginal law, maritime and admiralty law, citizenship, immigration and refugee law, as well as civil lawsuits against the Federal Government, like my road construction case. The Federal Court's main office is in Ottawa, but it sits throughout the country. The Federal Court consists of a chief justice and thirty-six other judges, and the Federal Court of Appeal consists of a chief justice and twelve other judges. The judge for our case flew out from Ottawa.

The Federal Government required an upgrade and new construction of approximately 8.3 kilometres of road to access a radar site at Cumshewa on the Islands of Haida Gwaii in Northern British Columbia. Haida Gwaii literally means "islands of the Haida people." The island archipelago forms the heartland of the Haida Nation, upon which people have lived for 13,000 years. Haida Gwaii consists of two main islands: Graham Island in the north and Moresby Island or Gwaay Haanas, meaning "Islands of Beauty" in the south, along with approximately four hundred smaller islands. Haida are Indigenous people who have traditionally occupied the coastal bays and inlets of Haida Gwaii.

Cumshewa (meaning "rich at the mouth of the river") is a village of the Haida people located on Cumshewa Inlet on Moresby

Island. It is named for Cumshewa, an important Haida chief. Cumshewa is a remote location. The quickest way to get there is by airplane from Vancouver to Sandspit, and then by four-wheel drive to Cumshewa.

The government hired an engineer who had two years to produce plans and specifications for the construction of the road. The plans included 241 cross-sectional drawings indicating the assumed depth of stripping required to expose material suitable for the construction of the roadway, as well as a volume overhaul diagram, which set out the cuts and fills necessary to construct the road. The volume overhaul diagram gave critical information about the cost to build the road, as it indicated how much material had to be cut from the high points and how far that material had to be hauled to the low points to even out the rugged terrain so a road could be built.

John only had a short time to tender a bid on the lump sum contract. He sent two men to do an inspection. It took all day just to get there. The next day, they drove a four-wheel drive up the part of the logging road that would need an upgrade and then walked up to the area of land that would become a new road leading directly to the radar site. They did not have the heavy equipment necessary to dig under the surface of the logging road.

John did not have the time to engineer the road. He relied on the information provided by the government—the cross-sectional drawings and the volume overhaul diagram—in making his bid. The engineer for the government had two years to prepare this information.

From the cross-sectional drawings, John assumed the average depth of excavation would be approximately 0.5 metres. From the volume overhaul diagram, John calculated the distances the material from the cut sections would have to be hauled to fill sections. Unfortunately, John won the bid.

It was a logistical nightmare to get all the machinery necessary to build a road to the remote radar site at Cumshewa. A much greater problem arose when they started to dig up the logging road to make the upgrade. It became obvious that the original logging road had been constructed with stumps and logging debris covered with dirt. On this base, a corduroy technique was deployed whereby logs were laid perpendicular to the road alignment at intervals and covered with gravel. Instead of stripping off 0.5 metres as assumed by the cross-sectional drawings, it was necessary to dig out waste material as deep as four to eight metres. We had photographs of backhoes disappearing into these holes as if they were digging all the way to China.

Since the stripping operations had to go much deeper than foreseen, this resulted in greatly increased stripping volumes; the stripping waste could no longer be side-cast, but had to be hauled away to distant waste dumps. All of this caused huge cost overruns.

A clause in the contract provided for a claim for increased compensation above the original bid, if there was a change in soil conditions. Notice was given to make this claim. John completed the contract and finished constructing the road, but the government refused to pay the increased compensation. I commenced an action for breach of contract, and in the alternative, negligent misrepresentation.

In my view, the clause in the contract that provided compensation for a change in soil conditions was written for situations just like this case. It was a lump sum contract; therefore, this clause was designed to remedy the situation where there was a substantial change in soil conditions unforeseen by the parties.

In the alternative, the government provided the cross-sectional drawings and a volume overhaul diagram to John. Therefore, it must have known these specifications would be relied upon, even though the documents referred to "assumed rock lines" and "assumed" stripping depths.

The trial judge disagreed. He cited the definition of soil from the dictionary where soil was defined as being "derived from disintegrated rock, broken down over geological ages by the action of weather and water." To the trial judge, soil did not include logging debris. I was incredulous. The clause in the contract stated a "change in soil conditions." Instead of dirt, there were stumps mixed with dirt. Isn't that a change in soil conditions? Don't stumps and logging debris decompose to become part of the soil? Doesn't this mean that soil is not just broken-down rock?

The lawyer for the government had told me he would successfully defend the case based on photographic evidence, taken before the road construction commenced, that displayed logs and logging debris clearly visible on the side of the upgrade section of the road. I didn't think this was evidence of what was under the road. In my view these photographs were irrelevant.

In the end, the government lawyer established the defence that John should have undertaken his own subsurface investigation in light of what was visible on the site. I didn't think this would win the day because the government had hired, at great expense, an engineering company to provide the engineering for the road. It had taken two years to prepare the engineering drawings and specifications. John did not have sufficient time to prepare new engineering specifications, as it could not be done in two weeks.

Sadly, the trial judge ruled that John could not rely on the change of soil conditions in the contract, or on the 241 cross-sectional drawings, or the volume overhaul diagram. Consequently, the action was dismissed.

We appealed to the Federal Court of Appeal. I felt confident we would succeed. Three years later, I was in front of the three judges of the Appeal Court. They seemed to understand my argument. They seemed to agree with my submissions. However, a month later, they rendered written reasons for judgment dismissing the appeal. It was a great disappointment. There was no use seeking leave to appeal to the Supreme Court of Canada, as this case did not have national importance, therefore, leave would never be granted. We had come to the end of the road, so to speak.

CHAPTER FIFTEEN

The Tongan

Kaivai Tukuafu's greatest dream was to touch snow. He yearned to let the delicate crystals melt in his hands and mouth. He longed to roll around in the snow and swing his arms and legs to make snow angels, just like he had seen in a movie. He wanted to pack some snow into a ball with his hands to throw in a huge snowball fight with numerous friends, snowballs flying in every direction. He imagined himself building a snow fort where he could retreat to make more snowballs to ready himself for another attack. He would even make-believe that he could build an igloo like the Inuit peoples traditionally did in the Canadian Arctic as he had viewed in a documentary.

The dream also placed him on a mountain in a blizzard with high winds, the snow swirling around his head so thick that all he could see was white, and he was left groping and floundering. It was clean and pure. It was blindingly bright. It was light he could not see.

In addition, he thought about the silence of the snow; walking quietly in the soft white powder, each snowflake with a unique design falling slowly, silently as if he were walking in a long-awaited reverie. Snow never fell on their island, as the average temperature in winter was 23°C (73°F) and in summer, 28°C (82°F). The temperature was always warm or hot.

Kaivai, meaning "mariner," was from a tiny fishing village by the sea in Tonga, where they could only imagine snow, having never seen it. As his name implied, he was from a long line of fishermen. His father was a fisherman; his grandfather was a fisherman; they had all been fishermen in his family as far back as anyone could remember.

Tonga is the only Polynesian kingdom in the Pacific since Taufa'ahau in 1875 declared itself a constitutional monarchy. Tonga was united under one chief in 1845. This must have been quite an achievement, because the mostly flat limestone islands are scattered over 700,000 square kilometres of the southern Pacific Ocean, which is about the size of British Columbia. The archipelago is also known as the "Friendly Islands," comprising 176 islands. Thirty-six of these are inhabited.

In school, Kaivai learned all these details about Tonga. He spoke the two official languages: Tongan and English. He knew the country's population was only 100,000 inhabitants. His family lived near the capital city Nuku'alofa on the nation's main island of Tongatapu in the village of Tatakamotonga on the eastern side of the lagoon of Tongatapu. For generations his family fished all year round in the crystal-clear waters for blue, black, or striped marlin, sailfish, mahi-mahi, big yellow fin tuna, and wahoo. They also cast their jigs for predators like blue fin and giant trevally, occasionally catching a shark.

The family home was comfortable, but somewhat crowded, as Kaivai lived with his mom and dad, four brothers, and three sisters. At twenty-one, he was the third oldest and still single. His two older brothers were married, but they still lived at home. The family just built an extra room onto the home for each of them.

Everyone in the family was large. They lived by the Tongan motto, "The bigger you are, that's beauty." Kaivai was the size of an offensive lineman in the National Football League, six-foot-four-inches tall and 310 pounds of thick muscle. He looked rather handsome with his long, full, wavy black hair, dark eyebrows and lashes, and warm brown skin. His face was heart shaped, broad across the forehead and then narrowing down to the chin. It was safe to say that he had a fine-looking face.

What was even more appealing was the glow emanating from his face. His kind of enthusiasm was contagious. He seemed to emit visible light, especially from his dark hazel-coloured eyes. The power of his voice was like the haka, a ceremonial dance in Maori culture performed with vigorous movements, stamping of the feet, and rhythmically shouted battle cries.

Kaivai planned on getting married to his childhood sweetheart, Saofa'i, who was the love of his life. He could not remember a time when she was not his best friend. They grew up together in the little fishing village.

The only time they had been separated was when he was on a mission on behalf of his Christian Church where he had been preaching the Gospel of Jesus Christ across the many Tongan Islands. He felt it was a great honour to represent Jesus. The main theme of his teaching was the love of Heavenly Father for all of His children and the love of the Saviour, Jesus Christ, for all the people of the earth. He had been taught Bible stories about the life of Jesus from the time he was a little boy. His favourite parables were "The Prodigal Son" and "The Good Samaritan." He taught that Jesus was the Good Samaritan, who would heal all wounds and pay the price to save every soul, as he was filled with mercy, forgiveness, and love. He had great faith in Jesus.

Having just returned from his mission, his plan was to visit a Tongan friend, Ruataata, in Richmond, British Columbia in December, where they would travel to the mountains nearby to achieve his dream of touching snow. When he returned home, he would marry Saofa'i and start a family. He believed strongly in love and marriage.

It was difficult to save enough money to purchase a flight to Vancouver, as Kaivai did not earn much money in Tonga. However, he didn't need a lot of money, as he ate the fish he caught from the sea and the vegetables his mother harvested year-round from her large garden beside their home.

In order to earn the money he needed, he took tourists fishing. Kaivai knew all the good fishing spots, and the tourists were very generous after taking photos of themselves with all the big fish they had caught. In a couple of months, he managed to save enough for a one-way ticket to Vancouver as well as a little spending money while he was there. Ruataata would take care of the rest, as he was in a position to earn a lot more money than anyone in Tonga—at least anyone that Kaivai knew.

Ruataata had married an adorable woman from Canada and had become a Canadian citizen. He and his wife, Catherine, lived in their own home, which was much larger than anything in Kaivai's little fishing village. His friend told him he would pay for the ticket home. Kaivai would stay with him and his wife in their home, and they would provide for all the food. It was the Tongan way, a very generous way of life.

All Kaivai brought with him on the flight was a small suitcase with some clothes and a little bit of cash. He knew that Ruataata would take care of the rest. During the flight, there was a minor mechanical problem, which resulted in the airplane making an unexpected landing in Hawaii, where they were forced to stay for the night. There was a woman on the plane with three small children who did not have enough money to pay for a hotel room, so Kaivai gave her all his money.

The Tongan culture rejects materialism. It was natural for Kaivai to give his money to this woman who needed it more than he did. If someone had told him they liked his watch, he would have given it away. It was part of his Tongan upbringing. He slept on the floor in the airport.

The next day the airplane landed at the Vancouver International Airport, which is located on Sea Island in Richmond, British Columbia. Ruataata was there to pick him up, but Kaivai never made it through customs. When the customs official asked him if he had a return ticket to Tonga, Kaivai answered he did not. When they asked him how much money he had, he answered he didn't have any money. When they searched his small suitcase, all they found were a few clothes. The Canadian officials formed the opinion that he was not a bona fide visitor to Canada, but a person seeking illegal entry into the country. He was sent to the lock-up, which was a small jail cell at the immigration office in Vancouver.

This is when I entered the story. I knew Ruataata and Catherine. They gave me a call, explaining all the details of Kaivai coming to Canada. I had never had an immigration case, and this would be the only one I would ever have in my career, but I thought it was a simple issue: Was Kaivai a bona fide visitor to Canada? The first step was to go and see Kaivai.

When I arrived at the immigration office, the guards described their experience with Kaivai. When they searched this giant of a man, he meekly submitted to their every request. They knew he could have thrown them around like a bunch of rag dolls. When they locked him in his jail cell, he began to pray to His Heavenly Father in the name of Jesus Christ to deliver him from bondage.

He prayed out loud in a powerful, but deeply sympathetic voice. It was a kind of voice and prayer they had never heard before. It felt like he was talking with God, who was with him in his cell.

Throughout the night when he wasn't praying, he was singing hymns of praise to God. The immigration officials were moved to tears as they had never experienced anything like this before. They felt as if his songs rose to heaven where they were received with joy by the angels. When he sang "Guide Me O Thou Great Jehovah," it seemed like the entire prison reverberated with the sound of his voice.

The prison guards became emotional as they described their unique experience with "The Tongan," as they called him. The climax came as the Tongan sang "Amazing Grace." The guards knew at that point that the Tongan knew Jesus. He didn't just talk about him, he knew Him. It was their greatest desire that he be released. They were glad I had come to get him out of that jail cell. The guard unlocked the door, and I entered into what the guards had called, "holy ground."

The Tongan towered above me. My whole body would fit into one of his shoulders. He lifted me off the ground with a firm, but gentle hug. Now I knew what the guards meant as I felt encircled by the love of Jesus while he held me. He put me down. He said: "Jesus has sent you to deliver me from this jail." I was overwhelmed. As soon as I got control of my emotions, we sat down on the small cot in his room to get his story. I took careful notes, but I would not need them, as I would remember every detail, since it was emblazoned in my memory. We were together for about two hours.

I needed to leave, as I had to arrange for a hearing before a judge to determine if the Tongan was a true visitor to Canada. If it was determined he was attempting to enter Canada illegally, he would immediately be sent back to Tonga without achieving his dream of touching snow. The earlier I could set the court case, the better, as he had already lost two days of his two-week vacation. I reserved a time for the next day. The Tongan was ready to testify. Catherine and Ruataata were prepared to appear on his behalf. I was ready, but I felt a great deal of pressure.

I am always anxious when I appear in court, as my client is depending on me to win. In court, there is nowhere to hide. I must stand in front of the judge and plead my client's case. The stress is extreme just before I start to talk, but once I commence with my opening statement, I always swell with confidence as the words I have prepared and repeated in my head many times simply flow out of me. The anxiety was even higher in this case, as the Tongan told me I was "an instrument in the hands of God" to secure his release. He knew Jesus had sent me.

I believed everything the Tongan told me. Who wouldn't? He had such honest faith. The next day, I returned for the hearing. We appeared before the judge. The lawyer for the Federal Government sought to adjourn the case, so he could gather more evidence. I insisted on the urgency of proceeding immediately, given the limited time Kaivai had to visit Canada. Thankfully, the judge did not grant an adjournment, and the trial went ahead.

I called Kaivai Tukuafu to the stand. He was sworn in. I had him give his background regarding his family in Tonga, his life as a fisherman, and his time as a Christian missionary, and tell the judge about Saofa'I, whom he would marry on his return to Tonga. He produced a photo of his family and Saofa'i, which I handed to the clerk to give to the judge. I could see the judge studying the photos, thinking the Tongan had every reason to return home.

I had Kaivai explain in great detail his reason for coming to Canada—his dreams about touching snow. Studying the face of the judge as the Tongan spoke, I thought he understood.

The next part of the story we needed to cover was why Kaivai didn't have any money, and how he had given it all away to the woman with three small children at the airport in Hawaii. We also needed to explain why he only had a one-way ticket to Canada and not a return flight, as his good friend, originally from Tonga, would take care of purchasing the ticket for his return home and provide him with food and any money he would need during his stay in Canada.

I had Kaivai explain why he brought so few clothes, as Catherine had promised him that she would take him shopping to buy some clothes from British Columbia to take home with him. It would be exciting to be seen back in his fishing village with clothes from Canada.

I don't think anyone would not have believed the Tongan. Even the cross-examination by the government lawyer was feeble and sounded hollow. Still I had to be sure to win, so I called Catherine and then Ruataata to confirm the Tongan's story. These were solid Canadian citizens with good jobs. Also of importance, they owned their own home in Richmond.

I told the judge I had no further witnesses. The lawyer for the government did not call any witnesses. I summarized my case, emphasizing the critical point—this would be Kaivai Tukuafu's only opportunity to touch snow, as he would never again be able to afford to return to Canada. In my submissions to the judge I said: "The fulfillment of his dreams lies in your hands." After which, the judge smiled at Kaivai Tukuafu and declared: "I find that you are a bona fide visitor to Canada. You are free to go."

A great smile broke across the Tongan's face. He turned to me saying, "I knew Jesus had sent you to free me, thank you." He gave me another one of those hugs where he lifted me effortlessly off the ground. Remember I am only five-foot-seven-inches tall, so I disappeared into his massive arms. It was a loving hug I will always remember.

Just before the Tongan left for home, he told me about his dreams being fulfilled when he touched snow for the first time. The day after his release, Catherine and Ruataata took him up the gondola at Grouse Mountain. It was a sunny, clear day. High above towering Douglas firs, he described the breathtaking views of the City of Vancouver, Stanley Park, the sparkling Pacific Ocean, Gulf Islands, and most of all, the snowy peaks unfolding as he journeyed up the mountainside. When he reached the top he rushed forward to touch the snow. He found an area where the snow lay undisturbed, clean and pure. He touched the snow. He held it, as it melted in his hands. He let some melt in his mouth. He made a snowball and threw it at Catherine. She cried out, "I've been hit." Ruataata and Catherine made snowballs, hitting Kaivai many times. He loved it. It was everything he dreamed it would be.

The next day, they visited Mt. Seymour. It was a cloudy day with the snow falling softly. He tried to study each snowflake, as he thought it was a miracle of nature that each one was unique. He thought it was like the people of the earth, millions upon millions of them, but no two were the same. Yet Jesus loved them all. It was a spiritual moment walking quietly in the soft, white powder, as if in a dream.

Ruataata and Catherine shook him out of his dream when they took him tobogganing. It couldn't have been more exhilarating enjoying the excitement of tobogganing in the snow. It was also amazing to watch the people skiing and snowboarding. Kaivai marvelled at how the vegetation was green down in Vancouver and Richmond, while it was all white with snow on the North Shore Mountains, just a thirty-five-minute drive away.

The third trip to the North Shore Mountains was to Cypress Bowl, where Kaivai tried some cross-country skiing and snowshoeing. While they were snowshoeing through the forest near the top of the mountain, a blizzard struck. The snow swirled around him, just like in his dream. The freak storm only lasted about thirty minutes, but it left a lasting impression on Kaivai of the spotless and sparkling, white snow.

Catherine called me a few months after Kaivai Tukuafu returned home. He married Saofa'i, as promised. He remained a fisherman. They added another room to his mom's and dad's home for Saofa'i and him. But the big news was he wrote a song about his adventures in Canada. Most of the song was about the snow, but there was one verse that talked about how God had sent a spokesman to deliver him out of bondage. Kaivai played the guitar as he sang to his Tongan friends. I marvelled at the fact they were singing about me in faraway Tonga.

I never made it to Tonga to hear my song, but I think about the experience often. I remember the feeling of love I received from the Tongan. Of all the religious leaders and followers of the many denominations I have ever encountered, Kaivai Tukuafu, the Tongan, was the most Christ-like man I ever met. His faith in Jesus was the way he lived.

CHAPTER SIXTEEN

The Dog Was Worth More than the Man

Sam was a world-class athlete. He had won gold medals against the best competition in Germany, Austria, and Switzerland. He started his training at eight weeks of age in a sport for German shepherds called schutzhund, which is a German word meaning "protection dog." It refers to a sport that focuses on developing and evaluating those traits in dogs that make them more useful and happier companions to their owners.

The training started as a puppy learning to respond to seven directions: Sit, Down, Stay, Come, Heel, Off, and No. His owner, Carson, had a goal to train for at least fifteen minutes every day and then have short, five-minute sessions spread throughout the day. Carson had a wife and three kids, so he asked them to train the puppy to do these tasks in every room of the house.

Sam had hair as black as coal across his back, blending into chocolate brown and finally sandy blond down his sides. His face was ebony with mahogany brown around the edges. He was bred to have a sloping back from his head down to his hind end. His parents came from a long line of schutzhund champions in Europe. He was a handsome dog, bred for competition.

Carson trained Sam at a schutzhund club in Langley, British Columbia, where he lived. Sam had the perfect temperament for competition. He was obedient to his owner, right down to the smallest detail. He never lost control and always remained patient. He was aloof, but not aggressive. He was reserved, so he did not make friends immediately, but once he did, he was extremely loyal. He was easy-going with the family, but if a family member was threatened, he became strong and protective.

After a couple of years of training, Sam began some trials, where he participated in competitive events at which he was awarded titles as he passed the standard tests. The trials consisted of three phases: tracking, obedience, and protection.

The tracking phase tested Sam's scenting ability as well as his mental soundness and physical endurance. A "track layer" walks across a large field dropping several small articles along the way. Sam would then be directed to follow the track while Carson followed about ten metres behind. When Sam found each article, he would lie down with the article between his front paws. Sam followed the track carefully.

In the obedience phase, Sam was placed in a large field with a second dog. Sam was commanded to lay in the down position on the side of the field, while the other dog performed several heeling exercises, including heeling through a group of people. Then the dogs switched places. There were two gunshots during the heeling to test the dog's reaction to loud noises. An exercise that Sam enjoyed was running up a wooden A-frame about six feet high and then jumping over to the grass below. He also liked jumping other solid obstacles. The "send out" was exciting to Sam. Carson would direct him to run away straight and fast, and then lie down on command during the run. Sam was enthusiastic, as these exercises provided him with the physical and mental stimuli he craved along with the positive reinforcement that bonded him to his owner.

The protection phase tested Sam's courage in shielding Carson from potential threats along with his compliance and control in the heat of the moment. An assistant, called the "helper," wears a heavily padded sleeve on one arm. There are several "blinds," which are like small tents, on a large field that the helper hides behind. Sam was directed by Carson to search all the blinds for the helper. When Sam found the helper, he would bark, jumping up on his hind legs to prevent the helper from moving until Carson arrived. Sam was trained to never touch the helper in this exercise.

In the next exercise, Sam would stop the attack of the helper by biting on the padded sleeve. When the attack or an attempted escape stopped, Sam was commanded to "out" or release the sleeve. Sam knew that if he failed to release the sleeve when commanded, he would be dismissed. He had to show courage to bite the padded sleeve, but have the temperament to obey Carson when ordered out.

Following several years of training and competition, Sam was ready to compete at the highest level. He travelled with Carson to the place where the sport was invented and where the top German shepherds contended for the top honours in the world—Germany and Austria. Schutzhund was a fledgling sport in Canada, little known and little valued. However, in Germany and Austria, competing in schutzhund was like a professional hockey player being privileged enough to compete for the Stanley Cup in the Forum in Montreal against the Montreal Canadiens during the 1970s when they won five Stanley Cup Championships.

Against all odds, Sam became a world champion. He was renowned and celebrated throughout Europe, but still unknown in Canada, except among the schutzhund aficionados back home where he was famous.

Sam was in great demand for breeding in Europe. He had all the desirable genetic traits to sire future champions in a sport that was extremely popular in Germany and Austria, as well as many other European countries. The owners of the top German shepherd bitches in Europe pursued Carson to enter into lucrative contracts for stud fees for Sam's services. The rules of the sport prohibited artificial insemination. The Austrians and Germans would pay all expenses for Sam and Carson to live the life of luxury in Europe, as well as pay thousands of dollars for each stud service. The contracts were signed amounting to earnings of approximately $150,000 plus all travel and living expenses. Sam retired from competition.

A month before Carson and Sam were supposed to leave for Austria, they were involved in a motor vehicle accident in Kamloops, British Columbia. Carson was driving his green Subaru Forester SUV with Sam in the back in his dog crate made of heavy-duty, grey plastic with an extra strong steel wire door, when they were rear-ended at a red light. The young driver behind them was busy on his phone and never noticed the light had changed to red. He didn't even slow down.

The purpose of the visit to Kamloops was to simply observe a schutzhund competition and display Sam, the champion. Everyone was anxious to see the hero.

Carson suffered a whiplash injury to his neck and back. It appeared that Sam experienced a whiplash injury to his back as well, as he moved quite slowly with some limitations in his movements. In any event, they attended the event in Kamloops. Upon their return home to Langley, Carson brought Sam to his veterinarian. The veterinarian diagnosed Sam with a mild soft tissue injury. The prognosis was for a full recovery in a couple of weeks.

Carson also visited his family doctor who diagnosed him with a soft tissue whiplash injury. The prognosis for a full recovery was good, but the doctor was guarded when it came to estimating the duration of the injury. Carson went ahead with his plans to travel with Sam to Austria and then Germany to fulfill the contracts for stud services.

Sam arrived in Vienna without incident after a fourteen-hour flight from Vancouver. It was a prolonged period of time to remain in his dog crate. Vienna may have been famous for its cultural events, coffee houses, cozy wine taverns, and the Viennese waltz, but Sam was not impressed. He just wanted to get out into a grassy field and run. He was happy when they arrived at an acreage just north of the city where he could do just that.

The next day, Sam was introduced to a bitch in heat. Generally, the female will let the male mate her for a period of about three weeks. Sam was contracted to mate a different bitch every day for a month, which he was capable of doing. Sam started by sniffing the female. The female indicated she was receptive by standing still and holding her tail to the side. Sam mounted her but could not achieve penetration as he was not capable of getting an erection. The attempt was made over several hours, but Sam could not succeed in mating. It was a tragedy.

Carson took Sam to the next appointment, about a two hours' drive away near Salzburg. Sam and Carson could have cared less about this historic centre renowned for its Baroque architecture with twenty-seven churches and being the birthplace of Mozart.

The sole concern was whether Sam could perform. He could not. They returned, sadly, to Vienna.

Carson decided to try one more time at a beautiful setting in the Wachau Valley, a World Heritage Site due to its spectacular scenery, just an hour's drive from Vienna. Sam viewed the Danube River snaking through the valley past picturesque monasteries, grand castles, villages, and vine-draped hills, but he still could not perform. They would have to return home with their tails between their legs. It was humiliating.

As soon as they were back home in Langley, Carson took Sam to his veterinarian. The veterinarian completed a full physical examination of Sam and discovered the problem. It was a matter of canine penis anatomy. The veterinarian explained to Carson that at the time of penetration, the canine penis is not erect, and can only penetrate the female because it includes a narrow bone called the "baculum." Sam's baculum was fractured and could not be repaired.

How did this happen? Could the injury have been caused in the motor vehicle accident? Carson and Sam came to see me in Fort Langley for some legal advice. I examined Sam's dog crate. On the middle of the floor in the crate was a round protruding lip about an inch high and six inches across that I could see was used during the manufacturing process. I thought it was possible that Sam could have broken his baculum when he slid across the floor of the crate at the time of the accident. We went to see the veterinarian.

The veterinarian formed the opinion this was probable, providing me with an expert report. I started a legal action seeking damages for the injuries Carson suffered, but also for the financial loss caused by the inability of Sam to perform because of the broken bone in his penis caused by the motor vehicle accident.

I searched for legal cases across Canada and the common-law world; however, I could not find a fact pattern like this one. It was unique. This was exciting—to have a case that no other lawyer had tried, as far as I could find, anywhere in the entire history of the world.

I relied on the basic law of damages in a personal injury claim. The first claim by Carson was for pain and suffering and loss of enjoyment of life. The second head of damages was for economic loss. These damages refer to actual monetary losses. Carson lost contracts worth $150,000 due to Sam breaking his baculum in the motor vehicle accident. The insurance company had never seen a claim like this one before and refused to pay for the economic loss.

I produced the written contracts. The insurance company would not budge. The insurance company's position was that Sam could have broken his baculum during a competition, while jumping over an obstacle. I produced evidence that Sam had successfully mated with a female German shepherd in Langley just before his final competition before retiring. I also produced the video of that competition, which showed Sam clearing all the jumps by a wide margin. He did not snag his penis on any of the jumps.

The insurance company refused to allow the stud service contracts into evidence without someone from Austria or Germany attending the Supreme Court trial personally, as a witness, to confirm the truthfulness of the documents. I arranged for the woman who set up all the contracts to come to Vancouver to give evidence at the trial.

The night before the trial was to begin in Vancouver, I brought my witness from Austria with me to meet with the insurance company's lawyers. They were impressed with her evidence. The lawyers obtained instructions to offer $100,000 for the economic loss due to Sam not being able to perform, and $50,000 for loss of enjoyment of life due to the moderate whiplash injury Carson suffered, as well as legal costs. Carson instructed me to accept. We knew there would be uncertainties the trial judge would have to take into account in calculating the economic loss. The offer was not perfect, but it was just enough to settle this amazing case where the dog was worth more than the man.

I joked with the insurance company lawyers that if I was forced to go to trial, I would amend the pleadings to add Sam as a plaintiff and seek a generous award for his pain and suffering and loss of enjoyment of life. Just think of Sam's loss of enjoyment of life, as he was contracted to provide stud services to all the best bitches across Europe! The lawyers couldn't stop laughing.

CHAPTER SEVENTEEN

The Luck of the Irish

Frank was a self-described idiot, and what is more, he was proud of it. He was the black sheep—the youngest in a family with an older brother and sister who were both high achievers climbing the corporate ladder at the bank, while Frank sold used cars at a large lot in Surrey.

His siblings achieved high marks in high school, straight A's, while Frank couldn't have cared less. The education bureaucratic gurus just advanced him to the next grade each year because they didn't want to permanently damage his psyche. Frank thought these clowns were a bunch of morons. He knew they gave him a meaningless graduation certificate just to get him out of the system.

Frank lived at home with his mom and dad, while his older brother and sister established solid marriages with wonderful children. His mom still treated him like a baby, and Frank loved it. She made his meals, did his laundry, and made sure he got to work on time.

Washing cars for minimum wage at the used car lot was his first job out of high school. After several years of watching the salespersons, Frank learned a lot about sales and even a little bit about cars. The owner of the used car dealership gave him a chance to try sales. This is when Frank learned he had the gift of the blarney, and likely why he came to believe he was Irish (even though his mom told him they were from England).

Learning how to manipulate—or as Frank put it, "serve" customers—became Frank's strongest virtue. He was a wonder and became a successful salesman.

At thirty-two years of age, Frank's dad finally kicked him out of the house. His father said that his mother was too soft on him. Frank wondered, *What did he mean, "too soft"?* Frank was offended. He moved into a small apartment in Fort Langley. He would prove to his father that he could not only take care of himself, but that he could also sustain other, equally intelligent life. So, he bought a goldfish. He named his new pet, St. Patrick.

Frank worked each day from 11:00 a.m. to 6:00 p.m. at the used car dealership. He thought 11:00 a.m. was rather early, but he got used to it. He always picked up three egg McMuffins from McDonald's for breakfast, which he ate in the lunchroom at work. Of course, he ate donuts throughout the day from Tim Hortons. After work, he habitually ordered two cheeseburgers and a strawberry shake from the Dairy Queen just down the street. Later, if he got hungry back at home, he would chew on a big block of Kerrygold Dubliner, a hard-ripened cheese imported from Ireland. Only Irish, grass-fed cows were good enough for him.

Unsurprisingly, Frank was not in good shape. He was five-foot-eight-inches tall, weighing a flabby 210 pounds. His hairline was already receding, and he looked quite comical with poufs of hair on each side of his head and one on the top.

"Handsome" was not a word used to describe Frank, but he was pleasant-looking when he told a funny story with his trademark comical grin. He was quite the popular character at Donegal's Irish House, an Irish pub with award-winning cold beer, and featuring live music four nights a week. After a few pints of Guinness, Frank even had quite the singing voice. With his drinking mates, he could be heard all the way down the street singing "The Wild Rover," "The Craic Was Ninety in the Isle of Man," and "The Irish Rover."

Frank also had his own special way with women. It was such a way that they never went out with him twice. He would take his date to a slapstick comedy at the movie theatre, then to the pub for beer and songs. When they closed the pub at 1:00 a.m., Frank was in such an inebriated condition that his date would have to drive him home in his car and then catch herself a cab to get home. You can see now why he never had a second date.

One night, he was driving his red Honda Accord home after the proverbial two beers, when he ran into a problem. That problem was the Jack the Clipper barber shop. He turned left on the corner to his apartment; unfortunately for Frank, he turned a little too early and found himself barrelling through the large picture window of the barbershop, right into a row of salon chairs. He sat there in shock for many minutes, finally realizing he was not hurt, at which time he said to himself, "Boy, that was a close shave!" Fortunately, it was 1:00 a.m., so no one was having their hair cut, and not a soul was out on the street. Not a single person was there to witness the event. In a state of deep contemplation, Frank thought, "If a Honda Accord crashes into the barbershop, and no one is there to hear it, does it still make a sound?"

He slowly climbed out of his car, then sauntered along the three blocks to his home, humming an Irish drinking tune. When he arrived at his apartment, he got out his Paddy's Irish Whiskey and poured himself a drink. He believed, like the Irish, that whiskey meant "the water of life." About an hour later, he was still sitting at the kitchen table, slowly sipping on his drink, when the police showed up. Little did he know, ironically, that he was establishing a defence by having the officers watch him continue to drink.

The officers had a reasonable suspicion that Frank had alcohol in his body while he was driving, due to the fact that his red Honda Civic was inside the barber shop. The police were just driving by on their usual patrol when they spotted the unusual. They had to laugh as they had never seen a car in a barber shop before. Now they had seen everything.

The officers demanded that Frank accompany them to the police station to provide a sample of his breath. When they arrived, about fifteen minutes later, he blew three times the limit. Frank was charged with driving while impaired, and driving while his blood alcohol concentration was over 80 mg of alcohol per 100 ml of blood.

Frank's trial was about six months later in Provincial Court in Langley. Crown counsel for the trial was a lawyer by the name of Al, a pretty good friend of mine, since we had done so many trials together. After Al had called the two police officers, and I had finished my cross-examination, I called Frank to the stand.

It was on a Friday afternoon with just Al, Judge Andersen, Frank, and myself left in court. There was a severe thunderstorm happening outside. Frank gave his evidence that he only had "two beers" at the pub. He testified he just mistook the barber shop for the corner leading to his apartment. He then walked home and began drinking his favourite Irish Whiskey. He said he was on his third glass, when the officers arrived. It had been about an hour and a half since he entered the barber shop. It was another fifteen minutes to the police station before he was required to provide a breath sample.

Throughout the trial, the tempest with hurricane winds increased its onslaught upon the court house like a blasting assault, assailing, attacking, and bombarding. We had a clear view of the dark storm clouds swirling in a black vortex while the pouring rains slashed into the windows. It was at this point, during cross-examination by Crown counsel—just when Al asked Frank how many beers he had at the pub and Frank was in the middle of answering the usual, "two beer" defence,—that lightning struck along with a loud jolt of thunder, resulting in the lights going out. When the power was restored a few seconds later, Al looked up at the judge and said with a big grin, "I think this is a comment on the credibility of the evidence of this witness."

Judge Andersen and I had to laugh. We tried, but it was impossible to contain the laughter.

There was no evidence of Frank driving under the influence other than the result—that is, his red Honda Civic coming to rest in the barber shop. This hilarious outcome could have been caused by any number of factors, such as Frank's bad driving in the dark, poor eyesight, or singing Irish ditties with far too much gusto. Frank probably could not do two things at the same time, sing and drive.

In addition, the breath tests did not measure his blood alcohol content at the time of driving, as he imbibed three glass of Irish Whiskey after the mishap. The breath tests were performed about an hour and a half after the driving, so the results could not be relied upon to indicate Frank's condition at the time he was driving. Based on these arguments, I submitted that the judge must acquit Frank of all charges.

It was Al's turn to start his closing argument. Just as he was waxing eloquent, there was an even larger lightning strike with a greater boom of thunder. The power went out. The lights went out. We were standing in the dark.

Matching the tone of Al's earlier comment, I leaned over to the judge and stated with a straight face: "I think this is a verdict from a higher court." Al couldn't help it. The laughter exploded out of him in great convulsions. Judge Andersen and I could no longer hold it back either. We burst out laughing. It was a unique moment in the annals of legal history, for a criminal trial to cause so much merriment.

Judge Andersen quickly dismissed the charges. Frank put on his comical grin, then he asked me: "What was all the laughing about anyway?" Frank would never be accused of being a brain surgeon. He was just happy all charges were dismissed against him. He thanked me and then declared boldly, "It must have been the luck of the Irish!"

I didn't remind him he was English, as I knew this would fall on deaf ears. I also didn't tell him about the Irish potato famine, when the Irish were not so lucky. I knew he wouldn't believe it.

CHAPTER EIGHTEEN

Fort Langley: Historic Birthplace of British Columbia

It was Saturday morning, the first weekend in August—time for Brigade Days held each year at the Fort Langley National Historic Site. My wife, Beth, made blueberry pancakes for breakfast for me and our four children—James, Jessica, Jennifer, and Jane, so we could fuel ourselves up before making our annual pilgrimage to the historic event.

Raj, a good Sikh friend and client, originally from the Punjab in the northern region of India, always supplied us with all the blueberries we needed each year from his large blueberry farm in Langley. I did solicitors work for him, like land transfers and mortgages. Raj explained to me that Sikhism, the world's fifth most popular religion, is a monotheistic faith that teaches equality and service to others. He added that the motto of the Sikh religion states, "Everyone is the same." I thought about those few occasions when I had attended a Sikh temple and then eaten in its cafeteria. The hosts there told me that anyone could come and eat there, without any questions about need or religion. I think it is a great way to feed the poor; people from all religions are welcome. Clearly Raj's generous personality follows the tenets of his religion.

Raj invited us to a reception at his farm for his son's marriage. Under a huge tent with hundreds of his friends, he held a gigantic party. There I beheld the greatest kaleidoscope of colour I have ever seen, with all the women in their various embroidered, beautiful sarees: peach, maroon art silk, blue textured silk, salmon pink, Prussian blue, off-white silk, dark purple, baby blue, hot pink, red and gold, orange and green, bright yellow, and lavender.

The Punjab region is often referred to as the breadbasket of India and Pakistan. The weather is perfect for growing crops all year long. Punjabi farmers came to British Columbia starting in 1897. They built successful blueberry, cranberry, raspberry, and strawberry farms in the Fraser Valley. Many more followed, Raj, being one of them.

Raj was also in charge of the cranberry harvest in the low bog lands down by the Fraser River at Fort Langley, where there are many cranberry fields surrounded by dykes. At harvest time in the fall, the fields are flooded, covering all the cranberry bushes with water to a depth of about eighteen inches. Motorcycle-like machines with big tires (so they do not crush the cranberries) and beaters on the front are driven into the water. These "eggbeaters" churn the water up and loosen the cranberries from the vines. Each berry has four tiny pockets of air that allow it, once freed from its stem, to float to the surface of the water for easy gathering.

Punjabi farmers wearing hip waders enter the water at a specific corner of the field, and then corral the berries dragging floating beams, called booms, through the chilly water. The last time I was invited to witness the harvest with Raj, the sun was setting with crimson rays of light filling the sky, while a fiery flotilla of berries drifted across the water-flooded bog. It was incredibly beautiful.

Raj and I were standing on top of the suction machine that pumped the berries out, rinsed them with fresh water and separated them from the debris. The berries were immediately loaded into a truck and shipped to a processing facility for Ocean Spray.

Let's return to breakfast with the family. When all the blueberry pancakes were eaten, we loaded into the car and headed for Marina Park on the Bedford Channel in Fort Langley. From our parking spot, we gazed across the Bedford Channel to Brae Island, filled with campers, and McMillan Island, a reserve land of the Kwantlen First Nation. Once there was a channel between these two islands, but silt and debris gradually filled in the channel and combined the two islands. The main body of the Fraser River lies on the other side of the island.

We hopped out of the car and headed down to the edge of the river, where a crowd was gathering, waiting for the fur brigade to arrive. Finally, we saw the paddlers of a dozen canoes and a replica York boat that had travelled from Hope to Fort Langley, where they traditionally unloaded their cargo of furs and barrels. We witnessed a Kwantlen welcome song. We heard the exciting bagpipe and black powder salute. This traditional re-enactment portrays the annual return of fur traders in the 1800s, who transported the year's intake of furs from the interior and northern trading posts to Fort Langley. The goods were later delivered by ship to England.

We followed the procession up to the Fort, led by the Scottish bagpipes. The palisades of Fort Langley, standing tall, came into view. Inside the walls, timber buildings recreate the rugged 1800s when Hudson's Bay Company fur traders mingled with California gold prospectors. There, First Nations interpreters tell century-old tales while tending to fragrant fry-bread. At the Fort we saw enthusiasts from all over British Columbia camping for the three-day festival, many of whom were history buffs showcasing 1800s fur trade culture through dress, weapons, blacksmithing, cooking, barrel making, and music. There was even a spot where the kids could try their hand at panning for gold.

We learned that Fort Langley was established in 1827 by the Hudson's Bay Company. The area is the traditional home of the Sto:lo, meaning "river people," a group of First Nations people inhabiting the Fraser Valley along the Fraser River, who fished for salmon, stickleback, eulachon, and sturgeon. The Kwantlen band are Sto:lo people, living primarily on McMillan Island at Fort Langley.

The best part for the kids was when we sat down on our blankets to listen to the Irish fiddlers, Scottish bagpipes, French Canadian voyageur folklore and music, along with Kwantlen storytelling, all while eating bannock, poutine, and smoked salmon.

On top of the palisades, we watched with great interest the historic weapons demonstration. Powder was poured from the powder horn into a measure that determined the amount to be emptied down the barrel of the musket. The demonstrator pretended to place a lead ball on the muzzle of the musket, and then pretended to shove it down the barrel by a ram rod until it rested on top of the powder charge. In fact, the ram rod was used to ensure nothing was in the barrel of the weapon. A finer grade of powder was poured from a different powder horn into the pan of the musket, and the hammer was pulled back, making the weapon ready to fire. The whole process required around forty-five seconds. The weapon was then fired into the air with a huge blast of sound and a large puff of smoke.

Demonstrations of musket fire at the Fort changed after a very interesting case I elegantly call "The Shot in the Butt Case." A volunteer who participated in historic weapons demonstrations came to see me after he was accidentally shot in the buttocks, damaging his colon. Surgery was required, and poor Benjamin was unable to sit for months. What's more, he was the "butt" of many jokes. It was embarrassing and completely avoidable.

After some investigation, I discovered what had gone wrong. During the demonstration, when the ram rod was shoved down the barrel of the musket, a small piece of metal broke off. Of course, nothing was supposed to be in the barrel when the musket was fired—just some powder that would make a dramatic bang and produce some smoke. It was quite a surprise when Benjamin received the shot in his hind end. For Benjamin, especially, it was a terrible shock.

Benjamin was a short and chubby Englishman. He was just the kind of good fellow you would find at the Fort pub, an old-time watering hole with front porch seating and a classic pub grub menu of burgers and fries, as well as the best fish & chips in Langley. He maintained his English accent as spoken in the South of England, as it was so popular in Canada. With his posh accent, sympathetic chubby face, and large oval smile, Benjamin was a well-liked, charismatic character among the pub crowd.

I contacted the insurance company covering accidents at the Fort. We negotiated a settlement that resulted in a procedural change in future weapons demonstrations. After the shot in the butt case, no weapon was ever again pointed at anyone's butt—or any other part of their body—during historic weapons demonstrations, but rather they could only be fired high in the air, such as on top of the palisades, well above any person. Tort law was successful again in making Benjamin, his butt, and the public at large safer. Benjamin was happy with the settlement.

Returning to our family trip to the Fort on Brigade Days, we took photographs of James, Jessica, Jennifer, and Jane high on the palisade looking across the Bedford Channel to the Holy Redeemer

Church, a small, white Roman Catholic Church built in 1897 on MacMillan island, home of the Kwantlen First Nation. Beyond the Island, we had a wonderful view of the Coastal Range Mountains and the twin summits of Golden Ears. This was a breath-taking background to our photos.

Next, we watched a short, amusing film about the history of Fort Langley and how it was built by the Hudson's Bay Company for the fur trade with agricultural production in the surrounding area. However, in 1858, due to the influx of thousands of prospectors from California and Oregon during the Fraser Valley Gold Rush, Governor James Douglas proclaimed the establishment of the Crown Colony of British Columbia, preventing the area from becoming part of the ever-expanding United States. This proclamation is why Fort Langley is called "The Historic Birthplace of British Columbia."

Stepping into the cooperage, we witnessed a master cooper at his trade. His job was important as he shaped the pieces of white pine into perfect degrees of symmetry to be assembled into barrels. Since barrels were used as the main form of transport for the Fort's most valuable trade items, the demand for barrels was great, and the master cooper was the highest paid tradesman in 1857.

The barrels were filled with salted salmon that was shipped to Hawaii, and cranberries to California. Indigenous Hawaiians came to Fort Langley to help build the fort and paddle the canoes filled with furs. After the fur trade, the Hawaiians remained, settling in British Columbia.

In front of the Fort, we read the story of the SS *Beaver*, a paddle wheeler and floating trading post that travelled as far north as Russian America, which is now known as Alaska, and as far west as Vancouver Island. It was a steamship carrying trading goods for the Hudson's Bay Company from 1835 to 1888.

We also viewed the Spirit Square Panels, carved from red cedar, depicting a beaver, a salmon, and a wolf. Inspiration comes from the rich history of the Kwantlen, meaning "tireless runner." Oral tradition tells of a great Chief whose daughter gives birth to wolf puppies that transform themselves into human form and become descendants of the first Kwantlen families. It is said that the wolf blood gave stamina to the Kwantlen messengers, whose task was to run and deliver messages throughout and beyond the vast Kwantlen territories.

James, Jessica, Jennifer, and Jane were finally tired of my obsession with history. They had humoured me long enough. We walked over to the Bedford House for something to eat. As the name suggests, the restaurant overlooks the Bedford Channel and McMillan Island. The house was built by a local carpenter in 1908, used as a store for the Hudson's Bay Company, later used as a butcher shop, and then as a brothel.

As we ate our chicken cordon bleu, I commenced telling the kids some stories about Bernie, the owner of the French eatery. The large and loquacious Austrian came by to say "hello," and I introduced him to each member of my family. He greeted each one with great fanfare.

I recounted the story about the night Bernie was standing outside his restaurant when two rugby players from the Fort Pub across the street came over to talk. One of them sucker-punched him in the nose. Now the nose of a restauranteur is not just any nose. It is a highly-trained nose used in cooking fancy French cuisine. We discovered who the culprit was and then sued him.

The punch had broken Bernie's nose. More importantly, he had consequently lost his sense of smell—so essential in the art of cooking. We sued on the basis of the intentional tort of assault and battery. We also made a claim for punitive damages, due to the outrageous nature of the attack.

We figured Bernie's nose would be worth millions! At the examination for discovery, the defendant produced his bank statement. He did not have a lawyer, as he could not afford one, and he did not have any other assets. He worked at a menial job earning just enough for a single young ruffian to survive. We took all the money he had, which wasn't much—perhaps it amounted to about $5,000—and settled for that. There was no use wasting more time and money on that buffoon.

Beth and the kids thought the story was very funny. Bernie was just passing through, so I asked him to get the framed photograph of him with his inflamed broken nose. He returned, showing them the photo of his humungous schnozzle. Everyone laughed.

I then recounted the story of how we used that photograph in another legal case involving Bernie. A young man had reserved a table in a very romantic spot by the window in Bernie's restaurant. Outside the window were lovely rhododendrons and azaleas in full bloom; some were purple, others red, orange, white, pink, and yellow. The foliage was a deep green.

Just beyond the flowers were magnificent red cedar trees and the gently flowing Bedford Channel. The Jacob Haldi Bridge spanning the Bedford Channel of the Fraser River was in full view. It was the perfect setting. The young romantic desired this exact table, because he was going to propose to his girlfriend. His imagination was set on that very spot; no other spot would do.

When he arrived with the love of his life, the table was taken. The waiter proposed a table with a similar view, right next to the one he had fancied. He was furious. It was not the table he reserved. He demanded to see the owner. When he was told Bernie was not available to see him, he ran up the stairs to Bernie's office.

Bernie was sitting behind his desk. The young man advanced toward Bernie in a violent manner. Bernie had a cattle prod on his desk, so he picked it up and jabbed the young man with it. The young man fell to the floor and started his retreat down the stairs. Bernie followed behind him, thrusting the cattle prod into his back a couple of times as he went down the stairs, just for good measure.

The police came by the next day and arrested Bernie for assault. We fixed a trial date in Langley Provincial Court. At the trial, I called Bernie to give evidence. Our first line of defence centred on the young man trespassing up the stairs into Bernie's private office, affording Bernie the right to fend off the trespasser. Our second and main line of defence was self-defence.

The Crown called the young man to give his evidence. They entered photographs of the two red marks on the young man's chest and four red marks on his back. The cattle prod with two electrodes on the end was entered as an exhibit.

I called Bernie to the stand. He explained that he was quietly doing necessary bookkeeping for the restaurant when the young man opened the closed door, entered the room, began shouting about his reservation for a certain table, and then violently advanced toward him. Bernie testified he thought the young man was attacking him. He just happened to have the cattle prod on the desk, because he used it to chase dogs away from the garbage beside the restaurant. He thought the young man was going to punch him in the nose, like the rugby player had done a few months before.

I had Bernie produce the framed photograph of his inflamed broken nose from the rugby player attack. Bernie explained he was filled with fear this would be another violent assault against him. He just wanted to defend himself. What about the two extra prods as the young man ran down the stairs? Bernie said he was in such a state of terror that he didn't know what he was doing. He just wanted to be sure to fend off the attack. I argued the law that a person defending himself could not "measure with nicety the blow."

Bernie was a middle-aged man in bad shape, about six feet tall and 185 pounds. The young man was twenty-five years old, athletic, and muscular, but only five-foot-nine-inches tall and 170 pounds.

When we were finished, the judge scratched his head and said to me: "Mr. Kearl, this is a close one. The defence of fending off a trespasser does not hold any water, but self-defence may win the day. The framed photograph of the accused's broken nose leading to his frenzied state of mind casts the slightest doubt in favour of the accused. Case dismissed."

It had been a long day in Fort Langley, the historic birthplace of British Columbia, but a great day. We had a lot of fun. We even learned a lot of history. We laughed about the shot in the butt case and Bernie's two brushes with the law, as we tucked the kids into bed, repeating the phrase, "Sweet dreams. Sleep tight. Don't let the bed bugs bite."

ROBERT B. KEARL

Our Family, 1990
Back Row: James, Beth, Jane, Robert
Front: Jessica, with Jennifer in front

CHAPTER NINETEEN

Pilgrimage to Paisley

May Donoghue entered the Wellmeadow Café with her friend that historic day, August 26, 1928, in Paisley, Scotland. Little did she know at the time she would transform the law, not just in Scotland and the UK, but all over the world that fateful day.

May Donoghue's companion ordered and paid for her drink, a bottle of ginger beer. The cafe had purchased the beverage from a distributor who had purchased it from David Stevenson, the manufacturer. The ginger beer came in a dark bottle. What was inside was not visible from the outside. May Donoghue drank some of the contents, then her friend poured the remainder into her drinking glass.

The remains of a snail in a state of decomposition fell from the bottle into her tumbler. This is why this case is known as the "Paisley Snail" or "Snail in the Bottle" case.

May Donoghue fell ill and decided to sue the ginger beer manufacturer, Mr. Stevenson. The orthodox view at the time was that Mrs. Donoghue had no sustainable claim in law, as she had no direct connection to the manufacturer. Injuries resulting from defective products were claimed on the basis of a contract of sale between the seller and the consumer. Donoghue had no contractual relationship with Stevenson, nor had she with the seller, as her friend had purchased the ginger beer.

Donoghue's lawyer made the novel argument that Stevenson owed a duty of care to her to ensure that snails did not get into his bottles of ginger beer, and that he had breached this duty by failing to provide a system to clean bottles effectively. In trial, a witness testified that snails and snail trails were frequently found around where the bottles were stored. This testimony supported the allegation that the bottles were left in places where snails had access to them, which was a breach of duty that caused Donoghue's subsequent illness.

The House of Lords held that the manufacturer owed a duty of care to Mrs. Donoghue, which was breached, because it was reasonably foreseeable that failure to ensure the product's safety would lead to harm to consumers. There was a sufficiently proximate relationship between consumers and product manufacturers. The world-famous 1932 case of Donoghue v Stevenson revolutionized the law of negligence or what is sometimes called the law of torts. Mrs. Donoghue's monumental victory, all that time ago, established that a manufacturer of a product owes the consumer a duty of care, thereby placing the onus on the manufacturer to ensure their product will cause no harm to consumers.

The case laid the foundation for the "neighbour principle," that a person should take reasonable care to avoid acts or omissions that they can reasonably foresee as likely to cause injury to a neighbour. This opened up the door to claims of negligence in a wide variety of circumstances.

The "reasonable man of ordinary prudence" is the central figure in cases of negligence. This is a model standard to which everyone is required to conform. She or he is the good citizen, setting a higher standard of conduct than was required by the law before Donoghue v Stevenson. The effect of this new law of torts, following this leading case, raised the behaviour of the individual in regard to their relationships with everyone else, thereby, protecting everyone.

I think I should like to make a pilgrimage to Paisley in recognition of this landmark decision. Paisley was a centre of the weaving industry, giving its name to the paisley shawl and the paisley pattern. Perhaps I could wear a colourful paisley shirt, the kind I wore in the 60s, the era of make love not war and flower power.

Similar to the snail in the bottle case, I have encountered many "May Donoghues" over the years and have used the precedent she established to protect the public. I had the hairball in the Nalley's Chip Dip case. A young lady with small children came in to see me. She explained that as she was eating some potato chips, she dug into a huge hairball hidden in the middle of the dip. She immediately threw up. She described how sick she was when she saw the hairball. Fortunately, she brought it in for me to see. I almost got sick just looking at it.

I sent a photograph of the chip dip with the hair ball to the chip dip manufacturer's head office, along with a description of my client's symptoms—how she hurled across the room and became horribly sick. I demanded immediate payment of $5,000, or else we would commence a legal action, which would attract the attention of consumer reporters on television and in the newspapers. We received the cheque the next day.

In a similar case, the teller at the Credit Union in Fort Langley bought a bag of chips. As she was eating the chips, she discovered a burnt bug among them. Again, I wrote to the head office and received the cheque for $5,000 the next day.

A really ugly incidence occurred to a father of three, who came to see me. He had purchased a large bag of walnuts from the bulk section of the grocery store. He put them away on the shelf, but when he came back to eat some a few days later, numerous moths came flying at him. He was duly disturbed and suffered from shock. His trauma led to difficulty sleeping caused by nightmares of hordes of flying moths attacking him. Again, the cheque was on my desk the next day.

Another disgusting instance of negligence occurred when a teenage boy on the high school football team from Fort Langley drank from his can of pop and then poured the remainder into a glass. Out plopped a small, dead mouse in the process of putrefaction. The tough guy heaved until there was nothing left in his stomach. He played on the offensive line, so he was quite a large fellow, yet he lost twenty-five pounds in a short amount of time after this disgusting incident—weight which he could ill afford to lose. He attended counselling for nightmares. We settled his case a few months later. I never again drank directly from a can. I always pour the entire contents of any can into a glass.

Along with the funds, each of the negligent parties in the above cases sent a letter of apology and promised to ensure it did not happen again. Almost always, the law of torts improves behaviour. People and companies do not like to lose money, so they develop better procedures to protect the public.

My wife's mother once purchased some pre-washed, bagged spinach, which she made into a salad. When she sat down to eat, after taking several bites, she noticed something on her plate that didn't belong. It was a huge, two-inch-long, dried-out, black beetle. She contacted the grocery store, who told her to phone the producer, who merely offered her three free bags of spinach. She never collected on those free bags, as she never ate spinach again. She should have contacted me.

A much greater potential for trauma occurred when a young mother bought her little child a pre-Christmas present. It was a video of Bozo the Clown. At least that was what was printed on the packaging. She took the present home to her child, who opened it and went into the basement to watch the video. When the mother checked in on the child about fifteen minutes later, she was horrified. Instead of a harmless movie about Bozo the Clown, she witnessed a naked young lady tied to an altar, being sacrificed by an evil man with a large knife held high above his head.

Fortunately, the mother arrived in the basement just before the video showed the evil man's blade coming down upon the screaming woman on the screen, and was therefore able to block her child from any further viewing. She brought the video with her when she came to see me. Some printing on the video cover disclosed that the packaging had been performed in North Carolina. I wrote to the company explaining all the circumstances and made a demand. The next day, I received the required cheque, along with a letter of apology, explaining how the video had been packaged in error. The company recalled a few hundred videos of pornographic horror, all mistakenly wrapped in Bozo the Clown covering. They expressed their appreciation that we had caught the error so early. The sincere promise was made it would never happen again, because they would double-check their packaging procedures.

The mother was traumatized, but fortunately it seemed she had arrived before the child (who may have been too young to understand) suffered any severe emotional distress. She did not notice any change in the child, and neither did the family doctor. If they had, we would have demanded far greater compensation, including a generous amount to cover the costs of counselling.

In the law of negligence, the classical pronouncement of what duty means is found in the words of Lord Atkin's "neighbour test" in Donoghue v Stevenson: "The rule that you are to love your neighbour becomes in law you must not injure your neighbour."

The famous question remains, "Who is my neighbour?" Lord Atkin responds: "Persons who are so closely and directly affected by my act that I ought reasonably to have them in contemplation as being so affected when I am directing my mind to the acts or omissions which are called in question."

I believe you may now understand why I must make a pilgrimage to Paisley. Mrs. May Donoghue of Glasgow, a person of modest means but great determination, was willing to fight all the way to the highest tribunal in Great Britain, the House of Lords. She is not only a product of Scottish legal mythology, but a real person. It must have been because of her firm belief in the importance of the principles established in her epic case that she continued to persevere until she won.

CHAPTER TWENTY

Greed, Like a Swarm of Locusts

Upon the death of a testatrix or testator (a legal term to describe a person who makes a will), sometimes there ensues an immediate and eager scramble for their assets. Most people love money. The scripture says the love of money is the root of all evil. This is certainly true when it comes to greed.

I heard a good joke a long time ago from someone misquoting this scripture, saying it is not the love of money that is the root of all evil, but the lack of money. You can judge for yourself which principle applies to the following three cases.

Ronald was an elderly man, eighty-five years old, five-foot-nine-inches tall and a frail 138 pounds. He had grey hair on the sides and at the back of his head, but he was totally bald on the top. His freckled face was heart-shaped, with eyes that sparkled when he was amused. But, when he was angry, those green eyes glared unrelentingly. Usually, he was well groomed and clean shaven.

Ronald was in his second marriage. His first wife had passed away from cancer after forty-three, happy years together. They had raised their son and daughter to be loving children, siblings, and now parents. He enjoyed his three grandchildren.

Still, he became lonely. Six years alone at home seemed like a long time. So, he joined a book-of-the month club, which is where he met Wendy. Wendy was always cheerful and friendly. Her first husband had died five years earlier. She had four grown children who were always too busy to come around. She lived all alone in her townhouse.

Ronald and Wendy discussed some of the books they enjoyed, such as *To Kill a Mockingbird, The Grapes of Wrath,* and *Brave New World,* at Wendel's Bookstore & Café while they sipped their "Dark Roast Death Wish Coffee." Over time, they became inseparable. Ronald decided to propose at their favourite ristorante, Mangia E Scappa, meaning dine & dash, eat & run, or eat it and then beat it. At that time, he was seventy-three years old, so it wasn't all that easy to get down on one knee, but he made it.

Wendy was a slightly plump seventy-year-old, who stood at a small five-foot-one-inches tall. She had short blonde hair with bangs over her vertical, smooth forehead. With long eyelashes, high cheek bones, and narrow facial shape, she was quite attractive. Ronald thought she was unforgettable, and that deep down she was the kind of woman who couldn't be anything other than her real self. She was authentic.

Wendy answered, "Yes." They were delighted, each of them thinking about how they could make the other happy. They were thankful for each other. Though every day would not be a perfect day, they could still always find some good in it. Wendy and Ronald were committed to each other; they were connected, giving, and respectful.

Wendy's four adult children were violently opposed to the marriage. They hated Ronald just because he was marrying their mother. It was not because they paid any attention to her, themselves, because they didn't. Perhaps, they just thought it was time she gave her estate (worth around $500,000) to them.

Ronald's children and grandchildren were supportive. They could see how happy their dad had become since he met Wendy and what a good person she was. They were delighted to attend the wedding and accept Wendy into the family. By contrast, Wendy's children begrudgingly came, all-the-while making their displeasure abundantly clear.

Wendy and Ronald decided they would travel while their health remained relatively good. Ronald sold his small bungalow, worth $450,000, so they could enjoy spending this money travelling the world. They lived together in the townhouse owned by Wendy. Ronald placed all his money on the sale of his home into a joint bank account with Wendy. They decided together on what furniture they would keep.

Wendy and Ronald were off to see the world. They started with a cruise through the Caribbean, then the Mediterranean, and finally, Alaska. Hawaii, Mexico, and Florida became destinations they enjoyed regularly. When they had been married twelve years, they planned a driving trip from Vancouver, British Columbia, down the coast of Washington, Oregon and California, to San Diego, where they had made reservations to stay at a five-star hotel on the beach.

While Ronald was driving through San Francisco, a car cut him off on the freeway and caused a terrible motor vehicle accident. Tragically, Wendy was killed. Ronald was heart-broken. He wound up in the hospital with moderate whiplash injuries. While still in the hospital mourning the death of his wife, Wendy's children broke into Wendy's and Ronald's townhouse and stole everything in it.

When we went to trial in the Supreme Court of British Columbia, the judge made it clear that the evidence Wendy's children brought forward was not credible. His view was reinforced by the vulture-like attitudes they demonstrated after the death of their mother, when they descended on her matrimonial townhouse, like swarming locusts, removing everything in sight and leaving it as empty of possessions as a psychopath's heart is of empathy. The judge found it was just pure greed on their part.

Wendy's children had produced a will naming themselves as executors and sole beneficiaries of their mother's estate. I spoke with the two witnesses, who testified that the will was blank when Wendy signed it. Her children must have filled out the will at a later date.

The judge granted a declaration that the will was null and void, and that Ronald was entitled to apply for letters of administration of his late wife's estate. Furthermore, a reference was made to the registrar to determine the value of everything taken from the matrimonial home, which would stand as a judgment against Wendy's children. Ordinarily, in estate litigation, costs are payable out of the estate, but the judge was so incensed at the high-handed manner of the defendants' actions, that he ordered them to personally pay all legal costs.

Ronald recovered in full everything he was entitled to, and justice was done. Of course, this could not bring back his wife, nor ease his loneliness. But, he did receive solace and comfort from his children and grandchildren, who also loved her. Sorrow is soothed and new beauty blossoms in sharing grief's heavy load with loved ones and heartfelt memories.

The second case of greed involved a sister and brother. Kevin and Emilia were raised by their parents, Wesley and Vivian, in Chilliwack, British Columbia. While they were young, their parents made wills giving everything to each other, with a gift over to their two children equally, if they passed away in a common accident. The will also provided that if Kevin or Emilia predeceased their parents, the one-half share intended for the deceased, would instead be divided equally among the children of the deceased. In the event there were no children, that share would go to their surviving sibling.

Emilia became a nurse. She married a doctor she met at the hospital in Chilliwack. They decided to move to Hawaii, where they had a lovely home overlooking the ocean. They never did have any children. Since she lived in Hawaii, she had very little contact with her parents, who continued to live in Chilliwack.

Kevin married Juliana, whom he met in grade twelve at the high school in Chilliwack. They had three lovely children and lived in a home on a small acreage, just a fifteen-minute drive from his parents' home. They saw his parents, Wesley and Vivian, every day. In fact, Kevin worked with his father, who owned the Dairy Queen in Chilliwack.

Kevin was a hard worker, just like his father. They worked together in perfect harmony, and soon they owned three Dairy Queen franchises in the Fraser Valley. Kevin was an integral part of the growth of these businesses, though they remained in the name of his father. It never crossed Kevin's mind that his father would ever die, as by all appearances, he was as healthy as an ox.

When Kevin was forty-one years old, tragedy struck. His father died suddenly of a heart attack at the age of sixty-four, while seemingly in perfect health. All of his assets were transferred to his wife, Vivian, in accordance with his will. Kevin continued to operate the three Dairy Queen franchises as usual, thinking all was well, as he had a wonderful relationship with his mother. He never thought about obtaining ownership of the businesses. He trusted completely in his mother.

Unfortunately, without her husband, Vivian began to rely more and more on her older brother, Andrew, who also lived in Chilliwack. Andrew was an officious intermeddler, who tried to dominate his sister, by intrusively offering help and advice. He couldn't understand how Kevin could have such a lovely home and nice cars. He formed the opinion, without any facts, that Kevin took advantage of his father and mother by taking an inordinate amount of money out of the businesses.

Kevin was still managing the companies full time, which not only supported his family, but also his mother, who was able to purchase anything she desired. However, her brother convinced her that Kevin was dishonest—a lying, deceitful son who was stealing all the money. Unbeknownst to Kevin, Andrew took Vivian to a lawyer to change her will. The new will gave everything to her daughter, Emilia, in Hawaii, and cut Kevin completely out of any inheritance. The will set out the reason for disinheriting her son, stating he had taken advantage of his father and mother by dishonestly appropriating the revenue of the three Dairy Queens.

When his mother died, some ten years later, Kevin was shocked to learn the businesses he had worked at all his life would now go to his sister in Hawaii who had not made any contribution. He came to see me in Fort Langley to see what could be done to rectify the situation. I brought an action to vary the will, as the mother owed a moral obligation to her son in all the circumstances of the case. We merely sought an equal division of the estate with Emilia, even though Kevin was instrumental in building up the estate, and may have been entitled to much more.

Kevin was being more than fair. In reply, his sister, Emilia, took the position that she should get it all. I could not believe that anyone could be so greedy. The estate was worth around three million dollars. Emilia was already wealthy, but no, another 1.5 million was not enough. She needed another three million.

We produced all the business records that proved Kevin did not take more out of the business than that to which he was entitled. At the trial in Supreme Court in New Westminster, the judge could see that our position was more than reasonable. He requested the lawyers meet with him in his private chambers. He expressed the opinion that if we did not settle, Kevin and Emilia would never be reconciled. Wasn't family more important than money?

We adjourned the trial for the afternoon to determine if we could settle the case. Emilia would not budge. Even after seeing the evidence that Kevin had worked all his life to build up the estate, and that he had only taken out of the business a reasonable wage, she continued to insist on the wording in the will that she receive the entire estate. We even proposed that Kevin would settle for 40% and give Emilia 60%. She persisted in her perverse greed.

The trial proceeded to its conclusion. The judge held that if the testatrix, Vivian, was not mistaken regarding her son's conduct, she would have provided for him equally, as evidenced by her prior will. In addition, considering the substantial efforts in the family business, there was no doubt in the judge's mind that a moral duty was owed by the mother to her son. An order was made dividing the estate equally between the brother and the sister. They never spoke to each other again. The judge was right. Emilia's greed was the great destroyer.

A third case of greed involved two brothers. The younger brother, Charles, was forty-two years of age and still living at home with his mother, Hazel, who was a widow. The older brother, Jordan, was forty-four years old, married with two children, and living in his own home with his wife. Hazel owned her home clear title and everything in it. Along with her husband, they had worked hard to pay off the mortgage, along with every other debt.

Charles did not contribute one cent to living at home with his mother. Hazel paid for the food, all utilities, and all needed home maintenance costs. Hazel began to suffer from poor health, including reduced cognitive abilities, even though she was only sixty-six years old. Charles took advantage of these problems to convince his mother to put the home, worth around $800,000, and her bank account, with cash in the amount of $150,000, into joint ownership, so that when Hazel passed away, the house and money in the bank would be his. Jordan knew nothing about this.

Hazel had a peculiar habit, which was known to the two brothers; she kept a lot of cash hidden in her home. They knew it was around $60,000, but neither of them knew where it was hidden. Charles followed his mother carefully in an attempt to discover the hidden cache. One night, he watched his mother close the bedroom door. He listened carefully with his ear to the door. He heard the rustling of clothes in the closet, then a creak in the floor. The next day, when his mother was not around, he searched her bedroom and discovered a loose floorboard in the closet. Hidden underneath, he found his mother's secret savings.

Shortly thereafter, Hazel died from an accidental fall down the stairs. After the funeral, Jordan obtained a copy of the will, which divided her estate equally between the two sons. However, now he learned there were no assets left in the estate, as his younger brother Charles owned everything. Jordan came to obtain some legal advice from me.

We commenced a legal action alleging undue influence, or alternatively, that the transfers were only effective to convey legal title, not a beneficial interest; therefore, we argued, the home and bank account were intended to fall into Hazel's estate to be divided equally between her two sons. The transfer of the land and the bank account were not accompanied by the usual declaration that Hazel intended the beneficial ownership to be transferred to Charles. Hazel's true intention was disclosed in her will, which divided her estate equally between the two brothers.

As part of the examination for discovery, Charles was put under oath to tell the truth, the whole truth, and nothing but the truth. He swore on the Bible. I asked him about his occupation and income. He testified he earned $2,000 per month cleaning carpets. He stated this was his only source of income. He produced his income tax returns verifying his testimony. I asked for his bank statements. They were produced many months later, just before the trial.

The bank statements showed his $2,000 per month income from carpet cleaning, just as Charles had testified, and as was confirmed in his income tax returns. But, Charles was not too bright. Those same statements also disclosed that he had made cash deposits, starting shortly after his mother's death, in the amount of $5,000 per month for twelve months.

At the trial, during cross examination, while Charles was under oath to tell the truth, I had him confirm his only income was $2,000 per month. He testified he had no other income. I put his evidence to him at the examination for discovery where he testified of the same facts. I then went through every cash deposit of $5,000 and asked, "where did the money come from?" I put it to him this was the cash his mother hid in the house. He finally admitted that it was. I said he was a liar and had committed perjury at the trial and at the discovery. He agreed. It was the only time in my career I had a witness admit he was a liar, even though many of them lied.

It was all over. The judge declared the transfer of the home and the bank account only transferred the legal title, but the beneficial interest was held in trust for the estate. In other words, the assets—the house and the bank account—fell into the estate to be divided equally between the brothers in accordance with the will. In addition, the judge ordered Charles to pay Jordan $30,000, one half of the cash he stole from the closet. Finally, the only penalty the judge could impose was to order actual legal costs against Charles, personally, for his outrageous conduct. Although he admitted to lying under oath, Charles was never charged with perjury. I guess Crown counsel had bigger fish to fry.

I don't know how Charles could live with himself. How could anyone try to steal from his brother—or sister—or any family member, for that matter. It just goes to show how greed can destroy a person's conscience and soul. Clearly, greed is a pestilence that consumes everything in its path without logic, or mercy, or love.

CHAPTER TWENTY-ONE

The Long and the Short of It

Hank

My partner, R. Henry Easingwood (Hank), liked to eat his food while it was hot, which is why he ate so fast. When we went for lunch at the Lampliter restaurant, located on Glover Road, the main street in Fort Langley, John Cherrington and I would often joke that Hank was frequently served his food first and had it finished before John and I had even started.

We regularly ordered the Fort Langley salmon, served in a unique style with cranberries and almonds, by the chef who was trained in Italian and French cuisine in Northern Italy. In fact, this is where the chef's wife, Nicoletta, who served us, was from. If Hank ordered the Belgium chocolate cake for dessert, then I couldn't resist ordering it as well. We loved excellent chocolate. Who doesn't?

Hank was married to Buffy, and they had three children. He was a family man and a sailing man. He navigated his sailboat throughout the Gulf Islands and up the coast as far north as Haida Gwaii. One year, he sailed across the Pacific Ocean to Hawaii. He said the waves off the Oregon Coast were as high as two-storey houses. I don't think I would like that, but he loved it. This is why every inch of wall space in his office displayed photographs of lovely sailboats heading into the wind and waves of the Pacific Ocean.

Hank was always the first person in the office early in the morning and often the last to go home at night. His legal practice consisted of complex commercial transactions—the more complicated, the more he liked it. I would find him in the library with charts spread out across the entire wall, setting out all the legal entities involved, the documents needing to be signed, and where all the paper work had to go. Piles of lengthy agreements, leases, and transfer papers would be neatly stacked across our large antique table in the boardroom. He enjoyed studying every word and then giving excellent advice to his sophisticated clients.

Hank was forceful, honest, and direct; some called it rude. He would not suffer fools gladly. We never had a serious disagreement that I can remember, but some of the staff were apprehensive when he barked out his orders.

Hank would have worked longer than John and I, but he suffered a painful death in stoic silence from colon cancer. His last days were spent at his beloved cottage on Pender Island with his family.

Hank Easingwood, Robert Kearl, John Cherrington

Mick

Mick, a junior lawyer at our law firm, worked with me on large construction cases involving dozens of boxes of documents and lengthy engineering reports. Due to my case load, I didn't have the time to read through all this material myself; besides, it was so tedious I wouldn't have been able to force myself to do it, so Mick had to do it. He was good at it and brought to my attention anything that was relevant to our case.

Mick also assisted me on a number of appeals from decisions of administrative bodies to the BC Supreme Court. He was very bright, as well as being excellent at doing legal research regarding these types of cases. One case involved our client, Malcolm Bond, who applied to the Council of the British Columbia Veterinary Medical Association, for approval of the name "Spay and Neuter Clinic."

Previously, a member of the Council received approval to use the name "Spay and Neuter Clinic." Yet the use of the name by Malcolm Bond was denied by Council on the grounds it was a "non-conforming name." It was a battle between our client, a veterinarian, and the governing body of a self-regulating profession with broad powers to control the rights of its members to advertise.

The first day of argument was heard before Justice Gow, in New Westminster. We were unable to complete the argument in one day, so we carried on the next day, in Vancouver. We were dressed in our robes with wing-collared white shirts and tabs. While I was waxing eloquent, Mick leaned back too far in his chair, which flipped over backwards, leaving Mick sprawling all over the floor, robes and all. It was a sight to behold—Mick lying there spread-eagle! Justice Gow and I began to grin, snicker, and then laugh out loud. Mick jumped up, brushed himself off, picked up the chair, and took his seat.

I concluded my argument that "a heavy duty rests on professional bodies to adopt appropriate regulations, without restricting unduly the freedom of expression of their members." Mick must have felt a tad chagrined from his fall. Fortunately, however, we had a good laugh over it. We also won.

Canada–US Border

I had a client from Arizona, a lady in her forties, who was injured in a motor vehicle accident in Northern BC. The insurance company denied her claim, saying the accident was her fault. Clearly, it was not. We commenced an action in BC Supreme Court.

My client drove up from Arizona for the trial. When she crossed the border, the guard asked her why she was coming to Canada. She explained that she was meeting with her lawyer in Fort Langley to make final preparations for a trial that would start the next day in New Westminster. He queried her regarding the name of her lawyer. She replied that it was Robert Kearl. The border guard then told her that she was very fortunate indeed, because Robert Kearl was the best lawyer in British Columbia, and that he had never lost a case!

When my client arrived at my office, she told me she didn't know I was such a famous lawyer, as even the border guards knew all about me. She was floating on cloud nine and very confident we would win our case, since she now knew that I was the best lawyer in British Columbia, having never lost a case!

In reality, it was quite the funny coincidence. I only knew one person who worked at the border, and as it turned out, my client happened to meet him. Like a fledgling actor seeking their next audition, I seize every opportunity for a good joke. A good sense of humour is part of life's greatest joys and comforts. So, whenever I see my border guard friend, I tell this story again, as we laugh and laugh. Happily, my client and I won the trial, preserving my perfect record!

ROBERT B. KEARL

Gemstones and Third Mortgages

In his briefcase, he carried small bags of gemstones, such as red rubies, green emeralds, blue aquamarine, yellow heliodor, pink morganite, purple amethyst, and opals; some were transparent, others translucent or opaque, with a background colour of white, black, or sometimes every colour of the visual spectrum. Attached to each bag of precious stones was an appraisal from an expert gemologist identifying and evaluating the gems.

In a second locked attaché case, he carried third mortgages on properties located all across the interior of BC, in the Cariboo, Kootenay, and North Coast regions, as well as real estate appraisals by professionals calculating the market value of each of the properties.

He called himself Angus MacGregor, a rather notorious con artist of the past. He stood out above all the others for his brazenness, as he ran a number of scams based on his claim that he was the ruler of an empire, called Poyais, in Central America (which in fact was a wilderness filled with malaria and other diseases).

Angus was tall and thin with a protruding nose and reddish hair. There was nothing in his appearance that would draw people to him, but when he started to talk in his flamboyant, confident style, he was very convincing. He was an incredibly good liar, who could play confidence tricks, exploiting victims using their credulity, naivety, compassion, vanity, irresponsibility, and greed. He was a real grifter searching for his next mark.

It was a fairly fast swindle with no need to involve a team, props, sets, extras, costumes, or scripted lines. It just required a victim who was desperate to sell his property and gullible, inexperienced, and greedy.

Matty was a handsome young man, whose rich parents had gifted to him a beautiful house in West Vancouver (a district where only millionaires live), when he was only nineteen years old. Matty worked in his father's business, helping him manage a chain of furniture stores. He lived a sheltered life. He didn't even do his own laundry, which his mother took care of each week.

Without telling his parents, he decided to sell his house, valued at two million dollars at the time, and worth around five million dollars as I write this story. His choice to sell was motivated by his desire to use the money to purchase a large, hundred acre hobby farm in the Fraser Valley, complete with a horse training track, barns, and a lovely country home. He did not realize it was not a good time to sell, as the market was slow and falling. At first he listed the property with a real estate agent, but it did not sell for the price he wanted, so he decided he would save the real estate commission and sell the home himself. He figured he was smarter than any real estate agent anyway. This is when he met the flim-flam man operating under the name Angus.

Angus appealed to Matty's vanity, building him up as the most clever and attractive young man he had ever met. Angus satisfied Matty's pride with flattering words about him being superior to and more deserving than others. Angus said he would give him more than the fair market value of his home, but not in cash. Rather, he offered something even better: gemstones and third mortgages worth a total value of three million dollars, not just two.

Matty began to feel an intense and selfish desire for wealth. He became obsessed with getting more and more money. It became an overwhelming urge affecting all his thoughts during the day and all his dreams at night. He withdrew from his parents and friends as he and Angus discussed all the things he could do with his money.

Matty did not obtain advice from anyone else, as Angus was successful in gaining his trust. Matty's home was transferred to Angus, and in return, the gemstones and third mortgages, along with all appraisals, were given to him. Angus quickly flipped the property and transferred the funds to an offshore account. Matty quickly learned that he was unable to sell the precious stones and third mortgages, as promised. He came to me in Fort Langley for legal advice.

We sued Angus for fraud, which is when I discovered he had used this same scheme on a dozen other deals completed in the last few months. I took the gemstones to several gemologists in Vancouver, who provided their opinions that the gemstones were only commercial grade and therefore worthless. I engaged a reputable real estate appraiser I knew, to determine the fair market value of the properties whereon Matty had taken third mortgages; there was no equity, the mortgages were worthless. All of the appraisals were fraudulent.

Angus was so bold that he remained in British Columbia to defend the lawsuit, but the assets were gone. At the trial, Angus was found guilty of fraud, and a judgment for the amount of the money lost was made against him. It was only then that he disappeared, along with his ill-gotten gains from all those he had swindled.

I met with the Commercial Crime Unit of the Police Department and provided them with all the evidence they needed for a criminal conviction for fraud against Angus, but they did not seem interested. He was gone with the money, and that was the end of the story. He was never brought to justice.

Slander

My client Mia, was an experienced female nurse, single, around thirty-eight years old, and living on Vancouver Island. She became aware of criminal charges against a male family doctor for sexually assaulting young boys, which was in all the local papers. The case went to trial, and the court found the doctor was innocent, for there was no legitimate foundation for the charges. Although Mia didn't work directly under the doctor, she occasionally crossed paths with him in the hospital. She often observed his condescending behaviour towards her fellow nurses—the way he dismissed their opinions and read patient charts with an upturned nose. Mia felt deeply uncomfortable in his presence, like there was something predatory in his demeanor and behaviours. Other nurses felt the same. While the charges against the doctor were dismissed, Mia still felt in her bones that he was guilty.

After the doctor was acquitted, a close female friend asked Mia for advice on finding a family doctor for herself and her two young boys. When she specifically asked Mia, as a friend and nurse, for her opinion if this particular doctor would be suitable, Mia replied, "No, he is a pedophile."

Unfortunately, the doctor learned what Mia had told her friend about him and sued her for slander, a false spoken statement damaging his reputation. There are five key elements in a successful lawsuit for slander: it must be a statement of fact; it must be published—meaning communicated to another person; the statement must cause injury; it must be false; and the statement must not be given in circumstances of qualified privilege.

The first four elements were clearly established. Therefore, the only possible defence was whether qualified privilege applied to the statement, meaning, was it lawful for Mia to give her opinion to her friend? Her friend was asking advice about a doctor, because Mia was a nurse—a position qualifying her to give an opinion on whether he would be a good doctor for her friend and her friend's two young boys. This was the defence we advanced.

However, qualified privilege is defeated where the person suing for defamation proves that the person who made the defamatory statement acted recklessly or with malice. Malice is usually proven if the defamatory statement is communicated to others outside of the privileged communication. I felt we had a good defence of qualified privilege, as long as Mia only told her friend—who asked for advice—and no one else. She assured me this was the case.

We went to trial in the Supreme Court of BC, in Victoria, where the lawsuit was filed. It was a pleasant venue, unlike the heavy traffic in Vancouver and up the Valley. In Victoria, there was so little traffic that, even during what they called rush hour, I could drive right up to the courthouse and park outside on the street without any difficulty.

The trial was going well. It was big news in the Victoria papers, where I was described as a big-time Vancouver lawyer defending a nurse for accusing a doctor on the island of being a pedophile. I called the paper to inform them I was just "a little guy from the tiny village of Fort Langley, the historic birthplace of BC."

Just when it appeared we would successfully defend the legal action on the basis of qualified privilege, Mia admitted in cross-examination that she told many of her friends the doctor was a pedophile, and even volunteered this information without being asked.

Mia had told me that she didn't tell anyone else. I told her our defence rested on this fact. I emphasized to her, in no uncertain terms, that the defence of qualified privilege would be defeated by malice if she had told anyone else the doctor was a pedophile. As you can see, it was understandably a great surprise to me when Mia made the admission in court. I suppose being under oath to tell the truth, the whole truth, and nothing but the truth, finally weighed upon her conscience. She told the truth for the first time and lost the case.

The judge ruled that qualified privilege would have been a successful defence, but communicating the slanderous statement to others constituted malice, so we lost our defence. Damages were awarded in the amount of $30,000, which was a reasonable sum in the circumstances. The slander was of the worst kind, but it was only communicated orally to a few people.

A Great Cross-Examination

Mrs. Godsend was a little old lady. I think she was about eighty-nine years old, but still as sharp as ever. She had a great desire to restore her old, dilapidated matrimonial home in Abbotsford, for emotional reasons, but she did not have the money to do it. Her neighbour, Andy, was a real handyman and friend who had helped her fix things in her condo many times without asking for any compensation. He owned a couple of fast food joints, so he had the time and the money. Andy was middle-aged, married with four children, and a leader of a Christian congregation.

Mrs. Godsend asked Andy to restore the old house, but he refused, saying it did not make economic sense, as it would cost more to fix the home than it was worth. She kept after him to do it anyway, while he repeatedly rejected the idea.

In a final attempt to return the old home to its former glory, Mrs. Godsend said she would transfer the house to Andy on the promise he would complete the restoration work. That way, the home would be his, as she realized the amount he would have to spend would also amount to the fair market value of the home. She realized Andy would not receive a windfall. Andy finally agreed.

The land was transferred to Andy, and he completed all the work to the satisfaction of Mrs. Godsend. Mrs. Godsend then sued Andy for the return of the home, taking the position that the money he spent to restore the home was a gift. Andy came to see me to defend the legal action.

At the trial I commenced my cross-examination of Mrs. Godsend by asking whether she had completed high school. She said she did not, but at the examination for discovery a number of months earlier, she had said that she did graduate from high school. I put the discovery transcript to her, including the portion where she was sworn to tell the truth, to which she replied that she did graduate from high school. I asked her why she did not tell the truth to the court, even though she was under oath. First she said she did graduate from high school, then she said she did not. What was the truth?

She got very angry and started speaking with a loud voice, contrary to the little old lady who presented herself as someone who would be easily influenced and manipulated. Up to that point, she could only answer questions that were loud and clear, due to her poor hearing and understanding. Yet when I walked away from her in the courtroom and whispered these questions toward the back of the court, not even toward her in the witness box, she yelled back the answers, saying this questioning was irrelevant. She attacked with, "What difference does it make whether I graduated from high school?" She became increasingly belligerent, argumentative, and stubborn.

I was as surprised as the judge when Mrs. Godsend displayed her true character. I responded to Mrs. Godsend's question that this trial was all about who could be relied upon to tell the truth.

My cross examination made it obvious that this was not a case about a little old lady being taken advantage of by a younger businessman, but an elderly woman using her age as a weapon to attempt to deceive Andy and the court. The case was dismissed.

A Small Stream Under the House

The newborn baby cried continually in the home of a lovely young couple who were excited about the recent purchase of their first home together. Their excitement was only dampened by the day-by-day increasing congestion they experiences in their noses and throats. Before long, new symptoms started to appear. They couldn't understand what was going wrong, and their family doctor wasn't able to solve the mystery; why were they all so sick all the time, when they used to be so healthy?

Then, mold started appearing from behind the baseboards. They had an expert do an inspection of their home, who determined that it was black mold, thereby making their home unfit for habitation. This black mold is what caused the young family's chronic symptoms of illness: chronic coughing and sneezing, irritation to the eyes and mucus membranes of the nose and throat, rashes, chronic fatigue, and persistent headaches. The young family had to move out and live in a hotel.

This is when they came to see me for legal advice. I studied an old topographical map of the area, before any houses were built, and discovered that a small stream used to run right where their house was built. The builder had constructed their home on top of a watercourse.

Unfortunately, I could not sue the builder as he had gone bankrupt, so our only recourse was to look to the municipality for redress. How could the municipality have approved a house to be built above this small creek, without sufficient perimeter drainage? This was the issue.

The municipality denied any liability. Therefore, I commenced a lawsuit for the cost to repair the damaged house, the costs incurred due to the necessity of the young family having to live in a hotel, and damages for pain, suffering, and loss of enjoyment of life. I knew that once I started the lawsuit, I would be entitled to be provided with all relevant documents, and in particular, the inspection report of the perimeter drainage by the municipal inspector. This was the document that I hoped would establish our claim for negligent inspection.

When I received the list of documents by the municipality, I studied the list, and then requested a copy of all documents. "Eureka!" I shouted for joy when I discovered the document I could rely upon to win the lawsuit. The report on the inspection of the perimeter drainage disclosed that the drainage system had already been covered up when the inspector arrived, and he relied on the word of the builder that it had been designed and built properly to carry the water away from the house, thereby preventing it from seeping in through the basement walls.

In fact, the necessary perforated pipe with a mesh sock covering it to keep the soil out, installed underground, circling the perimeter of the house and surrounded with plenty of gravel, had not been designed and built as required for a home with a waterway running underneath it. The tiny holes needed to allow the water to enter the pipe, where it could then be drained away from the home's foundation, were critically important, but were not to be found.

The writing was on the wall—the municipality would lose big time, including paying all the legal costs. We won. They settled.

Yee-Haw!

The entertainment company advertised the ride as the best activity for a Western-themed event: a mechanical bull, fitted with a Western-theme, safely surrounded arena, and the latest speed-limiting control box. They said it was a must-have for a dry grad. Many corporate functions also rented it. The operators assured Kyle it was safe for all ages, and that they would make sure everyone had an enjoyable ride.

Kyle was athletic, six-foot-two-inches of rugged muscle. He was thirty-nine years old, with a loving wife and two young daughters, whom he adored. He loved his job selling exercise equipment—the best treadmills, elliptical trainers, exercise bikes, and many other products—to fitness centres right across the country. He was able to demonstrate the operation of all the equipment he sold at a very high level, since he was in such great shape.

Kyle rented the mechanical bull for a fun community function. Kyle would take the first ride to show everyone how it was done. The operator assured him the ride was ready to go. Kyle didn't know what his femoral artery was, nor about its function to carry oxygen-rich blood away from his heart, or its location at the top of his thigh, in an area called the femoral triangle. The femoral triangle can be found just below the groin, right in the crease where the abdomen ends and the leg begins, and the femoral artery runs all the way down to the knee. A person can bleed to death in just five minutes if the femoral artery is severed, and the hemorrhaging isn't stopped. Kyle did not know this.

Unfortunately, on this day, riding the mechanical bull known as Bruiser, Kyle's physical prowess and his cowboy hat would not help him in the slightest. As soon as he mounted Bruiser, the bull began to spin wildly, and Kyle's legs slid along the side of the bull and up over its head. At this point, Kyle felt instant pain in the upper part of his right leg, and then blood began spurting everywhere. Mercifully, there was a doctor in the waiting crowd who saw what happened, or else Kyle probably would not have lived to tell the tale. Somehow his leg slipped across a sharp protrusion, which was not supposed to be there, and cut his femoral artery.

The doctor was able to control the bleeding long enough to get Kyle to the hospital, only a five-minute drive away, which saved his life. At the hospital, he immediately underwent surgical repair of the blood vessel. Even though the procedure was successful, it was still unknown whether he would suffer a partial or complete loss of movement or sensation resulting in some degree of permanent disability in the leg.

Kyles's recovery was slow, but after many months of pain and suffering, it was complete. Shortly after the injury, Kyle consulted me in my office in Fort Langley. Obviously the entertainment company was responsible for his injury and the resulting damages, such as loss of income, pain, and suffering. Fortunately, the company carried insurance for these types of events, so I was able to negotiate a favourable settlement, in a reasonable period of time, after Kyle had recovered and the damages could be quantified.

Bruiser was true to his name, as Kyle took more than a bruising on that wild ride. The consequences were certainly more than Kyle had bargained for when he first shouted "Ye-haw," while hanging onto Bruiser with his left hand, right hand waving his white cowboy hat high in the air to the cheers of the waiting crowd. Unsurprisingly, no one who witnessed the spectacle took a ride that day—nor any other day—on a mechanical bull.

Popeye on Adrenaline

It was on the six o'clock news that day. There he was, Jeremiah, in full colour, rushing around, directing the first responders to push all the onlookers back, since the propane tank in the back of his van could explode at any moment. Such a blast would have enough force to launch debris from the tank, itself, and its surrounding objects as far as a block away.

Jeremiah drove a propane-powered van, filled with the construction tools used in his building business. He was often heard to say, "I am a builder, not a bullfrog!" He was a big fan of Three Dog Night singing "Joy to the World." Often, he would sing this tune, imagining he was the prophet Jeremiah, from the Bible, singing to unite all the people of the world in happiness.

He was short and stout with big jowls, and he liked to wear green, so he did look something like a bullfrog. On the news, he was jumping around and gathering his tools from off the road after he had been involved in a big rear-ender crash. The rear doors of his van had been crushed by a blue Ford pickup truck driven by a young hooligan who didn't have the sense to watch where he was going.

Picking up some heavy ladders that he had secured to the roof of his van, but were now strewn across the pavement, he raised them over his head, like a muscle man—something like Popeye would have done—in full view of the rolling cameras on the news. Many times his hands were raised above his head, lifting this thing or that. Of course, those evil people at the insurance company were always watching.

Jeremiah came to see me regarding a personal injury claim. Among his injuries, the most lasting and problematic was the pain in his right shoulder, caused by the dislocation of the acromioclavicular, or AC joint, where two bones meet. One of these bones is the collarbone, or clavicle, while the other is the scapula or shoulder blade.

The insurance company defended, taking the position enunciated by their doctors, that it is impossible for a person to lift their hands above the head, let alone carry heavy ladders above the head, when the AC joint is dislocated. The insurance company insisted the dislocation occurred sometime, somewhere, after the accident, but they had no evidence as to where or when.

The insurance company trotted out a copy of the video in the news report as proof Jeremiah did not dislocate his AC joint, as he carried heavy ladders above his head and moved around as if he wasn't even injured. At trial, as I knew the judge was a hockey fan going back to the 1950s, I cited the example of Tim Horton, famous defence-man of the Toronto Maple Leafs, playing hockey after breaking a leg. It was all a matter of adrenaline pumping at the moment.

The judge agreed. Adrenaline could allow a normal person to have super human strength in the heat of the moment. It was probable that Jeremiah acquired Popeye strength with the flow of adrenaline through his veins. He was also singing "Joy to the World," which really pumped him up.

The insurance company appealed, but the three judges in the Court of Appeal agreed with the trial judge in Supreme Court; maybe they were hockey fans too. In any event, the explanation of Popeye strength for a short time due to an adrenaline rush won the day.

Five Accidents, One Trial

They say bad luck comes in threes. Unfortunately, for my young client, Michelle, bad luck came in fives! She was a single, young lady, only twenty-one years old, so how could she be involved in five car accidents when she had only been driving for two years?

In the first accident, she was a passenger in the back seat when the driver, for some strange reason unknown to anyone, turned east onto the railway tracks running along the Bedford Channel at Fort Langley Marina Park. It must have been a terribly bumpy ride as they bounced over each railway tie. Unfortunately, travelling west on the same track was a train locomotive pulling ninety-seven cars, fully loaded with coal, headed for Roberts Bank on the coastline of the Strait of Georgia in Delta, British Columbia, to be shipped to China. It resulted in a head-on collision between the car and the train; the car was thrown off the track, like a speck of dust, while the train continued on its way as if nothing had happened. Both the driver and the front seat passenger were killed. However, Michelle, sitting in the back seat, somehow survived—though with fairly significant whiplash injuries.

The second accident occurred as Michelle was parking in front of Beatniks, an excellent restaurant in Fort Langley, when she was rear-ended. Just think how disappointing it must have been to be looking forward to biting into a juicy Beatnik's burger, but instead to have some random Toyota Corolla biting into your back bumper! Rear-ended indeed! What a bummer!

The third time Michelle felt the wrath of the road, she was traveling north on Glover Road, at 88th Street, into Fort Langley. While she was stopped at a red light, she was rear-ended again.

In the fourth incident, Michelle was turning right to drive up to the historic fort, when she was rear-ended for the third time. In each of the rear-end collisions, Michelle sustained minor whiplash injuries to her neck and back. Sometimes I think maybe some of my children would prefer a whiplash injury to visiting the Fort one more time (since my history obsession led me to take them over and over again). I doubt Michelle would agree.

The fifth accident occurred in front of the 50s Diner in Fort Langley. Michelle had stopped with the traffic, but the driver behind her, who was drinking a strawberry milkshake, spilled some on his lap, looked down, and rear-ended Michelle. What a way to shake things up!

By now, the most debilitating injury to Michelle was the fear and anxiety that all vehicles were "after her." Michelle could not drive a car, ride in a car, or walk close to the road where cars were travelling, as she was overcome with an all-consuming fear that all cars were deliberately committed to hitting her. Every vehicle she saw overwhelmed her with the feeling they were designed to cause her harm.

I commenced a legal action against each of the drivers at fault, who were represented by insurance company lawyers. We sought damages for her personal injuries and joined all five to be heard at the same time in a single trial. Five accidents in one trial! It was not only astonishing to me, but also to the judge. A generous award was ordered by the judge to be paid by the insurance companies for Michelle's psychological trauma and physical injuries, as well as the cost of treatment and past and future wage loss. It was a unique trial, a sort of five in one.

Unbeknownst to me at the time, I would later appreciate the empathy I gained for Michelle's—and all my MVA clients' emotional traumas—as I witnessed my own teenage grand-daughter work towards overcoming her fear and anxiety, after being a passenger in a car accident.

Kindred Spirits

The young woman was coming to the close of her high school days. It was the end of grade twelve, a time for celebration and graduation parties. Claire was slender, weighing 105 pounds. She was five-foot-two-inches tall and had long light brown hair and twinkling green eyes. Claire had an effervescent personality with an attractive face and figure, which resulted in her being extremely well liked in her high school.

Claire's best friend was Penelope, who was slightly taller at five-foot-four-inches and somewhat stronger and more athletic, weighing 130 pounds. Her blonde hair was short, which brought attention to her cute, round baby face with big brown eyes. She was nothing short of adorable.

Penelope and Claire were inseparable companions. They were often seen strolling down the halls of the high school, laughing and chatting with everyone they passed. The two of them were probably the most popular girls in the school, not only with their fellow students, but also with the teaching staff. Their teachers found them to be highly intelligent, flexible in their thinking, adaptable to change, and able to effectively manage their emotions.

Claire and Penelope met when they started grade one in a little brown school that only taught grades ones to three. There, they bonded together and became, as Anne of Green Gables would say, "bosom buddies" and "kindred spirits." They loved to read together and analyze and craft their own works, shaping their written stories, creating persuasive and argumentative essays of their own. Each of them excelled in the Honours English class they enjoyed together.

The two of them not only enjoyed innovation and imagination in their writing, they also were delighted to participate in drama class. They were often chosen for leading parts in the school plays, as they were talented in creating characters, understanding them, and performing them realistically. Drama enhanced their verbal and nonverbal expression of ideas and their artistic abilities, and helped them to develop self-discipline, confidence, and team work. It also bonded them closer together.

One lovely spring day in June— a day that felt more like summer than spring as the sun shone brightly, and the pink blossoms, which had dreamily drifted from the Japanese cherry trees were already replaced by the fine greenery of verdant leaves— Penelope and Claire attended a graduation party. The party was at a popular spot, the gravel pit, where the extraction of gravel had ended many years earlier. The young ladies knew there would be a lot of drinking, which they were not really in to, but sadly decided that fateful day to go anyway.

As they joined a large group gathered at the edge of the gravel pit, Claire and Penelope didn't think much about the many cars coming and going nearby, driven by teenage boys with an unrealistic view of their ability to drive while drinking. Then it happened, the greatest tragedy of Claire's life. While the rays of the sun brought radiant light and warmth, with dozens of the graduating class of that year laughing and consuming copious quantities of alcohol, a foolish boy, who had been drinking too much, lost control of his car and careened into the group. He hit a few students who bounced off his car and then tragically ran over Penelope right in front of Claire, who was only a few feet away. Claire sprang forward and held Penelope lovingly in her arms as she died.

How do you explain such a tragedy? How do you describe the sorrow felt by Claire? What a disastrous conclusion to a beautiful life. All that was left for Claire was grief, disbelief, shock, and denial. Claire was numb for weeks and could not speak. Eventually, she began to feel pain and guilt. She constantly thought about why she took Penelope to that party. She felt Penelope's death was her fault.

With the effluxion of time, Claire's personality completely changed as she became filled with anger, and then a debilitating depression set in. Claire felt she had fallen into a deep, dark pit, where there was no light and no escape. She was not capable of feeling any hope. She could not accept Penelope's death. She felt there was no life without Penelope.

Claire's parents brought her to see me at my office in Fort Langley, where she recounted her story. She could not speak about the death of her best friend Penelope without uncontrollably weeping. Her family doctor had referred her to a psychiatrist and a psychologist for treatment. I requested expert reports from each of them with a diagnosis and prognosis that could be relied upon in court regarding the psychological trauma caused by the fatal car accident.

Claire did not suffer any physical injuries in the motor vehicle accident, but the psychological harm was more debilitating to her than any injury to her body. It was one of the saddest cases of my legal career.

The law provides recovery for psychological damage when the claimant witnesses an accident and the resulting severe injury or death of another. The law does not allow recovery when the claimant was not an actual eyewitness to the event. For example, if the accident was described by telephone right after it occurred, it is deemed by law to be too remote, so there can be no recovery of damages, even if the psychological injury was the same as if the claimant had witnessed it.

The circumstances of Penelope's death, dying in Claire's arms, and the effect upon Claire on the death of her best friend, caused even the hardened insurance adjuster quantifying the claim to shed many a tear. The adjuster made an offer greater than any that had ever been made in British Columbia, up to that point in time, for purely psychological injuries suffered by a claimant only witnessing an accident and not being injured physically in the accident in any way.

We settled the case, but Claire never did recover as long as I knew her. They say that time heals all wounds, but Claire said this was not true. Time did not erase the sorrow, despair, and depression caused by the death of her best friend. I have not seen her for many years, but I hope she finally achieved some degree of peace and happiness. The conclusion of this story is unsatisfying, as the end comes so abruptly, like Penelope's life.

Nuisance

My client, Barbara, a middle-aged lady with a husband and four children, was driving down a country road in the middle of a hot day in summer, with her driver's window down to enjoy the cooling breeze. At the same time, a tractor was driving down the grassy shoulder of the road, with a roadside mower attached to cut the long grass in the adjacent ditch.

As they passed each other, a rock with a circumference of approximately six inches struck her with great force on her temple on the left side of her head. It was a freak accident.

Lamentably, Barbara suffered from the worst luck possible that day. Upon her return home, she continued to suffer from excruciatingly painful headaches, so her husband took her to the hospital where they diagnosed her with a serious concussion. The continuing headaches, poor concentration, and memory loss, eventually led the neurologist to render a diagnosis of post-concussion syndrome.

Fortunately, Barbara kept the rock that had hit her and brought it to my office when she came to see me for legal advice. It was also important to our case that, at the time the incident occurred, she had informed the tractor driver of the head injury she had incurred due to the rock being thrown by the mower. The driver told the owner, who informed his insurance company, and an insurance adjuster did an investigation, concluding the facts were just as Barbara had described.

This was the type of case where the law imposed strict liability, that is, compensation would be awarded without the need to establish the defendant's fault, as it constituted a public nuisance—an act that endangers the life or health of the public. Since there were no defences to this nuisance, the case was eventually settled once we were able to establish the full damages upon Barbara's full recovery.

Taekwondo

Taekwondo, which originated in Korea, is the art of self-defence. Recognized as one of the oldest forms of martial arts in the world, it reaches back over 2,000 years. The name is descriptive of this form of self-defence technique since "tae" means foot, "kwon" means hand, and "do" means art.

In-Su, his name meaning "preserving wisdom," taught taekwondo at a prestigious martial arts school in Toronto. The owner of the school was Dae-Hyun, the translation being "big show-off," and he certainly was a man with a huge ego.

In-Su decided to move to Vancouver, on the other side of the country, as he loved the scenery and the weather there. Toronto winters are brutal. Upon his arrival in Vancouver, he started a school teaching taekwondo, but back in Toronto, Dae-Hyun was furious that he had left. When Dae-Hyun learned about In-Su's new school in Vancouver, he commenced a lawsuit against In-Su, alleging In-Su had no right to set up his own school to teach taekwondo.

In-Su consulted me in my office in Fort Langley for legal advice. It was my opinion we had a strong defence, since the non-competition clause in his contract of employment with Dae-Hyun could only apply to Toronto and its surrounding suburbs, but certainly not Vancouver, British Columbia. I thought it was a frivolous lawsuit meant to intimidate my client. Therefore, we defended vigorously.

When the trial date finally came around, Dae-Hyun surprised me at my law office, after regular work hours, when everyone else had gone home, by barging into my personal office. His unannounced arrival, without his lawyer, was grossly inappropriate and unusual. Obviously, I had forgotten to lock the door. I hadn't thought about it, as Fort Langley is generally a very safe community.

Standing in front of my desk, Dae-Hyun tried to intimidate me, telling me I had better advise my client to pay him a lot of money "or else," as he had a black belt in taekwondo. I stood up as tall as I could—which isn't very tall as I am only five-foot-seven-inches—and yelled at him to get the hell out of my office or I would call the police. He left. Needles to say, I locked the door. I called his lawyer in Vancouver, but of course he had no idea his client was doing something so outrageous.

The next day, when the trial was to commence, Dae-Hyun was nowhere to be found. No doubt his lawyer had advised him he had no case. His lawyer showed up, apologizing to the court, and the case was dismissed with costs.

Over time, In-Su built up an internationally recognized taekwondo school in the Vancouver area and became renowned as a great teacher and coach. One of his star pupils was Seo-Jun, meaning "talented," a nineteen-year-old woman, who became a world champion in the fly weight division for those with a weight of 108 pounds or less.

Competing in the Olympics, Seo-Jun landed a kick to the head of a Chinese competitor, which would have qualified her for the next round and a chance to win a gold medal, but the Russian judge failed to award her the points. I watched the video, and even I could see she had won the match, but there must have been a deal between China and Russia. In-Su wanted me to commence a lawsuit on behalf of his star pupil, but I advised him it would be a waste of time and money.

When Seo-Jun retired from international competition a few years later, she appeared as a stunt double in many TV shows and movies filmed in Vancouver, whenever the script called for martial arts. I thought it was hilarious that a young woman weighing less than 108 pounds could take the place of big, strong men and do their fighting for them.

In order to bring this story to a romantic conclusion with a happy ending, Seo-Jun and In-Su were blissfully wed and remain joyfully together to this day.

Medical Malpractice

Ruth was forty-five years old and happily married with four children. The oldest two children were married with children of their own, while the younger two were still living at home. Ruth was glad that she was not an empty-nester, as she enjoyed the company of her children. These feelings of love were reciprocated by all her children and her three grandchildren. Her husband felt the same.

Ruth had always struggled with her weight, which may have contributed to a hernia and pain in her belly, including the area just above her stomach, as well as an ache in her back, which was diagnosed by an ultrasound as a gallbladder infection. A bulge in the area on the side of her pubic bone, causing pain and discomfort, especially when bending over, coughing, or lifting, was diagnosed as a hernia.

Open surgery was recommended by the specialist to repair both problems at the same time. The surgical incision is one of the most crucial steps in any surgical procedure. It is always essential to determine the proper location of the incision for optimal visualization, especially in this case where the surgeon recommended that it was safe to repair the hernia during gall bladder surgery. Ruth's case took place back in the day when open surgery was used to remove the gallbladder, whereas today it is usually performed laparoscopically.

The doctor explained to Ruth that gallbladder removal surgery and hernia repair are considered standard, safe procedures. He also assured her the risk of complications are rare, so there was no need to worry. Ruth and her family were apprehensive anyway, but she decided to proceed based on the many assurances given by her doctor.

However, during the course of what was considered a routine procedure, the surgeon mistakenly damaged the abdominal aorta, causing massive internal bleeding. Ruth was rushed from the local rural hospital to the Royal Columbian Hospital in New Westminster, twenty minutes away. There, the specialist put clamps above and below the damaged aorta to stop the blood flow, as there was no doctor in the rural hospital who could perform this procedure.

Tragically, Ruth left the hospital paralyzed from the waist down. It was a shocking result when this surgery was considered "routine." It had never happened before, but it did happen to Ruth, who was left without the use of her legs.

We brought a lawsuit for medical malpractice against the doctor and the rural hospital. To succeed in a medical malpractice case in Canada, the plaintiff must not only prove the doctor was negligent, but in addition, that the doctor had deviated from standard medical procedures. Medical malpractice in Canada is one of the most difficult types of cases to prove.

With great difficulty I found a surgeon who provided a written opinion that the doctor who performed the surgery on Ruth used the wrong surgical incision, which would constitute a deviation from standard medical procedure. In his opinion, the doctor should have used a midline incision, as this would have provided for optimal visualization to make the proper repair of the hernia and remove the gallbladder. Yet he used a subcostal oblique incision.

Shortly before trial, the defence settled the case. I thought they had settled because the doctor had used the wrong incision, but years later, the lawyer acting for the doctor informed me that they had actually settled because of the twenty minute delay Ruth had faced in travelling to New Westminster to reach an expert who could put the clamps on the aorta. The defence thought the negligence lay in the fact that the local hospital did not have this capability, and that this delay is what caused the paralysis.

I felt lucky that we had obtained a favourable settlement for Ruth, even though I didn't even know why we won. I guess the reason we won didn't matter to Ruth; it was just important that the funds were available to help offset the loss of use of her legs. No amount of money would compensate Ruth for that loss, but at least the funds would help.

From time to time, I think of Ruth, who went into the hospital for a routine operation and came out paralyzed from the waist down. Maybe this is why I avoid hospitals and often joke about my reluctance to see doctors. Perhaps this is an irrational fear, but we are often influenced by our emotions. Even a lawyer has emotions!

CHAPTER TWENTY-TWO

The Love Triangle

The newspaper headline declared in large bold letters: "Shoot Out At High Noon." Reading the first paragraph of the article disclosed the truth of the old saying, "Don't take a knife to a gun fight." The man with the knife lay dead on the ground, while the fellow with the rifle fled the scene in his blue Ford F-150 full-size pickup truck.

I was at the courthouse in New Westminster, when my partner called me in the Barrister's Lounge to say the son of a good client of the firm was in lockup at the police station in Abbotsford, located about a 45 minute drive east on the freeway from New Westminster in the Fraser Valley. Apparently someone was dead, so I headed out as soon as I finished arguing my case in Supreme Court.

Arriving at the police station, the officer informed me that a drug dealer, Dwayne, well known to the police, was killed by a young man, whose name was Samuel. Samuel had a clean record, never having been in trouble with the law before. Samuel was arrested for murder. The police officer set me up in a secure private room to interview Samuel.

The first thing I noticed about Samuel as he walked toward me was how tall he was. Since I am only five-foot-seven-inches tall, Samuel, at six-foot-two, towered over me. As we sat down at the desk, I took out my paper and pen. I noticed Samuel was trembling; in fact, I think every inch of his slender frame was shaking almost uncontrollably. I learned he was only nineteen years old, the youngest child of five children, raised on a large raspberry farm in the area known as the "Raspberry Capital of the World"—Abbotsford.

His father escaped Eastern Europe when Soviet tanks invaded Hungary in 1956 because the leaders of that nation threatened to withdraw from the Warsaw Pact and reject communism. Over 2,500 Hungarians and 700 Soviet troops were killed in the conflict, and 200,000 Hungarians fled as refugees, Samuel's mother and father being two of them.

Samuel's parents emigrated to Abbotsford, where they started their raspberry farm. Due to their hard work, their farm became very successful. Their four oldest children were married with children of their own, and were model Canadian citizens. Samuel came as a surprise seven years after the fourth child, so while the first four children had experienced hard work and thrift on the farm, Samuel lived the life of abundance.

Samuel had natural, long, blond hair with blue eyes. The upper half of his face was fairly broad, the cheek bones were high, and the lower jaw quite prominent. He was a handsome young man with a pleasant personality, polite and agreeable. I could not imagine how this youthful man standing in front of me could have killed anyone. As I got into the details, I learned it was the strange consequence of an odd love triangle.

From the police, I obtained details about the dead victim, Dwayne. He had started dealing illegal drugs at an early age in the town where he grew up: Cache Creek, a small town about 350 kilometres northeast of Vancouver, British Columbia, on the Trans-Canada Highway. Cache Creek is located in a famous area of the gold rush in the Thompson Okanagan region, in the midst of cactus and tumbleweed with a desert-like climate.

Dwayne's favourite pastime was to head into the desert brush and shoot snakes, gophers, squirrels, and anything else that moved. Throughout high school, Dwayne provided speed, pot, cocaine, and crack to anyone who had the money and the desire to buy, which meant he was well known to the RCMP as the local drug dealer.

Using speed, Dwayne felt energized and excited; however, the after-effects included mood swings, difficulty sleeping, and tiredness. The pot made him feel relaxed and talkative, but he often felt anxious, paranoid, and forgetful. "White Lady," which is what he called crack cocaine, made him feel confident and strong, but the problem was he became dependant on this expensive drug, which provoked him to resort to all manner of crime and violence to feed this gnawing addiction.

Dwayne was caught in that all-too-common no-man's land of middle childhood, with an older and a younger brother. There was a difference of three years with each of his brothers, so they didn't have anything in common. His mother died of advanced breast cancer when he was in grade nine. He never spoke about his mother, probably because she suffered a long, painful death.

Dwayne's father remarried a year later to a widow who also had three children—two daughters, one a year younger, the other two years younger than Dwayne, and one son the same age as Dwayne's younger brother. He had no connection with his step-mother or his new siblings, even though they were kind enough. He admired his father, but unfortunately chose not to follow his example of kindness and selfless service to others. He felt his father paid more attention to all the others. As each year passed, he distanced himself from the family more and more. Drugs became his life. He became a real loner.

When he was in grade eleven, the family moved to Delta, in the Lower Mainland, one of the suburbs of Vancouver. Dwayne was happy with the move, as this gave him a larger market for the sale of illegal drugs, allowing him to expand his product line to include LSD and ecstasy.

Dwayne experimented with LSD, which distorted his perceptions of himself and the world around him. The colours were brighter, the sounds were sharper, and his senses seemed mixed-up as he thought he could hear colours and see sounds. He liked the feeling of being weightless and disconnected from his body. However, he didn't notice the long-term effects of paranoia and depression.

Ecstasy was a popular drug, as it created a feeling of euphoria, increased physical energy, and sociability, but when the pleasurable effects started to wear off, Dwayne was left with panic attacks, anxiety, paranoia, and hallucinations.

One of Dwayne's customers in his high school in Delta was a fellow student named Charlotte. Charlotte's father was abusive, which resulted in her being vulnerable to manipulation by the worst people around her, as she was also desperate to feel the love and acceptance she was denied by her father. Her overwhelming desire was to escape to anywhere, at any time. Drugs were a great way to achieve her getaway, which led her to becoming dependant on drugs, and to Dwayne keeping her in supply.

When they graduated from high school, Charlotte and Dwayne moved in together, renting an apartment in Delta. Their pain attracted them to each other—each seeking to fill a cavernous void of need carved out by trauma and ruinous coping mechanisms. Dwayne treated Charlotte like dirt, just like some wrinkled, dirty, and smelly piece of clothing one throws in the hamper when it needs cleaning. Charlotte, conditioned to feel like she deserved the abuse, didn't even notice.

Two years later, they moved to a house they rented in Langley. Dwayne was dark and swarthy and of average size and build, therefore, he was forced to rely on weapons to intimidate everyone around him. His favourite firearm of choice was the double-action Smith & Wesson 29, 44-calibre Magnum revolver—"the most powerful handgun in the world," used in the 1971 movie *Dirty Harry*, by Clint Eastwood.

Dwayne thought he was Dirty Harry. The RCMP knew all about Dwayne's methods and his drug dealing. The police were just waiting for him to use one of his guns, so they could put him away for a long time, since small-time drug dealers like Dwayne did not get long sentences in the Canadian justice system; but if they used a weapon, it was a very different story.

Dwayne's live-in girlfriend, Charlotte, looked much different from him, as she was thin, small, and frail at the best of times, with long, dull, scraggly, light brown hair and a mousy appearance. Her behaviour was the opposite of charismatic, as she appeared timid, shy, and nervous. Yet through it all, she could evoke feelings of sympathy in others—the kind many people experience when they see a helpless, abandoned kitten and feel an overwhelming need to rescue and protect the poor creature. Samuel was one of these people.

This is where the love triangle began. Samuel explained to me he enjoyed smoking marijuana. However, as he did not want to be recognized purchasing the drug in Abbotsford, he travelled to Langley to obtain his supply from Dwayne. Sometimes Dwayne was out, so he was left to make his purchases from Charlotte, and they became good friends.

During his many visits, Samuel often observed how Dwayne treated Charlotte, and he didn't like it. It was clear Dwayne had an inflated sense of his own importance, a deep need for excessive attention and admiration, and a lack of empathy for Charlotte. He was a classic narcissist—the kind of person who did not have the ability to experience and show love. He was selfish, callous, and cruel.

Whenever they were alone, Samuel would encourage Charlotte to leave Dwayne, assuring her there was a better life, and what is more, she could escape the cycle of abuse in which she was trapped. "Do you want to live like this all your life?" he would ask.

He told her about an abused women's shelter in Abbotsford, where she would find all the help she needed, explaining she could trust the staff in the shelter, as they had assisted many abused women in the past. Samuel knew this, because his mother was a volunteer worker there, which meant she had told him many stories about the numerous women they had rescued.

After many months of trying to persuade Charlotte to leave Dwayne, Samuel finally succeeded. It came right after a terrible experience, when Dwayne was in one of his many foul moods. That night, Dwayne punched Charlotte in the face and then placed his Magnum revolver in her mouth and threatened to pull the trigger. His dark, evil eyes cast their malevolent glare with such force upon Charlotte, that she determined in that instant she would flee, if she survived.

The next day, Dwayne left to carry out some business, allowing Charlotte to carry out her escape plan by phoning Samuel, who drove her to Abbotsford. From a public phone, she called the women's shelter, who sent a female counsellor to pick her up and take her to their secret location. Charlotte felt she had entered heaven when she was surrounded in the home by kind and caring women, who sincerely wanted to help her. She was grateful to them and to Samuel for persuading her to take advantage of all this support.

When Dwayne came home later that day, he was livid, as he could not find Charlotte. He wondered what had happened to her—not as a concerned partner, but more as if she were a piece of furniture he owned. He was determined to find her and make her pay. No doubt she would have to surface again, and when she did, he would drag her home where she belonged, as Dwayne believed she was his, to do with as he pleased.

Many months later, Charlotte was able to leave the women's shelter to live in her own small apartment in Abbotsford, paid for by some local charity. For the first time in her life, she knew what normal felt like. A few weeks later, she decided to give Samuel a call, arranging a rendezvous at the White Spot, a local restaurant in Abbotsford, as she enjoyed the legendary burger and fries. It felt good to be treated like a human being.

Samuel and Charlotte continued seeing each other. Sometimes it was dinner and a movie, or five-pin bowling, or shopping at the mall. Sadly, Dwayne had his tentacles out looking for Charlotte. Finally, one of his customers spotted her and followed her home. This important information earned this customer several free samples of drugs. Dwayne planned his revenge.

Dwayne set up a stakeout in the park just up the street from Charlotte's apartment, where he maintained secret surveillance in his car in the parking lot, hidden behind the trees. One evening, he saw Samuel come by to pick up Charlotte. Dwayne was furious, bordering on manic. He experienced intense energy, racing thoughts, and extreme, exaggerated delusions about what he would do to the two of them.

Dwayne always carried several weapons hidden under the carpet of the trunk of his car. As his eyes furiously searched his stash, eventually falling upon a large butcher knife, his thoughts turned to his plan. Holding that butcher knife in his hands, he decided he would wait until Charlotte and Samuel returned and then threaten Samuel with the heavy-duty, stainless-steel blade, made for slicing and skinning meat. He thought about how good it would feel to cut him open. He would then deal with Charlotte.

Three hours later, when Charlotte and Samuel returned, Dwayne was disappointed, as Samuel did not get out of his car. Samuel just dropped Charlotte off at her apartment, and then drove away. Dwayne rushed forward, brandishing the shining blade. Charlotte screamed as she rushed into her apartment building, the door locking behind her. Dwayne shouted he would kill Samuel and then come for her. Charlotte disappeared up the elevator to her room, locking the door behind her, trembling with fear. Dwayne vanished as quickly as he had appeared.

Charlotte called Samuel to warn him regarding the threats on his life made by Dwayne. It was hard to get the words out given the terror that had overcome her mind. Eventually she collapsed on her bed, but sleep would not come. Again and again, she saw the long, shining knife plunging toward her. She left the lights on and watched late night talk shows all night long. Samuel assured her he would immediately go to the police station to report Dwayne's threats, so she would be protected. She should just stay in her room until the police arrived.

Samuel went to the police station in Abbotsford and filed a complaint. The officer took careful notes, and then placed the paper on a large pile of papers on his desk marked urgent. The officer assured Samuel they would send out a car to protect Charlotte and arrest Dwayne.

Little did Samuel know that as he drove home, Dwayne was following him, and again the next day, Dwayne was watching when Samuel took Charlotte to a coffee shop. While Samuel and Charlotte were drinking coffee, Dwayne slashed the tires of Samuel's truck. When Samuel and Charlotte returned to the parking lot, Samuel could see his shredded tires and knew instantly that it was Dwayne. But, Dwayne was nowhere in sight.

Charlotte phoned the women's shelter, which resulted in one of the staff coming to pick her up. Samuel had his car towed to the Kal Tire, where he was forced to purchase new tires. He called his work to let them know he wouldn't return until the next day. Samuel also called the Abbotsford Police Department, but they didn't seem interested in a case of slashed tires. He demanded to know if Dwayne had been arrested, as promised, but it didn't seem like anyone knew what he was talking about, nor did anyone seem to care.

Samuel worked at a nursery. He had his father's nurturing touch as far as growing plants. The owners and his fellow workers liked Samuel a lot, as he was so helpful and easy to get along with. Samuel decided to go to work the next day, but he would take a rifle, which was fully licensed, and mount it under the back window of his truck just in case he needed to defend himself. The rifle was loaded. He knew about Dwayne's collection of guns—especially the Magnum revolver that was waved about when Dwayne wanted to intimidate someone.

Samuel was well accustomed to his Remington Model 700 bolt-action rifle, as he went target shooting with his father quite regularly. The Model 700 was reliable and accurate.

Samuel parked his truck in the lot across the street from where he worked. He told all his fellow workers about Dwayne's threats to kill him, as well as the fact that Dwayne had slashed his tires the day before. They all felt Dwayne was dangerous and were on the lookout for this evil man, keeping a careful watch over Samuel's truck.

While Charlotte recovered from her trauma at the women's shelter, Dwayne broke into her apartment. He had a sinister plan. He removed all of Charlotte's towels and clothes and cut holes in the areas that had something to do with sexuality, like the breasts and the crotch. Meticulously, he folded the clothes and towels so the areas he had cut out would not be seen until Charlotte went to put the clothes on or use the towels. It took him three hours to carry out his malicious and perverted plan, but he felt it was well worth the effort. It was the ultimate intimidation. Creating fear in a victim through terrorization was the only activity Dwayne truly enjoyed.

When Charlotte returned to her apartment the following day to retrieve her clothes, with one of the ladies from the shelter, she discovered the wicked plot. Her whole body began shuddering as her fear and anxiety put her into shock. The lady from the shelter had previously thought she had seen everything that vile and nasty men could do to women, but she had never before seen such a disturbing design. Every piece of clothing, even the towels, had been carefully cut and folded to have its maximum effect.

Charlotte called Samuel to inform him what Dwayne had done. Samuel was young and inexperienced. He had never met pure evil before. Even though he lived at home, he failed to do the one thing that might have assisted him—get advice from his parents. He mistakenly thought his parents would only condemn him, not help him. He knew they would disapprove of him smoking marijuana and starting up a relationship with Charlotte. What he failed to consider was the fact that his parents loved him, just like they loved his brothers and sisters. They would have gotten over their initial disappointment, and then provided the aid he needed, for he was truly in over his head. But, he didn't ask.

Samuel instead called the police again the next day to see if they had arrested Dwayne. They had not. He then determined the police would not protect him, so he would have to protect himself.

At work that day, one of his co-workers spotted someone hanging around Samuel's truck. He called to Samuel, who went running out to confront the individual. Sure enough, it was Dwayne. Dwayne hopped into his red Ford Mustang and sped down the street. Taking the matter into his own hands, Samuel decided to chase after him in his truck. After two blocks, Dwayne turned right, into a large, empty gravel parking lot across the street from the Shell service station. Samuel stopped in the lot as well, about 120 feet behind him.

Dwayne slowly got out of his car and sauntered leisurely toward Samuel. Samuel stepped out of his truck and opened the back door so he could reach in at any time to retrieve his loaded rifle. When Dwayne was about twenty-five feet away, he raised his right hand, which disclosed he was holding a large knife. His pace accelerated toward Samuel. Samuel quickly pulled out his rifle, firing two shots in rapid succession. When Dwayne fell to the ground, face in the gravel, Samuel jumped into his truck and drove away. The sun was beating down high in the sky, as it was noon in the middle of July.

There were many witnesses to the spectacle of the crazy guy who brought a knife to a gunfight. Some of those witnesses were tourists from Oregon and California, just driving by, who thought it was part of Hollywood North making a movie. The service station attendant finally figured out the whole debacle was real, and called 9-1-1, when the guy on the ground never got up.

Ten minutes later, a fire truck arrived on the scene, followed by an ambulance, and finally the police. Dwayne was pronounced dead at the scene. While the police gathered statements from the many witnesses, a call came in to the police headquarters in Abbotsford. It was Samuel.

After Samuel sped away from the scene, he headed down the freeway and then stopped at the mall in Abbotsford. First, he called Charlotte to tell her what had happened, asking her what he should do. She told him to call the police, so he did. What happened next was pure keystone cops—humorously incompetent policemen, as recorded in the police monitoring system, trying to find Samuel after he had already turned himself in and described in great detail where he was in the mall, so they could arrest him. It seemed like fictional slapstick, but it was real.

Even with each new and accurate direction given by Samuel as to his location, the police could not find him. This went on for half an hour. One could not help but smile listening to the recording. Finally, he was arrested and taken to the police lock-up. This is where I met with him to obtain these details, as well as the particulars provided by the police and the witnesses.

Samuel was taken to Oakalla Prison, next to Deer Lake in Burnaby. The Oakalla Prison Farm, opened in 1912 and boasting 185 acres of land, was initially designed to hold 150 men and 50 women. By the 1950s, however, the population was well over one thousand. In its early days, it was a working farm, as the prison had its own dairy, vegetable gardens, and livestock. Eventually, all these good ideas of working on a farm to rehabilitate the prisoners were abandoned as the population of the jail expanded.

During its long, strange history, forty-four prisoners were executed at Oakalla. Others underwent electroshock therapy against their will. In 1959, the last execution in British Columbia took place at Oakalla. Following a bloody riot and mass escape in the late 1980s, Oakalla, BC's most notorious jail was closed down in 1991 and developed into new residential housing.

Oakalla was a hard place to do time. My first legal task was to obtain Samuel's release from custody until his trial. I prepared an affidavit, but I was required to obtain Samuel's signature on the legal document. This meant it was necessary for me to enter that dreaded place. It was a sobering moment when I passed through the outer fence and was searched at the guard house. Next, I was searched again as I entered the main cell block. The dark feeling here was palpable, like entering an eerie place in the Twilight Zone.

I took a look around. It felt like the walls were closing in. I sensed it would be tough to long for sunshine and grass. I imagined being prevented from walking in meadows and forests—with their veritable feasts of colours—and instead being able to see nothing but the grey, cold stone of the prison walls. What about the loss of freedom to walk hand-in-hand with a loved one to the river or lake and dive into the cold, clean, fresh water? How important was it to share with family and friends the warm light of the sun, the warmth of its touch only surpassed by their touch? How brutal was the isolation in a prison cell barely ten feet by eight feet, all alone, without a single window and no relief from the stench of stale air? Pure hatred was built into the design.

I met with Samuel in a private office. I asked him how he was doing. He pleaded with me to get him out of this hell hole. I said I would try. I had him sign his affidavit. I asked if he was sexually assaulted or brutalized in any way by the other prisoners. He replied that before he arrived, all the prisoners knew he was there because he killed a man, so no one even came near him. I brought greetings from his mom and dad who loved him, as well as his brothers and sisters.

Samuel knew his father had retained me to act on his behalf, as Samuel didn't have much money. He was grateful to his father and longed to hug his mother. At this moment, I was his only link to the outside and freedom. He didn't want me to leave, so I lingered for a time, but I really wanted to get out of that place as fast as possible.

A few days later, I appeared before the Chief Justice of the Supreme Court of British Columbia to obtain Samuel's release pending the trial. Samuel was not a flight risk, as evidenced by the fact he had turned himself in. He also lived at home with his parents, who owned a large raspberry farm in Abbotsford, who could guarantee his attendance at court.

In addition, he had a very concrete defence, self-defence, meaning the use of force to protect himself from being murdered by Dwayne. The presumption of innocence is a fundamental legal principle, meaning that every person accused of any crime is considered innocent until proven guilty. The chief justice had no difficulty releasing Samuel until the decision of innocence or guilt was pronounced at the trial.

I had many lengthy discussions with Samuel about what to do now. I thought he should elect to be tried by a judge and jury. In order to get a conviction, the Crown would have to convince twelve people, beyond a reasonable doubt, that Samuel was not entitled to the defence of self-defence. Samuel agreed to follow my advice.

The next step was to fix a date for the preliminary inquiry, which is where the Crown presents its evidence, the defence can cross-examine the Crown witnesses, and a judge determines if there is sufficient evidence to have a trial. It was fixed for six months later in Provincial Court in Abbotsford.

I knew there was plenty of evidence that Samuel killed Dwayne, so the case would certainly be committed to a trial in Supreme Court in New Westminster about a year later. However, it is important to cross-examine all the Crown witnesses at the preliminary inquiry, so all the facts that would be used in the case—for or against Samuel—would be clear.

The tourists from Oregon and California were called. It was clear from their evidence that Dwayne first advanced toward Samuel, while Samuel merely stood his ground. In addition, they saw Dwayne raise his right hand, and they saw the knife in this hand raised in a menacing fashion. The knife was large, and it flashed in the sunlight. The tourists also testified that when Dwayne raised his right hand with the knife, he quickened his pace toward Samuel. They observed that at no time did Samuel advance toward Dwayne, and that it was only at the last moment, that Samuel reached into his truck, pulled out the rifle, and shot Dwayne twice. They were clear in their recollection of the facts, because they watched carefully what they thought was a movie.

The evidence of the tourists clearly established that Samuel killed Dwayne, but it also laid the foundation for self-defence. If

I could establish that Samuel acted in self-defence, then he would be acquitted of all charges. He was charged with first-degree murder, which is a homicide that is both planned and deliberate. He could be convicted of the lesser included offence of second-degree murder, a deliberate killing that occurs without planning, or another lesser included offence of manslaughter, being a homicide committed without intent. Or, he could be acquitted; the jury would decide.

First-degree murder carries an automatic life sentence with no possibility of parole for twenty-five years. The minimum sentence for second-degree murder is life in prison with no parole for ten years, but sentences can be as long as life in prison without parole for twenty-five years. Manslaughter carries no minimum sentence, but the judge would usually impose a sentence in a range from five to seven years in jail.

The next evidence came from an expert who described how Dwayne died. The first shot hit him in the right shoulder, which swung his body around, so that the second shot, coming from a bolt-action rifle, 1–1.5 seconds later, hit him in the back, travelled through his heart, and killed him in minutes. The first shot only injured him, but the second shot killed him. This was a serious problem. I was aware of this, as the Crown had already provided me with the expert report. I had reviewed the report with my expert, but the consensus was that the evidence in the report was solid.

My cross-examination of the police was a great embarrassment to the Abbotsford Police Department. They acknowledged that Samuel made the complaint that Dwayne was attempting to kill him and had even filed the report in the urgent basket, but the paper was lost in the shuffle, and the police never did do anything. This was an important fact for my defence, as it provided further evidence that Samuel was forced to protect himself. This explained why he was driving with a loaded rifle.

Yet what posed the real problem (in addition to the fact that Samuel's second shot—the one that killed Dwayne—hit Dwayne in the back) was that Samuel had been the one to jump in his truck, and pursue Dwayne, with a loaded rifle. Would the jury accept his evidence that he only wanted to confront Dwayne to settle things, as he didn't want Dwayne sneaking up and shooting him in the back? Was it a planned and deliberate attack or self-defence? The Provincial Court judge committed the matter to trial.

I discussed at great length with Samuel the Crown's case. Samuel was licensed to carry a rifle, but not a loaded rifle. Why did he travel everywhere with a loaded rifle? Was it because he planned to kill Dwayne, because he loved Charlotte? When the first opportunity to kill Dwayne arose, he drove after him in his truck for two blocks, stopped in the parking lot behind Dwayne, got out of his truck, and when Dwayne exited his car, opened the back door to his truck so the rifle was available. Then, when the opportunity arose, he shot Dwayne, not just once, but twice, with the second shot—the kill shot—hitting Dwayne in the back.

The Crown would emphasize to the jury the loaded gun, the chase, the confrontation without any retreat, and then the killing by shooting Dwayne in the back. Why did he not get back into his truck and ride away?

Crown counsel were certainly credible on motives, perhaps three of the strongest: revenge, fear, and love. Samuel could have been motivated to kill Dwayne by any one of those motives—or perhaps by all three.

In reply, I would argue that Samuel had every right to defend himself. Dwayne had threatened to kill him. He had displayed the butcher knife, followed Samuel and slashed his tires, cut Charlotte's clothes in a grotesque fashion, and was a known drug dealer who beat Charlotte whenever he wanted. He was known for violence—and he had the weapons, including his beloved 44-calibre Magnum revolver—to carry out his threat to kill Samuel. Additionally,

Samuel had reported the murder threat against him to the police, showing Samuel believed that Dwayne was trying to kill him.

Dwayne initiated the conflict by making the threats. Dwayne made an attack in the parking lot by raising a knife, which was an immediate threat to Samuel's life. Dwayne advanced toward Samuel to carry out that threat. When Dwayne raised the knife, Samuel did not have time to get into the truck and drive away. He only had time to pull out his rifle, which he used to defend himself from a deadly knife attack. The degree of force used by Samuel was objectively reasonable under the circumstances. Samuel felt threatened with imminent death. In defending himself from a deadly knife attack, he was justified to use the deadly force of a rifle. He did not have an opportunity to retreat. Samuel had a reasonable fear of death. All of the necessary requirements for self-defence, allowing Samuel to use the gun, were present.

Samuel thought that Dwayne had continued to advance toward him after the first shot. He did not comprehend that the shot hit Dwayne's shoulder, then spun him around so that his back faced Samuel. He did not realize that Dwayne was no longer advancing toward him. The second shot came 1–1.5 seconds later. In a state of fear, taking two shots was reasonable.

It was also reasonable to chase after Dwayne in his truck, as the terror of Dwayne stalking him was overwhelming. Did he have to wait until Dwayne snuck up on him and shot him in the back to defend himself? By then, it would be too late. The police were certainly no comfort.

I advised Samuel that if the jury believed him about why he chased after Dwayne and why he took a second shot, he would likely be acquitted. Samuel was a pleasant, likeable person, so I thought the jury would believe him. However, there was the chase and a shot in the back. Anything could happen.

With this uncertainty hanging over his head, Samuel authorized me to speak with the Regional Crown in New Westminster to see if they would be amenable to making a deal. I met with the Crown and proposed they take a guilty plea to manslaughter and withdraw all further charges. I reviewed all of the facts with Crown counsel, who was sympathetic, but wanted to talk to the police before making a decision. A month later, when we met, Crown counsel explained that the police told him: "We don't care if you take a plea to littering, because Dwayne was just a pile of garbage. We were happy to get rid of him. Samuel did us a big favour."

The Crown said they would take a plea to manslaughter, even though the only defence didn't really fit the plea. Either Samuel planned the killing and it was murder, or it was self-defence and he should be acquitted. It was all or nothing. However, given the position of the police and the practical problems regarding the cost of a lengthy trial and the availability of court time, the offer was made. The Crown said they would ask for five years in jail. I said I would ask for three years.

I met with Samuel. It was a long conference as I went over all the facts, possible outcomes, and our chances of success. He did not want to risk a murder conviction where he might spend twenty-five years in jail. This would destroy his life. With a jail sentence of three to five years, he would be out in two to four for good behaviour. He could do that. I was instructed to make the deal.

A sentencing hearing was set back in Provincial Court in Abbotsford. I had a favourable pre-sentence report, which outlined many good things about Samuel. I spent all day going over the facts of the case with the judge. I could tell that I had aroused some sympathy. Samuel's mom and dad, and his brothers and sisters, were in the courtroom. Dwayne's parents were also there. They learned a lot about their son that day. I have always felt sorry for them, and I wished they were not there. But facts are facts; Dwayne was a perverted narcissist who brought about his own demise by his threats, intimidation, and violence. Dwayne had reaped the whirlwind that he had sown.

The judge ordered a sentence of three years, which was a favourable result. The next day, Samuel's father came to my office. He pulled out his cheque book and signed a blank cheque, explaining that he was very pleased with my work, and that I could fill in whatever number I wanted. He felt I had saved his son's life. He expressed such gratitude that I will never forget the moment. He wept for his son.

Samuel's father was quite a wealthy man. Canada had been very good to him. But, the money meant nothing to him next to the life of his son. I charged the normal amount for my time and for a job well done. I was happy with the result.

Two years later, Samuel came to my office in Fort Langley. He had just been released for good behaviour. He said he served his time in a federal penitentiary, and that "it was not too bad." He trained in welding while he was there and got his ticket. It was odd to train as a welder, since he loved growing plants. Yet he found the focus and concentration required to fuse two materials together at stunningly high temperatures—the fabrication process—helped the time to go by quickly.

As when he was locked up before, no inmates ever bothered him, because they all knew he was serving time for killing a brutal drug dealer. In contrast, he explained, the child molesters and snitches could not survive in the general prison population, as even the worst criminals had some standards.

Samuel thanked me again. He told me he would follow his parents' advice from now on, as he now understood how much they loved him and how much smarter than him they were. He also had high praise for his brothers and sisters.

I didn't ask about Charlotte. There was a pause in the conversation when he said, "I was caught in a terrible love triangle. I think I loved Charlotte, but it was based on a desire to protect and save her—save her from Dwayne and from herself. I don't know where she lives now. She never kept contact with me in prison, so I don't think I will ever see her again."

We said our goodbyes as I thought about this strange love triangle that caused so much grief.

CHAPTER TWENTY-THREE

Spare the Rod and Spoil the Child
(Proverbs 13:24, 29:15)

In my line of work, it is important to put myself in the shoes of my clients to truly seek to understand what motivates their actions, so I can build a compassionate and logical defence for them. When Pierre came to me, we were in similar stages of life. He was about the same age as me, with two children. I had young children of my own as well. Being a parent is very difficult, and there have been many times that my own children have tried my patience. When Pierre told me his story, I imagined myself seeing what he saw and experiencing what he felt. In this next story, I write in the first-person as Pierre to demonstrate how I would sometimes engage in theoretical empathetic exercises, especially when a client showed tremendous remorse.

My mother named me Pierre—Pierre LaPerriere. Pierre is a French form of the name Peter. Pierre originally meant "rock" or "stone" in French. She tells me I was christened in the Cathedral in Caen, located in Normandie, in Northern France. My mother named me after the most famous Apostle of Jesus with the hope I would always follow them both—Jesus and Peter.

My mother's name is Marie, named after Mary, the mother of Jesus. She often repeats the story of how I cried out as a baby while the priest made the sign of the cross on my tiny forehead at my christening, where he gave me my name. I bawled even louder while the priest gave readings and prayers for me and my parents and then anointed me with oil.

After the christening, I was baptized into the Catholic faith to free me from the original sin I was born with. My mom says the sprinkling of water is like a vaccine against sin.

It was fitting that—given my name—the baptism necessary for me to be saved was carried out in the Cathedral of Saint-Pierre, constructed in the early thirteenth and sixteenth centuries, the largest building located in the heart of the city.

My mom also baptized me Pierre, as she often taught me that Jesus used a play-on-words when he declared: "You are Pierre and on this rock I will build my church" (Matthew 16:18). I was taught this meant that Peter is the rock upon which the church is built. Inside the cathedral dedicated to Saint Peter is a stained-glass window with Peter carrying a large key. My mom explained that Peter carried this key, because he was in charge of opening the gate to heaven for all those who qualified to enter therein. I lived in fear that I might not be eligible, as the alternative was to be cast into a lake of fire and brimstone, always burning, but never consumed. They say God is a God of love, but I guess only if I follow His rules.

It didn't really make any sense to me. I just knew that my mom loved me no matter what I did. Wouldn't God be like that?

Mom lit a candle to the Blessed Virgin each time we visited the cathedral, presenting her prayers to Mary and asking her to pray for us. Her petition always commenced with the words, "Remember, O most gracious Virgin Mary, that never was it known that anyone who fled to your protection was left unaided."

I don't remember my father, as my mother told me he left when I was quite young. I don't know why he left or where he went. He just left. I am an only child, so it was just me and my mom.

Mom worked hard cleaning the homes of the rich people of Caen. When I was ten years old, she decided to immigrate to Canada, because she thought this would give me a better future. We settled in Quebec City. It took quite a while to adapt to Quebecois French and to learn English. The winters were long and bitterly cold in Quebec City, unlike the moderate climate we were accustomed to in Normandie. This led Mom to decide that we would move to Vancouver, on the West Coast of Canada, where the winters were mild, just like our home in France.

Eventually, we settled down in Maillardville, the largest French-Canadian Community on the West Coast, located in Coquitlam, a suburb of Vancouver. The Festival du Bois in Maillardville is the largest and most attended Francophone festival on the West Coast of Canada. Sitting on the green grass of Mackin Park in early spring, surrounded by cherry blossoms in full bloom, we listened to Canadian folk and French Celtic music artists perform, and ate the traditional foods, including tourtiere, poutine, smoked meat sandwiches, maple taffy pole, and maple sugar pie. Of course, we wore the official Festival du Bois headgear, a green toque embossed with a frog.

At the age of twenty-four, I married a girl from Surrey, and we moved to Langley, just up the Fraser River Valley from Vancouver. I had graduated from the local college, in accounting, and had been working for a couple of years with a large accounting firm. The early years of our marriage flowed smoothly, like the gentle, warm, spring rains in Vancouver. We had two sons (nine and five years old) when everything fell apart. My wife decided she longed for a more exciting life than I could provide, so she left me. She said I was about the most boring person she had ever met. Somehow love turned to hate. I didn't understand why, just like I didn't comprehend why my father left me and my mom.

My wife dragged me off to Family Court, where she could air all our dirty laundry. I just stood there in silence while she did all the talking. The only thing I understood is that our two boys would stay with me every other weekend.

On one of those weekend visits, my sons and I were watching *Star Wars* and eating pepperoni pizza, when my older son began to beat on my younger boy for no good reason. The older son was much larger and stronger, so I told him to quit it. He started up again and again. After the third warning, I lost my temper and hit him hard with the palm of my open hand against the side of his face and head. His cheek turned red, and he began to cry. I felt bad.

I knew it was a sin. Each Friday night I entered a confessional booth, greeted the priest, and said: "Bless me Father for I have sinned. It has been seven days since my last confession." My mother taught me the intent of this sacrament is to provide healing for the soul as well as to regain the grace of God lost by sin. In this way I could avoid eternal punishment, and Saint Peter would open the gate to heaven for me when I arrived there. I was always anxious regarding the state of my soul in relation to God. I searched my memories continually to be sure I confessed every sin.

The next day, after the boys returned to their mother, the police showed up. The policeman asked me if I beat my son. It was like confession to a priest, so I told him I did hit him hard with my open hand on the side of his face, causing his cheek to turn red.

The officer asked if I did this often. I answered that this was the only time I had ever struck him in the head, explained the circumstances why I did it, and expressed my sorrow for losing my temper. I knew it was a sin, so I would also confess my wrongdoing to the priest the next Friday.

The police officer apologized and told me he would have to arrest me for assault, as he was directed by an overzealous, female Crown prosecutor, who had received the complaint directly from my wife. The policeman admitted he didn't like it, as he thought this prosecutor was a man-hater, just like my wife. He told me to go and get a good lawyer.

This is when I met with Robert Kearl at his office in Fort Langley. I knew him, as he had completed the conveyance on the purchase of my family home when we first moved to Langley. He was not like any lawyer I had ever met or imagined from watching television. Robert was happy that I used the French pronunciation of his name. He loved French culture and the French language. He told jokes, then laughed at them so enthusiastically that I just had to laugh too. He spoke of going to court, that is, the tennis court. He pointed out the twin peaks called Golden Ears, and then told me stories about how he had climbed to the top several times.

I did not have a good impression of lawyers generally, but I liked Robert, and I knew he would do everything he could for me. He said he would start by meeting with the Crown to convince them to stay the charge, as he felt I should not be saddled with a Criminal Code conviction for making a mistake that almost every parent made at some point. He had four children, so he understood my frustration with my oldest son.

Robert explained to me that what I did was an assault, but the Criminal Code had a provision that allowed parents to use force to discipline their children, provided the force used was reasonable. The issue was whether I had used reasonable force. He also made the point that if the Criminal Code was used every time a parent struck out in anger, then most Canadians would be criminals. He thought it was a ridiculous charge in the circumstances.

I had never been in trouble with the law before. I knew a criminal conviction for assault on my record could have serious repercussions, especially adversely affecting my career in accounting. I relied on Robert to do everything he could to clear my name.

Two weeks later, I met with Robert again in his office. He was frustrated, as the prosecutor would not stay the charge. She was leading a crusade to convince Parliament to change the law and eliminate the provision in the Criminal Code of Canada that allowed parents to physically discipline their children. She told Robert, "All these violent men should go to jail." She said she would make an example of me by setting a precedent for such crimes—that jail was appropriate.

My sons continued to visit with me every other weekend. My wife attempted to eliminate my access to the children, using the charge of assault against my son like a blunt instrument used to bludgeon me, but the judge would not go along with it. She accepted the fact it was an isolated incident, so it would be in the best interest of the children to continue to see their dad. I was grateful for her compassion.

The trial commenced in Supreme Court in New Westminster about nine months later. I felt sorry for my son, who was forced by his mother to testify about how I hit him. In cross-examination, he told Robert that he had forgiven me long ago. He cried, explaining he did not want me to be found guilty and go to jail. He said it was his fault, not mine, because he was beating on his little brother even after several warnings.

As the boy testified, I could see compassion in the eyes of the judge. I knew Robert had to give him a way to avoid giving me a criminal record. After I testified in my own defence, admitting to all the facts, it was time for the argument. Robert submitted that the corporal punishment administered by me upon my oldest son was reasonable within the exception set out in the Criminal Code. I could see the judge was struggling with the idea of a hard hit to the side of the head being reasonable, so I was glad Robert added, that in the alternative, if it wasn't reasonable, it was an isolated incident that would not be repeated, and that any parent, including me, did not deserve to be sanctioned with a criminal record. Robert suggested an absolute discharge if the judge felt he must convict. The absolute discharge would act as if the assault had never occurred. I would not have a criminal record.

The prosecutor was livid with Robert's suggestion, insisting I should be punished for a violent assault on my son. But, the judge was well known to Robert, who said he knew him as a compassionate and reasonable person, so I was not surprised when the judge quickly convicted me, but ordered an absolute discharge.

I thought the judge acted like what he thought God was like, granting mercy and forgiveness like my mother. I told Robert that I thought the prosecutor was filled with the wrath of hell and acted like some of the worst sermons I heard in church.

Crown counsel would not give up. She said she would appeal the sentence. There could be no mercy granted. Violent men should go to jail where they belong, no matter what the circumstances. Robert spoke with her superiors, who assured him there would be no appeal. It was finally over.

It was quite the ordeal. Robert and I had lunch at the French restaurant in Fort Langley to celebrate. Robert's French was a little bit rusty, so though we spoke in French, we still broke into English quite often. I appreciated his kind friendship, but also his determination in court. It seemed to me he would keep talking until the judge agreed with him. Fortunately, it didn't take all eternity (like the burning in hell they preached about in church) to obtain justice and mercy.

CHAPTER TWENTY-FOUR

Ethylene Glycol Intoxication

Ethylene Glycol is an odorless, colourless, sweet-tasting syrupy substance, commonly encountered as automotive antifreeze. Animals are drawn to its sweet taste and die from licking it off of garage floors or driveways. Quinn lived in Chilliwack, not too far from his mother, who lived in Langley. Unfortunately, he probably should have been even closer to his mother's influence, as one day, responding to a dare from his friends, Quinn decided to drink some antifreeze. None of them knew how toxic it was. He foolishly drank approximately eight to ten ounces in his friend's garage.

Quinn did not know that four fluid ounces of ethylene glycol would be enough to kill an average-sized man. His friends reported his initial symptoms as intoxication, euphoria, and stupor. He rushed out of his friend's garage and drove away in his muscle car, a purple, two-door Chevrolet Camaro convertible.

Poor Quinn didn't get far, as he crashed into a parked car a few blocks down the road. The police attended the scene of the crash, where they formed the opinion that Quinn was driving while impaired due to his slurred speech, glazed over eyes, and failure to walk the line without stumbling. He was arrested and taken to the police station in Chilliwack.

While he was in jail, Quinn began to experience vomiting and abdominal pain. When the officer in charge checked on him, he determined Quinn was suffering from a decreased level of consciousness, headache, and seizures. Chilliwack RCMP took him to the hospital, where Quinn told the nurse that he had consumed eight to ten ounces of antifreeze, which was the first time consumption of this poison was mentioned to anyone. The nurse reported this to the doctor, along with a suggestion to have Quinn's stomach emptied.

However, the doctor did not believe the nurse. He thought Quinn was drunk from the consumption of too much alcohol, and that if Quinn had consumed any antifreeze, it would have been such a small dose that it would not be toxic. As a result, the doctor failed to conduct any tests or carry out any physical examination.

Fourteen hours later, Quinn was dead.

Quinn's mother, Lorraine, came to see me at the office in Fort Langley, as she was determined to sue the doctor. I explained the law to her. The death of her son, according to the law, was not worth anything, as he was not supporting her financially at the time, nor was he expected to do so in the future. I advised her not to sue, as it would be a waste of time and money. Nevertheless, she instructed me to commence a lawsuit, as it was more than just a matter of principle; it was also a question of justice, even if there was no financial recovery. I commenced the action on behalf of Lorraine in the Supreme Court of BC in Vancouver, suing the doctor for negligence.

The suit alleged that Quinn would have survived had the doctor taken appropriate and standard medical procedures for ethylene glycol intoxication. The statement of claim submitted on Lorraine's behalf sought unspecified general, special, and exemplary damages for the loss of support, guidance, and love of a son, including the trauma and mental anguish suffered by the mother on the loss of her son, and all legal costs.

On behalf of Lorraine, the mother, I attended the coroner's inquest into Quinn's death in Chilliwack to enable me to cross-examine all of the witnesses and ensure we would get to the truth. The expert witnesses explained how the ethylene glycol poisoning affected the central nervous system, metabolic processes, and the kidneys. When it breaks down in the body, it forms chemicals that crystallize, and the crystals collect in the kidneys, causing kidney failure and brain damage. It was the opinion of the doctors that Quinn died of kidney failure.

The experts also testified that treatment consists of using an antidote called fomepizole, which is a medication given by injection into a vein. It acts to inhibit the breakdown of the toxins, and if injected at the early stages, leads to a complete recovery. It was the opinion of the doctors called at the coroner's inquest that if the antidote had been given immediately upon Quinn's arrival at the hospital, it was likely he would have made a full recovery.

The truth was visibly manifest, with no doubt about the doctor's negligence. That was enough for Lorraine; she felt a sense of relief believing she had succeeded in achieving justice for, not only her son, but for herself, as a mother. She said to me: "It is not right that a son should die before his mother. It is too painful." She then withdrew her lawsuit, as it would not bring back her son.

Although the lawsuit was brought to a close, the tragedy for the mother remained.

It was our hope that, rather than punish the negligent doctor, he would learn from from his mistake, and that this tragic experience would shed light on this type of poisoning, so that a similar tragedy would not befall another mother. Lorraine felt she had achieved her purpose.

The coroner's inquest was carried out in the light of day, before the public and the press. It had attracted a great deal of publicity. The death of Quinn would not be forgotten—not by the police, the medical personnel, the public, and certainly not by Lorraine, the mother.

Special note #1. In Canada, medical malpractice is a difficult area of the law, as it is not enough to prove the doctor was negligent, it must also be proven that the doctor's conduct did not accord with standard medical procedures. This is an added protection given to doctors that is not given to any other profession.

Special note #2. In British Columbia, there has been a review and discussion for decades to reform the *Family Compensation Act* to allow for damages when a spouse or child dies due to the negligence of another—not only for the financial loss—but for the incredibly terrible pain involved in the loss of a loved one. Children can claim damages for a loss of love, guidance, and affection of a parent, but this is the only non-financial loss that can be claimed. The grief associated with the loss of a family member is difficult and can even be incapacitating. It can interfere with all aspects of one's life, including work. It can require medical and psychological attention. In short, it can have financial ramifications. Should the law be reformed to include these claims?

CHAPTER TWENTY-FIVE

Fort St. John in Winter

I flew into Fort St. John, British Columbia, in the middle of winter, when it was −20°C, and the wind was howling. In this climate, if any part of my skin was open to the weather, it would freeze within a few minutes. Fort St. John is located at Mile 47 of the Alaska Highway, and it is the largest city between Dawson Creek, British Columbia and Delta Junction, Alaska. Established in 1794 as a trading post, it was constructed to service the fur trade. It is the oldest European-established settlement in present-day British Columbia.

However, as my plane climbed over the Rocky Mountains, then descended, I noticed Fort St. John and the Peace River Country surrounding it looked more like the prairies in Alberta, where I was raised. With the wind chill at −59°C, it seemed like January in Calgary, when Mom fed me toast to dunk into hot cocoa, a deliciously warm liquid, for breakfast, just before I ventured out, all bundled up, for my walk to school.

Even the news in Fort St. John originates from Calgary, as the area is part of the oil patch, with plenty of jobs in the oil and gas industry, like Northern Alberta. The head offices of these oil and gas companies are located in Calgary. While I was there, some of the locals mentioned that there was a movement for Fort St John to become part of Alberta. But, the idea never picked up enough steam to become a realistic possibility.

I rented a car, at the airport, with the necessary engine block heater and cables, which would be essential to plug into the electrical outlets at the parking stalls located at the hotel and everywhere else in town; otherwise, the car would not start in the morning. However, the car rental people failed to tell me about an important detail.

When I arrived at the hotel, I plugged my cable into the outlet, checked in, and took my one small bag up to my room, as I would only be there a few days for the coroner's inquest. When I returned to drive to a restaurant, the cable was gone. The car rental company gave me another cable at no charge as they failed to inform me I had to drive onto the cable, leaving it under the tire after it was plugged in, so it could not be stolen. I guess stealing cables from unsuspecting visitors was big business in Fort St. John.

The next morning I drove to the Provincial Government building and law courts, located in the centre of Fort St. John. I was surprised to arrive at a modern, three-storey, concrete and glass structure. The windows were horizontal and recessed with a flat roof line. The building housed the Supreme Court and Provincial Court. The coroner's inquest, an inquiry into the cause of death of my client's husband in a tragic motor vehicle accident, would be held in the largest courtroom, as there would be media and many members of the public attending.

Coroners always request a post mortem to be carried out by a pathologist to determine the cause of death. An inquest will be held if the cause of death remains unknown after the initial examination, or there is reason to suspect the death was violent or unnatural, or if the deceased died in prison.

The inquest is an inquisitorial process rather than an adversarial one; this means that it is an investigation, not a trial with contested opponents. The coroner hears evidence from the witnesses, and I was there to cross-examine those witnesses in order to be certain the truth would be revealed.

It is important that an inquest be held in public to find the answers to a limited but important set of questions: Who was the deceased? When and where did they die? What was the medical cause of their death? It is held as soon as possible after death, and in this case, it was only four months later.

The possible verdicts in a coroner's inquest include: death by natural causes, accident, suicide, unlawful or lawful killing, industrial disease, and open verdicts where there is insufficient evidence for any other verdict.

My client, Abbie, lived with her husband, Hal, and their three children, in Grande Prairie, part of Northwestern Alberta, near the border with British Columbia, about a two-and-a-half-hour drive from Fort St. John. Hal worked as a bus driver for Greyhound in Fort St. John, driving to all the cities and small towns throughout Northern BC and Alberta.

At the inquest, we learned that Hal was driving from Fort St. John to Dawson Creek at five o-clock that fateful early morning. The Greyhound was thirty-five feet long with fifty-five seats, but at the time, it held twenty-four passengers. Tyson was a young guy who had been drinking and taking drugs all night long at a friend's house on the other side of town. At five in the morning, he decided to head for home, speeding down the road in his red 1964 Ford Fairlane Thunderbolt. His speed was estimated at 120 kilometres per hour in a 50 zone.

TALES AND TORTS: STORIES OF A COUNTRY LAWYER

In the centre of town, Tyson drove right through the stop sign, not expecting to find anyone on the road that early in the morning. Disastrously, Hal was driving the Greyhound bus down main street at a leisurely pace of 50 km per hour with his window open on a lovely July morning. Tyson hit the driver's side of the bus at 120 km per hour, exactly below where Hal was sitting. The tremendous impact spun the bus around and tipped it over onto the driver's side. Hal's head was outside the window when the side of the bus hit the pavement, crushing his head and killing him instantly. The pathologist also reported that Tyson died instantly as well, as his abdominal aorta and thoracic aorta were ripped from his heart upon impact as he decelerated from 120 km per hour to a standstill in one moment.

The pathologist was a crusty lady, conveying a certainty in her sworn testimony that left no doubt about what had happened. The medical cause of death was undeniable. The verdict was death by accident.

Abby's sister, who lived in Fort Langley, referred her to me for legal advice. Abbie retained me to act on behalf of her and her three young children. Hal was working at the time of his death, so he qualified for Worker's Compensation either in BC (since the accident occurred there) or in Alberta, because that was where he lived. Tyson was not working, so Abbie had an election of whether to take Worker's Compensation or commence a civil suit against Tyson and collect the settlement from his insurance company.

The first inquiry I made regarded Worker's Compensation. The benefits were more generous in Alberta, but initially I advised Abbie to proceed against Tyson's insurance, which would result in the recovery of a greater monetary amount. Furthermore, if Abbie elected to proceed with Worker's Compensation, she could not proceed with the civil suit unless authorized by Worker's Compensation. However, I checked with the Worker's Compensation Board in Alberta, who authorized me to bring a civil suit, even if Abbie elected to collect Worker's Compensation in Alberta. They were very sympathetic with Abbie's situation with three small children, so they agreed to pay a percentage of Hal's wage loss to the widow commencing immediately, and allow me to bring a civil suit. Further, surprisingly, they agreed they would not seek reimbursement for the amount the board would pay out to Abbie. This was an incredible deal and entirely unique.

In light of this agreement with the Worker's Compensation Board of Alberta, we elected compensation with the board which paid a percentage of Hal's wages to his widow each month, and simultaneously commenced a lawsuit against Tyson to collect on his insurance in British Columbia.

The next hurdle to cross became clear shortly after I commenced the lawsuit for the loss of support Hal would have provided to his wife and three children over his working life. This was a considerable sum. However, Tyler only carried the minimum insurance of $200,000. I requested that Abbie provide me with a copy of Hal's insurance, and sure enough, for only $30 he had purchased under-insured protection up to two million dollars.

After collecting the $200,000 of insurance monies in British Columbia, I proceeded against the insurance company in Alberta pursuant to the under-insured protection clause in Hal's insurance. The result was a favourable settlement that would support Abbie for the rest of her life, and also provide a generous award for each of her children.

I am unable to articulate the satisfaction I felt in achieving this unique and outstanding resolution, in this case for Hal, whom I felt somehow was still with us in spirit, looking out for Abbie and their three children. The trip to Fort St. John in the middle of winter chilled me to the bone, but the outcome of my efforts warmed me to such a degree that the cold was a faint and cherished memory. I will always have a warm place in my heart for Abbie, her three children, and my trip to Fort St. John in the midst of a winter storm.

CHAPTER TWENTY-SIX

Premenstrual Syndrome (PMS)

Patricia suffered from PMS, as she felt severe depression, irritability, and tension before menstruation. It is likely she suffered from an even more severe condition called Premenstrual Dysphoric Disorder (PMDD) given the anger, suicidal thoughts, and panic attacks she experienced before menstruation each month.

Her only method of gaining any relief from these symptoms was to practise yoga, take a hot bath, and sleep. However, it was difficult to find the time to enjoy these activities, with a demanding husband and two active boys, Jarrett, aged seven, and Jeremy, eleven.

Her husband was a trucker, and he had just purchased a trucking business with twenty-one of the best, heavy-duty gravel haulers in the industry. It was a totally new kind of pressure—to run a successful business and not just drive a truck. Patricia's job was to do all the bookkeeping. It was an exacting and onerous challenge to keep up with all the paperwork.

Her two boys just loved to roughhouse, constantly engaging in boisterous play. Their relentless rowdiness sometimes drove her crazy. She loved them dearly, but it was impossible to enjoy a quiet moment in the home. At the same time, her husband, Bob, was under new and unyielding pressure to keep his twenty-one trucks on the road at all times on many different work sites to be sure to earn enough money to pay the mortgage. It was a logistical nightmare.

Patricia had a round face, chubby cheeks, and big brown eyes. She was not slim, but rather built like an apple. Her eyes danced when she smiled, which was most of the time, as she had a jovial personality, routinely laughing and joking about herself. It was the strange case of Dr. Jekyll and Mr. Hyde—loving and kind most of the time, then changing to anger and irritability for the five days before her menstruation.

Bob was an easygoing, kind-hearted man with a large beer belly hanging over his belt, even though he didn't drink. He was the first to dive into the freezing waters of Gold Creek on camping trips with his family. Running a business did not suit his personality, so it caused a great deal of mounting pressure.

Bob loved his wife dearly. He always joked that when Patricia walked out of the bathroom in the morning at home, she was the most beautiful woman in the world. However, her fine hair quickly lost its curl, and her makeup ran within the first hour, leaving her quite the mess. She felt bad, but Bob thought this was an endearing feature about his wife that he really enjoyed. He liked to tease her about it.

One day, when Bob was out on one of the work sites, Patricia was left alone at the office doing the books. She was getting more and more frustrated as the numbers did not add up. It was that time of month, so she was more than irritable.

While struggling with feelings of depression and anger, a woman burst unannounced into Patricia's private office. The woman complained that the truckload of gravel her husband ordered had not arrived. Why not? What was the problem? Didn't she know how to run a business?!

Patricia was overwhelmed. She told the lady to leave her alone. However, the woman just kept it up. Patricia screamed at her to get out. The lady continued to press forward, getting right into Patricia's space, with her face just inches away. The lady shouted, "Are you an idiot?" She followed with, "Just how stupid can one person be?" At this point, Patricia lost all control. Overcome with rage, she clenched her fist and struck the lady in the nose as hard as she could. It was a swift and powerful punch. I think it could be called a knockout punch.

The lady went down with a broken nose and blood all over her face and pretty pink blouse. She cried out in pain and then fled from the office, tears running down her cheeks and mixing with the red blood. She was filled with fear, thinking her attacker would strike again.

At first, Patricia felt triumphant, but then she was overcome with feelings of remorse. Ultimately, she was in a state of ambivalence, with simultaneous conflicting beliefs and feelings about what she had done. Mixed emotions swept over her like waves of grain blowing in the wind.

Later that day, the police arrived, charging her with assault causing bodily harm. It was humiliating to be arrested, hauled off to the police station, fingerprinted, and have mug shots taken. Patricia was released on a promise to appear, but all she could think about were ways of ending her life. Fortunately, Bob rushed home when Patricia recounted her story to him over the phone. Bob congratulated her on striking such a forceful blow. He hugged and kissed her, repeatedly saying he loved her, and she did not do anything wrong. He went so far as to say he was proud of her.

When Patricia was feeling better, a few weeks later, Bob brought her to my office in Fort Langley. At that time, a defence of PMS was unheard of, but I thought I would try it. I went out on a limb and shared my defence strategy: PMS. Whenever I mentioned PMS, it was ubiquitously thrown around as a misogynistic joke. Any time a woman displayed a degree of emotion deemed unacceptable, such as anger or sadness, common phrases diminished her experience: "It must be that time of the month;" "I guess Aunt Flo is visiting;" "Don't mind her, she's on the rag." However, after careful medical investigation, I determined that PMS is a medical condition, and I was willing to take a calculated risk.

Just like Bob, I was on Patricia's side—that lady deserved a punch in the nose. It was just unfortunate she suffered a broken nose. If the judge decided PMS did not constitute a complete defence to the charge, then at least it would create the maximum amount of sympathy for Patricia and form the foundation for my submissions in the alternative requesting an absolute discharge.

The trial was held in Provincial Court as the Crown proceeded on an offence called summary offences, these being less serious crimes where the maximum penalty is a $5,000 fine and/or six months in jail. Indictable offences are the most serious offences under the Criminal Code, and they come with more serious punishments.

The lady gave her evidence, and then Patricia told her story. In addition, I had an expert report from her doctor regarding her PMS. It was the doctor's opinion that the PMS caused Patricia's lack of control, causing her to become so angry that she struck the victim.

During argument, the Crown ridiculed my submissions that PMS constituted an absolute defence, as it had never before led to an acquittal in Canada. However, it had been used as a relevant factor in speaking to sentence. Likewise, provocation is not a defence at law, but goes to sentencing.

Given the circumstances, the judge was sympathetic to Patricia, feeling there had been severe provocation. I could see he liked Patricia. She was a very likeable person. I questioned her on the stand as long as I could, because I knew the more the judge heard from her, the more he would like her.

I was ahead of my time in attempting to establish PMS as a complete defence to the charge, but years later I would be vindicated, as it became approved by the courts as a defence. I think the judge was thinking about an appeal if he accepted PMS as an absolute defence, therefore, he found Patricia guilty, but granted an absolute discharge due to extreme provocation by the lady complainant and Patricia's PMS. He knew this was as good as an acquittal, since it made it like it never happened, and Patricia would maintain her clean record. The Crown was happy with the outcome, because in the end they liked Patricia too.

With the good company of William Shakespeare, I thought, *All's well that ends well.* Patricia, Bob, and I went out for a victory lunch.

CHAPTER TWENTY-SEVEN

Toby the Bull

He was proud to be a Texas Longhorn, well named with characteristic long horns extending to over one hundred inches from tip to tip. He strutted around in his green grassy field, very distinctive in his colouration of dark red and white. At 2,200 pounds, he was not afraid of anything or anyone, as the ground shook wherever he walked, and he believed all animals bowed down whenever he passed.

With horns so long he knew that people wondered how he could even keep his head up off the ground. Little did they know the sheaths of his enormous horns were hollow on the inside, and to him, they felt as light as a feather. He displayed his horns with grateful honour, like a badge of courage.

His genealogy was well known, as he descended from the first cattle introduced to the New World from Portugal and Spain. In his mind, he envisioned the Italian explorer, Christopher Columbus, bringing his ancient ancestors to the Caribbean island, making landfall in what is now the Bahamas, and more particularly the island he renamed San Salvador in 1492.

The Spanish reached the area that became known as Texas near the end of the seventeenth century. Eventually some cattle were turned loose on the open range, where they remained feral for the next two centuries. These cattle developed hardy characteristics, like extreme tolerance for drought and an ability to survive on the poor vegetation of the open range.

However, the leaner meat of the Texas Longhorn was not as attractive in an era where fat was highly prized. Consequently, the Texas Longhorn stock slowly dwindled, but was saved from extinction by enthusiasts, who loved the bull's history and distinct appearance.

Garth, Toby's owner, was just such an enthusiast. Garth brought Toby all the way from Texas to Langley, British Columbia, and gave him the name Toby. Toby thought his name was "Cool." It sounded like a bull with an energetic demeanour and a sweet personality. Garth told him that the origin of his name was the Greek word *Tobias*, meaning "The Goodness in God."

Garth called him "Toby, the Langley Longhorn." He lived in a beautiful verdant meadow with a wooden fence around it and a huge oak tree in the middle. The oak tree was seventy feet high and nine feet in width with branches reaching 135 feet in length. Toby loved to stand in the shade of this ancient oak that was certainly five hundred years old.

Toby was intelligent, easy to handle, and adaptable. He thrived in the hot dry climate of Texas, but was equally happy in the damp environment found in Langley, close to Vancouver, on the West Coast of Canada. Toby was twenty-eight years old with an easy-going way about him. He was accustomed to his owner, Garth, who took care of him and talked to him every day. Garth made sure Toby had plenty of food and water. Garth walked throughout Toby's pasture without any concern for his own safety.

Garth worked for an innovative high-tech company in Vancouver, which was a great location due to the lovely landscape, West-Coast lifestyle, and proximity to Silicon Valley. He returned to his hobby farm each evening, where he was greeted by his chickens, lambs, and Toby. It was just Garth and his farm animals, so he was never alone, and he never felt lonely.

The high-tech industry was expanding rapidly, so Garth decided it would be wise to invest in shares of some innovative companies. With this in mind, he attended his local bank to increase the mortgage on his land to acquire the necessary funds. The banker told Garth that a full appraisal of the land would be required before further funds could be advanced. Thus the following week, the bank made an appointment for Garth to meet with their appraiser at Garth's hobby farm, to make a professional determination of the market value of his small acreage with a 2,500-square-foot house and outbuildings for his farm animals.

When they arrived at Toby's pasture, Garth told the appraiser whose name was Leo, that it was safe for him to cross the enclosure on foot to reach the other side where there was a white wooden marker that set out the boundary on the west side of the property. Garth pointed out where the marker for the property line was located. Garth remained leaning against the fence, while Leo climbed over the barrier and started walking across the field.

Toby the bull was standing under the old oak tree in the shade as it was a hot July day. He eyed the intruder. Toby had never seen this stranger before, and he wondered what he was doing in his pasture. Instinctively, Toby started to charge across the meadow directly at the stranger. This odd fellow started running for the fence, so Toby picked up steam to run him down. The man panicked as he caught sight of the 2,200-pound bull bearing down on him at forty kilometres per hour.

Leo was just an average, middle-aged man in poor shape. At five-foot-nine-inches tall and 165 pounds, he could only muster up a running speed of eight kilometres per hour. About ten feet before he reached the safety of the fence, Toby ran right over him. Leo looked like he would never be able to peel himself off the ground again. He lay unconscious, pulverized in the dirt with four broken ribs, punctured lungs, a broken leg, other internal injuries, and a severe concussion.

Toby stood about ten feet away, staring at the man laying inert on the ground, proud of his handiwork. He quickly realized there was no need to strike again. At the same time, Garth came screaming as he sprinted across the field, yelling, "Toby, what have you done?" He reached the devastated body pressed into the soil and called 9-1-1 on his cell phone. The ambulance arrived ten minutes later, but Leo still had not recovered consciousness. He was taken to the hospital.

Fortunately, Leo regained consciousness on the way to the hospital, but it was clear the blunt trauma had caused damage to his brain tissue. Garth was devastated. He was overcome with remorse, sorrow, and guilt.

After a few weeks, Garth visited Leo in the hospital, where he expressed his deep sadness, regret, and grief for what had happened. He brought flowers, chocolates, and a card, but it all seemed so inadequate. Garth told Leo he had five million dollars liability insurance on his property, and that he should consult an expert personal injury lawyer to be fully compensated for his injuries, lost wages, and expenses.

This is when I entered the picture as Leo consulted me for legal advice at my office in Fort Langley. Since Garth told him it was safe to cross the pasture, liability was not an issue. It was just a question of the amount of damages to be recovered for the injuries caused by Toby the bull.

A year later, Leo had recovered from most of his injuries, but he likely would suffer symptoms of a mild traumatic brain injury for the rest of his life, including headaches, fatigue, memory loss, problems with speech, depression, irritability, and loss of balance. I obtained all the necessary medical-legal reports to document the injuries. Almost two years after the injuries were incurred, we arrived at a reasonable settlement with the insurance company.

I named this lawsuit the "Toby the Bull Case." It was unique in my legal exploits of forty years. Toby never attacked anyone before or after this incident. There is not a person on earth who can explain why he did what he did on that occasion. There are just theories about what he was thinking; however, the violence was completely out of character. Just remember to never enter a pasture with a bull in it.

It reminds me of a phrase I like, found in a novel by Tom Clancy called The *Teeth of the Tiger,* where a character in the story explains: "If you want to kick the tiger in his ass, you'd better have a plan for dealing with his teeth." Likewise, if you want to enter a pasture with a bull in it, you'd better be able to run faster than eight kilometres per hour.

CHAPTER TWENTY-EIGHT

Evil

Did you ever see the face of evil, or feel it crawling up your spine until the hair on the back of your neck stood on end? Did the very thought of it overcome you with fright so that goosebumps emerged, caused by contractions of small muscles all over your body? Did all of your hair follicles rise up, an involuntary reaction of your nervous system, causing you to feel you had to fight or take flight?

Did the vile smirk, malicious scowl, or venomous sneer of someone ever warn you of the depravity within? Did you ever discern wickedness in a loathsome grin or wrathful laugh? Did you ever see a smile that did not mean well?

Did you ever feel enveloped in darkness when someone entered the room, so much so that you found it hard to breathe? In the presence of this person, did you feel the dark emotions of sadness, emptiness, despair, and fear, and did you smell and taste something dreadful and nasty as you were gasping for air?

Did the darkness weigh heavily like dense fog in the black of night? Was the atmosphere charged with malevolence?

I have only experienced these feelings twice in my legal career. The first time was when I conducted an examination of a defendant, who murdered a young woman riding on the back of his motorcycle, and pretended it was an accident (as described in an earlier chapter entitled, "Was It Murder?"), and the second time was during the course of the case I am about to describe.

It all started in the Philippines, a country in Asia situated in the western Pacific Ocean, consisting of about 7,600 islands. At the northern end of the Philippines sits Luzon, the country's largest and most populous island. It is known for its mountains, beaches, and coral reefs, and is home to Manila, the national capital. It is also home to Quezon City, located on the Guadalupe Plateau, just eight kilometres northeast of Manila. Quezon City has a population of three million people, making it the most populous city in the Philippines.

Jeffrey owned and operated an orphanage for boys located in the squalor of the slums in Quezon City. Moderate economic growth in the last four decades in the Philippines has had little or no impact on the poor. Greater and greater inequality between the haves and the have-nots continues to divide the people further and further. There are no jobs for the poor, and high-inflation means conditions continue in a downward spiral, as it requires more and more money just to exist. The rich get richer and the poor just get poorer.

High levels of population growth, combined with greater levels of inequality and corrupt or incompetent government institutions, relegate the unfortunate children in poverty to remain there. With no hope of an education, there is no escape from the slums.

In contrast, Jeffrey was born and raised in West Vancouver, the city with the highest average income in Canada. His family owned many successful businesses, and he inherited a mansion on the slopes of the North Shore Mountains, with 5,500 square feet of opulence, a swimming pool, and a tennis court. Managers ran his businesses, leaving Jeffrey with a lot of free time, while he was earning an income of well over $400,000 per year.

Jeffrey had a wife and two children—Sarah, who was fifteen, and Dan, who was twelve. Jeffrey didn't spend much time with them, as he preferred to travel to take care of his charitable operations in Port-au-Prince, Haiti and Quezon City.

Haiti is perhaps the poorest country in the world. Jeffrey owned an orphanage for boys here as well. The population of Haiti is almost entirely descended from African slaves who won independence from France in 1804.

Haiti is home to miles of breathtaking beaches and crystal blue waters. Tourism once made it a popular destination; however, the only growth industry over time was crime. For tourists, the danger of high levels of violent crime, assault, armed robbery, murder, kidnapping, and rape meant they flooded to safer destinations in the Caribbean.

The main problem for the people of Haiti occurred after widespread deforestation led to flooding, dramatic rates of soil erosion, and subsequent declines in agricultural productivity. Haitians could no longer feed themselves in a land where, in the past, they raised an abundance of food.

When Jeffrey visited his orphanage in Haiti, he had armed bodyguards to protect him. While there, he always attended voodoo religious rituals. He was fascinated by this Haitian folk religion, sometimes called the national religion. He liked the core belief that God does not interfere in daily life, but that spirits do. Connection with these spirits could be obtained by various rituals, such as drumming, singing, dancing, and chanting, to encourage a spirit to possess one of the people of the gathering, thus communicating with all of them. Jeffrey found the chanting of those gathered, combined with the gyrations of the dancers, hypnotic.

At each of his orphanages, Jeffrey had a large bedroom with plush furnishings, which remained empty while he was away. Each orphanage housed about forty boys between the ages of eight and fourteen in a large dormitory with beds about four feet apart. There was a large kitchen connected to a room with long tables where the boys ate each day. Outside there was a small field where they played football.

Teachers arrived at the orphanages at 8:00 in the morning each day, conducting classes in the cafeteria, where the boys learned English, History, Math, and Science.

There are roughly two million orphaned and abandoned children in the Philippines, out of a total population of 108 million. The main causes for such high rates of orphans are natural disasters, teen/pre-teen pregnancy, lack of education, and the main reason—extreme poverty. In the Philippines, over 6% of the population live on less than $1.90 per day, 26% live on less than $3.20 per day, and 55% live on less than $5.50 per day.

Widespread corruption in Filipino politics and business prevents any opportunities for social mobility and increased income. Power is concentrated among influential families, offering the poor no chance of bettering themselves. As a result, there is a never-ending cycle of poverty that leads to parents having to give up their children in hopes they will have a better life somewhere else.

Under these conditions, where parents living in poverty are unable to care for their children, as they cannot afford food, clothing, shelter, healthcare, and education, Jeffrey's orphanage was in great demand. The boys that were there would do anything to stay there.

Conditions in Haiti are even worse. With a population of just over three million, it is estimated there are nearly 500,000 orphans in Haiti. The estimated number of orphanages is around 760, housing 32,000 children. So where are the other orphans? Child slavery is Haiti's silent secret. When a family can't take care of all the children, because there are too many mouths to feed, and they have no income, one child is often sold into slavery, so that the other children can eat. Around 300,000 Haitian children are forced by their families into domestic servitude, where they are basically slaves. In these circumstances, a place in Jeffrey's orphanage was a much sought-after position.

Jeffrey didn't spend his own money running these two orphanages, as all expenses were paid through a charitable organization that had donors across Canada and the United States. One of the organizations, located in Vancouver, British Columbia, that sent donations to the Philippine orphanage, sent a representative by the name of Christian to review the operation, to ensure the highest standards were maintained, in order to assure all donors that their money was being well spent.

Christian made arrangements with Jeffrey to meet him at the orphanage in Quezon City. When he arrived, he watched with interest as the boys received instruction from their teachers. The teaching was excellent, and the boys responded positively to their teachers.

At noon they had lunch, which was the largest meal of the day. The meal consisted of Sinigang, a sour meat stew, along with fried rice. The quality of the food was excellent, nutritious, and the portions were generous. Christian ate with all the boys, enjoying the meal and the company.

After lunch, Christian played an energetic game of football with the boys, which was a lot of fun. Then it was back to their studies, which proceeded in an organized and efficient manner, disclosing an excellent routine. Christian was a young father with two small boys, so he easily gained the confidence of the orphans as they ate, played, and studied together.

Christian was impressed with the cleanliness of the kitchen and how well the kitchen staff prepared the food. For dinner at 6:00 p.m. sharp, they prepared longganisa, a Philippine sausage with plenty of steamed rice. Of course, they had rice at every meal, which is the most important staple crop of the Philippines.

Mealtime brought everyone together, which meant it was a time to talk, and with forty boys, it was loud. After dinner, the boys had free time until lights out at 10:00 p.m. At this time each boy had to be in bed so he could rise again the next morning at 6:00 a.m. for chores before a breakfast of champorado, a chocolate rice porridge.

Jeffrey arrived after dinner, at which time he met with Christian in his private room. Christian reported how impressed he was with the routine established for the boys. Jeffrey thanked him for his kind attention. After a lengthy conversation, Jeffrey drove Christian to his hotel in one of the two cars available at the orphanage.

The next day, Christian returned by taxi at six in the morning, in order to share another full day with the boys. Jeffrey was there as well. They discussed the problems with many orphanages in the Philippines, where the quality of care was appalling, and how traffickers exploited some of them. They were familiar with unscrupulous people that used orphanages as a way to make money, preying on the most vulnerable people in the Philippines—the children. Jeffrey condemned, in the strongest language possible, the practice of sex trafficking children. He described it as a real problem in the Philippines, but it was also rampant in Haiti, where many orphanages were just fronts for rich people from the United States and Western Europe to traffic in children. Christian felt sick when he thought about this heinous practice and wondered how people could be so monstrously evil. This made him feel even more proud to be part of securing the funds for an orphanage that really helped the children.

Jeffrey suggested that they visit some of the scenic countryside surrounding Quezon City the following day, which would be Christian's last day in the Philippines. Christian felt this would be a wonderful opportunity, so in the morning, Jeffrey picked him up in a Jeep, which was one of the vehicles at the orphanage.

They began by exploring the marvellous rice terraces—they were stunning. They trekked around small villages containing dwellings scattered around spectacular and ancient agricultural landscapes, visiting the typical one-room houses where entire Filipino families slept on the dirt floor. The vegetation was very rich and diverse with verdant green tropical forests and abundant flowering plants, including ferns and orchids.

The roads were in abysmal condition with large ruts, pot holes, and one-lane bridges. Christian understood now why it was necessary to travel in a Jeep. As they made their way up a picturesque valley with steep mountainous slopes on each side, they came to another one-lane bridge traversing a raging creek.

At these bridges, vehicles travelling in one direction had to give way to vehicles going in the other direction. Christian noticed that all one-lane bridges were marked with signs posted, showing who should give way. Christian had never seen one-lane bridges before, but it was clear that as you came up to a one-lane bridge, it was necessary to slow down to check for any oncoming traffic before driving onto the bridge, whether or not it was necessary to give way.

The one-lane bridges made Christian nervous. Jeffrey did not slow down, but continued travelling at eighty kilometres per hour as he approached the bridge. He was not prepared to stop and proceed only if the bridge was clear of oncoming traffic. The sign indicated Jeffrey was required to give way. He did not. A jeepney came around the corner, entering the bridge in the opposite direction, and in order to avoid a head-on collision, Jeffrey veered off the bridge to the right, plunging his jeep onto the rocky bank of the creek, about ten feet below.

The jeep landed on the passenger door where Christian was sitting, which resulted in him receiving the most serious injuries. Jeffrey only suffered light scratches and bruises. Jeffrey climbed out of the driver's door, where he was met by the driver of the jeepney. They decided not to try to remove Christian from the jeep, in case movement aggravated any spinal cord injury. Jeffrey would remain with Christian, who was conscious, while the jeepney driver would carry on to Quezon City, about a half an hour's drive away, and send an ambulance.

When the ambulance arrived, they carefully lifted Christian out of his seat, through the open driver's door, and then drove to the hospital in Quezon City. The doctors in the hospital diagnosed Christian with a fractured scapula in his right shoulder, along with a broken collar bone, as well as a damaged humerus in his right arm. He had serious cuts and bruises all down his right side, as well as a large bump on the right side of his head. The rapid side-to-side movement of the back and neck caused serious and painful damage to the muscles. He also suffered a violent blow to his head, causing a traumatic brain injury, resulting in physical damage to the brain, including bruising, torn tissues, and bleeding.

A month later, Christian was able to fly home to Vancouver for further intensive medical treatment, which included psychiatric and psychological care for his brain injury. One year later, he was still suffering from pain in his right shoulder, neck, and back, but his greatest difficulty was with confusion and disorientation. He just could not remember new information.

Christian consulted me at my office in Fort Langley eighteen months after the accident. We decided to commence a legal action in Supreme Court in British Columbia against Jeffrey for his negligence, which caused the accident resulting in Christian's injuries. Jeffrey was negligent, as he did not slow down approaching the one-lane bridge; he did not drive with due care, as he did not see the jeepney coming in the opposite direction, entering the bridge first; and he did not yield to the jeepney as required by the sign on the road.

The first issue to be determined was whether the law of British Columbia applied, since this is where both parties to the action resided, or whether the law of the Philippines applied, as this is where the accident occurred. Legal research made it clear that the law to be applied was the law where the accident occurred—therefore, the law in the Philippines applied. The next step was to research the law in the Philippines.

The Philippines was discovered in 1521 by Portuguese explorer, Ferdinand Magellan, and colonized by Spain from 1565 to 1898. The Philippines is named after King Philip II of Spain. It is believed that the people Magellan discovered were Austronesian peoples, which constituted a family of languages spoken in the area extending from Madagascar eastward through the Malay Peninsula, Indonesia, Vietnam, Taiwan, throughout Maritime Southeast Asia, and the islands of the Pacific Ocean. Tagalog, the native language of the boys in the orphanage, and twenty million other Filipinos, is an Austronesian language.

As I studied the history of the Philippines, I discovered what I was searching for, as it was necessary to learn what law applied at the time of the accident. The law in the Philippines is the Civil Code established under Napoleon I, enacted in 1804. In British Columbia, cases are decided on the basis of the common law, that is, judges base their decisions on precedent of past decisions and, to a certain extent, common sense as understood at the time of the decision. In contrast, in the legal system in the Philippines, based on the Napoleonic Code, judges rule based on the legal code, and that's all.

Napoleon was a French military and political leader that ruled as Emperor of the French from 1804 until 1815. Napoleon dominated European and global affairs for just over a decade, while leading France in many wars, establishing a large empire that ruled over continental Europe before its collapse in 1815. Napoleon caused a great deal of death and destruction, but he did leave one lasting achievement—the Napoleonic Code. The Napoleonic Code contains ideas that underpin our modern world, such as meritocracy, equality before the law, property rights, religious toleration, and modern secular education.

The Napoleonic Code was adopted throughout Europe, including Spain, who enacted the code in its colony in the Philippines. It seems strange that a French leader, who ruled for only ten years, would have such a profound influence over the law in Spain and across the world to such a faraway place in the Pacific as the Philippines, right up to the present day.

My next step in the litigation was to find an expert on the law in the Philippines, meaning the Napoleonic Code, and the application of this law to my case. I found a lawyer in Vancouver, who practiced law in the Philippines, and then moved to British Columbia to carry on with his legal career. In his expert report, he concluded with the opinion that under Filipino law, Jeffrey was negligent and liable in damages to Christian. In this case, the Napoleonic Code brought about the same result as English common law. I always thought that it would, as it was just common sense.

Jeffrey did not carry insurance on his vehicles in the Philippines; therefore, any award would be paid out of his personal assets in British Columbia, which were considerable and more than sufficient to satisfy any award of damages made by the court.

A few months before the trial, I carried out an examination for discovery of Jeffrey at the offices of Begbie Reporting, across the street from the courthouse in New Westminster, located at Begbie Square. This square was named after Sir Matthew Baillie Begbie, the first judge in BC from 1858–71, who was unfairly known as the "hanging judge."

There were only four of us in the room: Jeffrey, his lawyer, the court reporter, and me. Jeffrey swore on the Bible that he would tell the truth, the whole truth, and nothing but the truth. The court reporter recorded every word of each question I put to the defendant and every answer he gave.

As my examination proceeded, I felt my hair stand up on the back of my neck. I was caught by surprise as I sensed a great evil in the room, and it emanated from the defendant. I seemed to know there was some deep depravity within this man—a vile, malicious, and loathsome secret hidden within. I did not know what it was, but it was real and so intense as to seem tangible to me. It created a darkness in the room so thick I could feel it, maybe cut it with a knife. The feeling was so strong that it seemed I could physically touch it, like a cancerous growth.

This feeling only lasted about thirty seconds, and then I felt a great sense of relief as it dissipated. However, I wondered what all this meant, keeping that thought in the back of my mind.

The defendant did not make any offers to settle the case. I prepared for trial, arranging my expert witnesses, the doctors, an accountant, and the Filipino lawyer, as well as my lay witnesses, my client, his wife, and a witness I was bringing over from the Philippines, who was an orphan boy at the time of the accident. He was familiar with the defendant's dangerous driving habits. This young man had a traditional Tagalog name, Bonoy, meaning "eagle." Bonoy left the orphanage when he was sixteen and had been living on his own the last three years. He was fortunate to obtain a job working in the fields for a rich American from Phoenix, who operated a huge pineapple plantation.

The list of my witnesses and a summary of their evidence was discussed at a pre-trial conference. The lawyer for the defendant didn't think it was necessary for me to go to the expense of bringing Banoy over from the Philippines, but he requested that I tell him when he arrived in Vancouver. I thought this was an odd request, but I told him that I would.

Bonoy arrived the day before the trial was to commence, and I met with him in my office. During this meeting, the defendant's secret was revealed. Bonoy told me that whenever the defendant visited his orphanage in the Philippines, he would bring one of the boys into his bedroom for the night. It was always a different boy each night. Bonoy had been chosen only once.

As he spoke, Bonoy began to sob uncontrollably, re-living the guilt and shame that still haunted him. He knew it haunted all the boys. Bonoy was adamant in his desire to expose Jeffrey for what he was, determined to find some way to bring it out during the trial. This is why he travelled all the way to Vancouver, to find redemption for himself and all the other boys.

Bonoy described the defendant's insatiable sexual appetite for young boys. The orphanage in the Philippines, and no doubt in Haiti, was a cover for his depravity. The defendant, Jeffrey, was a pedophile who gloried in his wanton debauchery. He was a degenerate who used children as sex slaves to satisfy his evil predilections.

Nothing is more wicked than abusing children who are not able to protect themselves. Jeffrey preyed on the most vulnerable. I think he is the most loathsome person I have ever met. No wonder I felt the evil within him.

When I called the lawyer for the defendant to notify him that Bonoy had arrived and informed him of what his client did to young boys, his quick reply was to doubt the credibility of this witness and state the obvious: It was irrelevant to my case of a negligent driver causing the accident that resulted in injuries to my client.

However, the next morning, when the defendant saw Bonoy with me at the courthouse, he finally made a generous proposal to settle the case. We did the deal with the devil. It cost him dearly.

I suppose he thought his wickedness would somehow be exposed for the world to see during the course of the trial. Perhaps he saw the hatred and desire for justice in Bonoy's eyes. Justice for Bonoy meant punishment for Jeffrey. Jeffrey did not want to take that chance.

Of course, Bonoy, recounted his story to Christian, who cut off all funding for Jeffrey's orphanage. Fortunately for the boys, Christian did take care of them by opening a new orphanage, ensuring each boy a place where they would be safe from abuse.

Christian made such a fuss in the Philippines, that Jeffrey was never allowed to operate an orphanage there again.

I made an appointment for Bonoy to meet with the police in Vancouver before he left for home. Bonoy told me he gave a complete statement regarding Jeffrey's immoral, illegal, and wicked conduct. I never heard another word about it.

I did see the face of evil that day in the examination for discovery. It was the face of Jeffrey.

CHAPTER TWENTY-NINE

Volenti Non Fit Injuria

I woke up suddenly in the middle of the night with a cold sweat running down the small of my back. The only thing I could remember about my nightmare was the lawyer on the other side repeating the phrase, *Volenti non fit injuria* ad nauseum, and the judge high up on the bench slamming down his gavel declaring in no uncertain terms: "You win, you win, you have spoken the magic Latin words; therefore, you win, you win, you win."

The phrase is well known among lawyers; it is Latin literally meaning "to a willing person, no injury is done." This common law doctrine holds that a person who knowingly and willingly puts himself in a dangerous situation cannot sue for any resulting injuries.

Essential to the legal maxim is that the risk must be known to the plaintiff, and that there is a voluntary assumption of the risk. It only applies to the risk that a reasonable person would consider possible as a result of their actions. Thus, a boxer consents to being hit, and to the injuries that might be expected from being hit, but does not consent to his opponent striking him with an iron bar or punching him outside the usual rules of boxing.

My client, James, was a competitive motorcycle and drag car racer. He entered an unusual race between a motorcycle and a snowmobile at the Mission Raceway Park in Mission, British Columbia. A collision took place in the staging lanes, where they were waiting to be called forward to race.

Prior to the collision, James executed a "Release and Waiver of Liability, Assumption of Risk and Indemnity Agreement." The single issue to be decided at trial was whether the release agreement precluded James' claim against Bryce, the driver of the snowmobile, and the British Columbia Custom Car Association, which was the organization managing the races.

James had been a competitive motorcycle and drag car racer, winning many cash prizes in the United States and Canada, for over thirty-five years. The collision between James' motorcycle and Bryce's snowmobile occurred in the staging lanes at the race track, which were included within the definition of the release agreement.

At the time of the collision, the throttle orientation on Bryce's snowmobile had been altered from the original position, in that it was installed in reverse, known as a reactive clutch; so, when it is started, if the throttle sticks, the snowmobile takes off. The throttle resembles a bicycle handbrake, but it operates in the reverse manner, so that if the driver pulls on the throttle, the speed of the vehicle will increase rather than decrease.

The snowmobile still had the skis on the front, but they added tiny wheels that enabled it to race down the track. The paddle belt was taken off the back, and a flat belt, like a flat piece of rubber, replaced it, so it would bite really hard on the track surface.

It was the end of May, when racing on snow was no longer possible, so snowmobiles were converted to running on a racetrack. It was going to be a drag race, a quarter mile run straight down the track. However, James was concerned that snowmobiles wouldn't run in a straight line, like a motorcycle or a dragster. James had never raced his motorcycle against a snowmobile before.

Bryce's snowmobile was fifty feet back of James' motorcycle when he lost control and ran him down, causing him serious personal injuries. James asserted that the throttle on the snowmobile was installed in reverse, and that if properly inspected, it would not have been allowed on the racetrack. He said that a reverse throttle causes the snowmobile to run at full speed, without the operator's control, and therefore, is extremely dangerous. He claimed he never assumed the risk of competing with a snowmobile with a reverse throttle.

It was agreed that Bryce's negligent operation of his snowmobile caused the collision with James' motorcycle; however, did the release agreement signed by James and the doctrine of *volenti* preclude any claim?

Bryce's snowmobile was inspected by an expert certified to examine drag racing vehicles. He found that the snowmobile complied with the requirements found in the rulebook, which did not prohibit the throttle modification. Thus the release agreement was enforceable.

There have been a number of British Columbia Supreme Court and Court of Appeal cases cited involving release agreements being held to be binding when dangerous activities were undertaken, like white water rafting. In white water rafting, there are obvious dangers. A spill means immersion in the frigid waters of the Fraser River, with the possibility of hyperventilation, hypothermia, or death by drowning. In these circumstances, it was found not to be unreasonable to obtain a signed release excluding negligence on the part of the defendant.

Other dangerous activities where people assume the risk include shark diving, biking across a desert, kayaking over waterfalls, bull running, heli-skiing, wing walking, limbo skating, cliff diving, sky diving, cave diving, and bungee jumping. Although some of these activities are so dangerous that no one should try them, some people still do. There are certain people that have always found new ways to push all boundaries to the extreme. A few select individuals have a whole new perspective on things to do before they die. They like to pick dangerous activities that might actually cause their death!

What about risky hobbies like scuba diving, mountain climbing, back country skiing, skydiving, hang gliding, paragliding, and racing?

Similarly, a drag race between a motorcycle and a snowmobile is obviously dangerous. The participants agree that by entering such a hazardous event, the participants may suffer bodily injury or death. In such circumstances, the release agreement operates to exempt the defendants from liability to the plaintiff.

The words from my nightmare came back to me—*Volenti non fit injuria*. The sweat was not just running down the small of my back, but it was pouring off my bald head, with the words repeated ad nauseum, "James has voluntarily assumed the risk."

CHAPTER THIRTY

The Farmers and the Fort Langley Floodplain

A massive Cordilleran ice sheet, roughly two kilometres thick, covered all of British Columbia from 75,000 to 11,000 BP. The ice sheet repeatedly advanced and receded. Tide-water glaciers ran down to the Strait of Georgia, and with so much water locked on land in ice sheets, the sea level was low. The glacial maximum occurred approximately 25,000 years ago.

Rapid glacial melting to deglaciation followed between 18,000 and 11,000 years ago, which led to the Cordilleran ice sheet retreat. The meltwaters and glacial outwash left unsorted materials such as silt, sand, gravel, and boulders produced by glacial erosion, as well as glacial abrasion, by which materials are dragged across the subglacial surface and dumped as the glacier melts.

The outwash, sands and gravel transported by rivers of melted ice and deposited ahead of the glacier, constitutes the material that Fort Langley is built upon. To state it clearly, Fort Langley is constructed on a foundation of a large pile of sand and gravel, pushed into place by a glacier, and left there as the glacier receded.

The glaciers retreated into the mountains, the sea withdrew, caused by a rebound of the land, and after the ice disappeared, the Fraser River extended its floodplain to surround Fort Langley. It is possible that some cataclysmic event changed the course of the Fraser River from running around Fort Langley on the south side, to the present channel flowing just north of the village.

The Bedford Channel, an arm of the Fraser River, flows on the northern edge of Fort Langley. The elevation of the land along the Bedford Channel is only a few metres above sea level and subject to flooding during the spring freshet, so an earthen dyke was built along the river's edge to prevent an inundation of the land each spring.

The western edge of Fort Langley, with a population of approximately 3,500, is built on the flood plain, while the eastern edge rises up a cliff approximately fifteen metres high. Below the cliff, dairy farms thrive on the flood plain, where the fertile soil produces an abundant supply of grass, which is bailed in the spring, summer, and fall, as feed for the dairy herds during the rainy winter season.

In the great flood of 1894, during the Fraser River's spring freshet in May, high water caused flooding, resulting in Fort Langley becoming an island for a few weeks. However, the dykes were strengthened over time, which prevented major flooding until 1948, when the dykes broke on June 2. Fort Langley became an island again as the Fraser's waters swept down Glenn Valley and over the Salmon River flood plain.

The Salmon River meanders back and forth across the flood plain just south of Fort Langley, then turns west, twisting like a snake as it winds north until it empties into the Bedford Channel. Due to the large dyke along the Bedford Channel and the Fraser River, the water from the Salmon River must be pumped over the dyke to reach the waters of the Fraser. A pump station at the mouth of the Salmon River was built to alleviate the flooding.

A new pump station with a screw pump was built in the 1990s, as this type of pump is much more fish-friendly than the one it replaced. There is a sensitive balancing act involving the Salmon River—the flooding, fisheries, and upland development all play a role. About thirty years ago, the Salmon River had 8,000 to 10,000 coho salmon returning each year to spawn. There is a counting station on the river south of Fort Langley, which recorded the decline in those numbers to 1,200.

Upland development in the Salmon River watershed over those thirty years increased runoff during rain storms, profoundly affecting the river and flooding of the Salmon River drainage basin surrounding Fort Langley. As the years passed and housing continued to be built along the small streams and creeks flowing into the Salmon River, combined with the removal of trees and other native vegetation, the rain water flowed more heavily and more rapidly into the Salmon River. This caused increased flooding over the years. The flooding surrounding Fort Langley became more frequent, but also much more destructive to the farmers' fields as the volume of water increased and the duration of the flooding lengthened.

The Township of Langley owns and manages the pumps; however, senior government officials in the Federal Fisheries Department wouldn't allow the pumps to be used to full capacity, except when the Fraser River was in full freshet. This affects the low-lying fields around Fort Langley, which are critical to area farmers.

It was at this point that the fourteen farmers owning land on the flood plain contacted my partner, John Cherrington, and myself, for legal advice. The farmers demanded that the Township of Langley operate the pump to prevent flooding whenever there was a rainstorm, not just during spring freshet. The majority of the land is used by family-run dairy farms, but there are a few blueberry farms as well. We launched a lawsuit against the township, demanding that the pump be used at all times, to prevent flooding that causes damage to the farmers' fields.

Historically, the Salmon River lowlands were beneath the water of the Fraser River, and they have been completely covered with water at times when the Fraser was in full flood—most recently in the flood of 1948. Dykes were built as well as pump stations to prevent the flooding. We were only requesting that these resources be used.

The township blamed the Federal Fisheries Department, which explained they were just defending the coho salmon in the Salmon River. I met with fisheries officials, high in an office tower in Vancouver, in an attempt to convince them to allow the township to operate the pump to alleviate the flooding, which would lead to a settlement of the lawsuit. I explained that flooding left the coho salmon on dry ground to die when the floods receded; therefore, it would only protect the salmon to allow the pump to run all year long. The fisheries officials responded that operating the pump disrupted the salmon beds where the coho spawned. We went back and forth on many issues, but I couldn't convince the fisheries officials to operate the pumps all year round.

We pressed ahead with the litigation. The next step was to acquire an expert report that would assess the increase in flooding over a thirty-year period of upland development over the Salmon River watershed. It was the most expensive expert report I had ever obtained. I think the cost was in excess of $90,000. The report involved hydrology, the geosciences, and the history of land development over a large area of Langley for a period of thirty years. Armed with this report, we had other experts evaluate the damages suffered by the farmers due to the additional frequency and severity of the flooding.

I remember the pre-trial conference before a Supreme Court judge in New Westminster, as he was fascinated by the many interesting and complex issues involved in the case. It took most of the day for me to explain the many disputes of fact and law. When I was finished, the lawyer for the township expressed a determination to arrive at some kind of compromise to settle the case. If it didn't settle, he would need to order an expert report in reply, which would be very expensive.

The cost of the litigation was spiralling out of control. The length of the trial was ballooning, given the court time required for the evidence of fourteen farmers, their damages, expert reports for each farmer on the issue of damages, and the massive expert report on liability. It was difficult to estimate the amount of time the defence would require, but it was beginning to look like the trial would last at least two months.

It was at this point that the township broke the stalemate by making a generous offer to cover the damages—past, present, and future—of the farmers and work to arrive at a more favourable compromise with Fisheries. It was nothing short of a miracle that the case settled.

To this day, the three sides are still trying to find ways to balance the competing issues of the environment, fisheries, development, and agriculture. John Cherrington and I were happy to arrive at an excellent resolution of the dispute for the farmers. It was a unique case—the case of "The Farmers and the Fort Langley Floodplain."

CHAPTER THIRTY-ONE

Tragedy on Chinese New Year's Eve

In the year 2017, the Chinese New Year, also known as the Lunar New Year, officially began on Saturday, January 28. The celebrations around the world started on Friday, January 27, the eve of the Lunar New Year. The New Year celebrations would traditionally end with a Lantern Festival on the fifteenth day of the lunar year, or February 11, 2017. At this time, people would go out to look at the moon, send up colourful flying lanterns, fly bright drones, have a meal and enjoy time together with family and friends in parks and natural areas.

The Lantern Festival can be traced back to 2,000 years ago. In the beginning of the Eastern Han Dynasty (25–220), Emperor Hanmingdi was an advocate of Buddhism. He heard that some monks lit lanterns in the temples to show respect to Buddha on the fifteenth day of the first lunar month. Therefore, he ordered that all the temples, households, and royal palaces should light lanterns on that evening. This Buddhist custom gradually became a grand festival among the people.

The two-week celebration welcomed in the year of the rooster. People born in a year of the rooster are very observant, hardworking, resourceful, courageous, and talented. Roosters are always active, amusing, and popular within a crowd, as well as being talkative, outspoken, frank, open, honest, and loyal. They expect others to listen to them while they speak. Vain and boastful, roosters like to brag about themselves. Li jing was nothing like this, as she was quiet, shy, and anxious. Her husband was her perfect match, as he was bold and confident, providing her with the security she needed to flourish.

Li jing was at home on Chinese New Year's Eve, on January 27, 2017, preparing all the traditional Chinese New Year's foods. She prepared fish, which symbolized an increase in prosperity, Chinese dumplings and spring rolls for wealth, glutinous rice cake for a higher income or position, sweet rice balls signifying family togetherness, longevity noodles for happiness and longevity, and good fortune fruit, a lucky food for fullness and wealth.

She also prepared the most traditional Chinese New Year's gift to give to her children in the form of a little red envelope with gold Chinese writing on the front and a small amount of money inside. Displayed on the kitchen table were tangerines and oranges, as they are popular symbols of good luck due to the association their bright and vibrant colours have with good fortune.

She dressed her twin, one-year-old boys, in bright red shirts as, red represents happiness, success, and good fortune. It is also the national colour widely used in relation to anything Chinese during festivals and important events like weddings. Li jing wore a bright purple qipao, a type of body-hugging dress of Manchu origin, high-necked, with the skirt slit partway up the side. The literal meaning of qipao is "banner gown," symbolizing beauty and elegance. The qipao is seldom worn except for special occasions.

Li jing was striking. She had the ideal shape for a woman's face in China—a thin, small face, with a delicate jawline ending in a pointy chin, with large, bright brown eyes. Her naturally black hair fell thick upon her slim shoulders and upper back. She was petite at five-feet-one-inch tall, weighing 105 pounds—dainty and adorable, like a young child.

Her two boys had names that fit them just fine: Yuanjun, meaning "joy," and Jian, which means "healthy." And they were joyful and healthy, always active and into everything.

The two boys and Li jing were waiting for Wang lei, her husband and father of the twins, to return home from work, so they could begin the celebrations. Li jing began to think about how she met her husband just four years ago at the University in Shanghai, China. Le jing was studying business and Wang lei engineering.

Shanghai, on China's central coast, is the country's biggest city and a global financial hub. It is the "showpiece" of the booming economy of China. With a population of over twenty-seven million people and a metro population of over thirty-four million, it contains almost as many people as all of Canada.

Love, romance, and dating were discouraged when people were young in China ever since the Cultural Revolution led by Mao in 1966. The emphasis was on studying, not dating, as the Chinese Communist Government focused attention on building up the nation rather than enjoying pleasures and freedoms. However, the students in Shanghai were exposed more to Western-style ideas about love and romance, so they dated more and engaged in more public displays of affection, such as holding hands. Li jing rejected the old ways and quickly fell completely in love with Wang lei. He became her best friend and lover.

They were married a year after meeting in Shanghai, in a large ceremony, with all the family present. The two of them enjoyed

Western ideas and culture, so they decided to move to Vancouver, British Columbia, where Weng lei would complete his studies in mechanical engineering.

Li jing studied the history of the Chinese presence in British Columbia, learning it started in 1788 when fifty Chinese workers and sailors were hired to work at a British Trading post in Nootka Sound, on Vancouver Island. But it was not until 1858, when gold was found on the Fraser River, that the first major migration of Chinese people came to BC.

She recognized in her studies that it wasn't easy for early Chinese Canadians to come to Canada. They faced a voyage of over 10,000 kilometres across the Pacific Ocean on ships that provided little in the way of comfort. Between 1885 and 1923, all people from China were forced to pay an expensive head tax to enter the country. This practice finally stopped in 1923, when Chinese immigration was banned completely.

Once in BC, Chinese workers were paid less and exposed to harsher working conditions than white workers. Additionally, laws limited their basic human rights: the right to vote, equal working opportunities, and the ability to own land. These early Chinese Canadians face great discrimination.

In spite of these hardships, Chinese Canadians persevered and fought for their freedoms to be recognized. Li jing felt honoured to follow in the path these Chinese pioneers blazed for her and so many others. Times had changed, and the Chinese were accepted as equals in Vancouver and British Columbia. In fact, she noted that 20% of the population of Vancouver was Chinese. Richmond, a suburb of Vancouver, boasted a Chinese population of over 50%, making it the city in North America with the largest proportion of Asians.

She had often heard it said in China that Vancouver had a second name—Hongcouver—because there were so many Chinese from Hong Kong in Vancouver. She felt this would be the place to live, as she loved Western culture, but could still keep her close connection with China.

Her twin boys were born in Vancouver as Canadian citizens. She was proud of this fact. She found Vancouver was an open and welcoming place for her family. The vestiges of discrimination were gone. She loved the freedom, the beauty of the land, and the people.

Thinking about freedom, she thought back to where she was born and raised in the Fujian Province, near the Taiwan Strait, also known as the Formosa Strait, a 180-kilometre-wide body of water separating the island of Taiwan from Mainland China. This was back in the time when the Communist Party of China maintained a strict one-child policy. It was the world's most extreme example of population planning. It existed from 1979 until 2015. The freedom of a democratic Chinese nation of twenty-four million people in Taiwan seemed so close, yet they were worlds apart from the communist regime in Beijing. Li jing longed for this freedom.

To enforce existing birth limits, the communist government could, and did, require the use of contraception, abortion, and sterilization to ensure compliance. Li jing was the eldest child in her family. Her father worked as a tax accountant for the government, while her mother was a housewife and businesswoman selling clothing.

When her mother became pregnant with a second child, they had to hide this from the Communist Party, as this was illegal. Her younger brother was born, but raised by an aunt who lived nearby who had no children, to avoid detection by the communists. If the Communist Party had found out, her father would have lost his good job with the government, and there would have been further serious punishments. Her parents courageously went on to have a third child, contrary to the law, and hid this younger sister with another family member.

The city Ningde, in Fujian Province, where Li jing grew up, was known as a small city, as it only had a population of 2.8 million people! She enjoyed the warm and moist climate and fertile land providing favourable conditions to grow and export mushrooms and tea. The area was famous all around the world for their China tea. She had fond recollections of the puppet lion dance, a cute and colourful Chinese lion dragon puppet with strings to make it look like it is walking and dancing.

The old people in Ningde practised the ancient religion of Buddhism, embracing karma, the law of cause and effect, and reincarnation, the continuous cycle of rebirth. Li jing didn't attend the Buddhist temples regularly, but she did like the idea of karma, meaning the good a person gives out will come back to them.

Li jing didn't like the proclamation by the People's Republic of China in 1949, under the leadership of Mao, establishing a policy of state atheism. She knew about the history. She desired freedom to think and live. Fortunately, she thought, the Communist Party changed, allowing the old, traditional religions, like Buddhism, Taoism and Confucianism, to thrive once more. She didn't think she was very religious, but she did believe in karma.

At twenty-two years of age, on the eve of the Chinese New Year in 2017, Li jing looked and acted more like a young adolescent. She relied on her husband for everything. He was only two years older, but he was confident and capable. He was fluent in English, while Li jing was not. He knew how to earn money and pay the bills and the mortgage on their home, while Li jing knew nothing about these details of daily life. She relied completely on him.

However, this was fine with her, as she trusted him implicitly, for as she said: "He is my best friend, husband, and lover." In return, Wang lei was totally devoted to her and their twin boys. He worked as a mechanical engineer in Vancouver, with a degree from the University of British Columbia, and faithfully returned home each evening when his work was done. He was intelligent, honest, and hardworking, as well as the sole bread winner for their young family.

Horribly and shockingly, tragedy struck on Highway 1 in the Fraser Valley of British Columbia, just east of Vancouver, on a provincial highway that generally travels in an east/west orientation, with four lanes of travel in each direction. At the location of the motor vehicle accident, eastbound and westbound lanes are separated by a large, grassy centre median. The posted speed limit on Highway 1 is 100 kilometres per hour. It was dark and the roadway was illuminated by street lamps. The roadway surface was dry and in good repair with no reported visual obstructions.

Investigation revealed that on January 27, 2017, at approximately 4:50 p.m., a 2015 Toyota Tundra was travelling eastbound on Highway 1, just west of the 176 Street on-ramp, when it collided with the rear of another vehicle. The Tundra went off-road left, entering the grassy median that separated eastbound and westbound traffic lanes. The Tundra re-entered Highway 1 in the westbound lanes (facing oncoming traffic) and struck Wang lei's vehicle head-on. The impact forced Wang lei's vehicle backwards into the concrete that bordered the roadway.

The RCMP Collision Reconstruction Investigation Report estimated that the Tundra was travelling at speeds between 118 kilometres per hour and 132 kilometres per hour and did not show activation of brakes prior to the collision. Wang lei's vehicle was estimated to be travelling at a speed between 108 kilometres per hour and 120 kilometres per hour. It was noted that approximately 1.45 seconds prior to the collision, the brakes were activated on Wang lei's vehicle, slowing the vehicle down to between 67 kilometres per hour and 72 kilometres per hour .

Tragically, Wang lei was pronounced dead at the scene at 5:13 p.m.

The particulars of the motor vehicle accident set out above are indicative of part of the cold, clinical opening statement of a lawyer at trial or in a mediation brief. But they do not tell the whole story of the pain and suffering, or the heart and soul of the case. It was my calling to bring all of this to light.

The RCMP attended at the home of Li jing that Chinese New Year's Eve of 2017. In the living room of her home, Li jing fell to the floor as she cried out uncontrollably in sheer agony, sadly surrounded by the vestiges of celebration, while being told the news that would forever change her life. She was inconsolable, overcome with grief, and sad beyond comforting. The police officers sat there in silence, feeling the absolute devastation of her suffering. They had brought news of ruin and overwhelming grief, which left them helpless in the face of Li jing's pain. Li jing was utterly shattered.

Two weeks later, Li jing met with me in the board room at our office in Langley. Her parents were with her, visiting from China. Her parents only spoke Mandarin, not a word of English. Li jing's English was rudimentary at best, and I didn't know any Mandarin, so I was glad that she brought a friend who was fluent in English and Mandarin to interpret for us. Li-Jing had been referred to me by a friend, who had been a client of mine some years before, regarding a personal injury claim. She wept when she described the tragedy of New Year's Eve. It was obvious she was lost and in great pain because of the death of her husband.

Fortunately, the Chinese Canadian community in Vancouver rallied around her, raising $30,000 to tide her over until I could obtain further funds from the insurance company, since she no longer had any income. She also had friends who assisted her in figuring out how to deal with the details of daily life, like paying bills and banking.

The following week, when we met, her parents were not present, nor was her interpreter, as I had a Mandarin-speaking lawyer from the firm present. Li jing described her despair, indicating she would have ended her own life by her own hand, except for the fact her twin boys needed her. She was suffering from severe depression, with persistent feelings of sadness and loss of interest interfering with any daily functioning.

I obtained some advance funds from the insurance company and referred her to a psychiatrist to help find the right medication to alleviate her depressive symptoms, as well as a psychologist to help her talk through her issues and make her feel like she was not so alone. I assured her that she could call me or come and see me at the office whenever her suicidal thoughts began to overwhelm her, especially when her psychologist was not available. We had many calls and appointments with me attempting to buoy up her spirits. She said it helped.

I commenced a legal action in Supreme Court on behalf of Li jing and her twin boys, Yuanjun and Jian. The claim was for the loss of financial support of Wang lei, her husband. I had an accountant prepare an expert report on the loss of support her husband would have provided to her and the twins over a working lifetime. It was a substantial sum of money.

In addition, the modest amount of $35,000 each was claimed for the twin boys for the loss of love and guidance of their father, which was the maximum sum established in the case law.

We set a trial date of two weeks in 2019, the earliest date available. The defendant relied on a very rare defence—the defence of inevitable accident. The onus was on the plaintiff, Li jing, to prove negligence on the part of the defendant, the driver of the car causing the accident, on a balance of probabilities.

Negligence on the part of the defendant was reasonably inferred by the rear-end collision with the vehicle in front of him. It was also reasonably inferred by the defendant crossing the grassy median and entering in the westbound lanes, striking Wang lei's vehicle. The defendant entered a guilty plea, in BC Provincial Court in Surrey, to driving without reasonable consideration for other persons using the highway. He was sentenced to a fine of

$1,300. A guilty plea is admissible evidence as an admission of liability. It is considered evidence of negligence.

At the examination for discovery, the defendant testified that on the day of the accident, he travelled from his home in Langley to Dr. Pollock's office in Vancouver for a vasectomy. Following the six-minute, virtually painless procedure, he was advised by the doctor's office that it would be safe for him to drive the forty-five minutes it took him to get home. The no-scalpel vasectomy involved the doctor locating the tubes that the sperm travel through from the testicles, and then making one tiny puncture, so the tubes could be reached, gently stretching the opening, and then lifting both tubes out and blocking them using heat cauterization.

The defendant provided an expert report which stated: "The occurrence of a faint greater than thirty minutes following a vasectomy is between 1–2/1000." The defendant remained at the doctor's office for thirty minutes after the procedure. He testified that he fainted on his way home to Langley from Vancouver, due to the vasectomy. In other words, the accident was not his fault. It was an inevitable accident.

Most people would think that simply proving the particulars of the accident would be enough to recover damages from the insurance company. The consumer buying insurance would think that the liability of the defendant was clear. But, it was not. The onus was on us to prove negligence on the part of the defendant.

It has been suggested in some legal texts—and I agree—that the defence of inevitable accident has no place in modern tort law. However, I didn't think it was possible for my client to wait another five years for me to overturn this perverse area of the law, in the Supreme Court of Canada.

During the examination for discovery, the defendant admitted a medical history that included hypertension and sleep apnea. He also admitted he was a regular marijuana user and smoked a package of regular cigarettes per day. He admitted to smoking marijuana early in the morning on the day of the accident and on the drive home from Vancouver to Langley.

When questioned as to the purpose for smoking marijuana, the defendant answered, "Just to calm myself and deal with stress." When asked if he was smoking while driving, he said, "I normally would smoke while I'm driving, yes."

The defendant was your average, out-of-shape, middle-aged man with a wife and two kids, living in Langley. His use of marijuana was not unusual, as it was recommended by his doctor to reduce stress.

The defendant did remember driving away from the doctor's office in Vancouver. About ten minutes from the doctor's office, he remembered passing the Mountain Equipment Co-op on Broadway in Vancouver. However, he had no further recollection of his driving after that, until the scene of the accident about forty minutes later when he said he felt himself faint. He said, because he fainted, he had no recollection of the accident itself.

The defendant also used his cellphone on the day of the accident. The cellphone records were produced showing an incoming call, and then an outgoing call of two minutes at about the time of the accident.

We held a mediation in June 2019 just before the trial in July. In preparing the plaintiff's mediation brief, I stewed over the uncertainty of proving the defendant was negligent in choosing to drive home, rather than have someone drive him, or taking a bus or taxi, when the expert report established that fainting only occurred in one to two cases in one thousand. One in one thousand is only 0.10%. Two in one thousand is only 0.20%. How could there be a finding of negligence in choosing to drive in these circumstances, especially when the doctor's office said he could?

It was at this point of high anxiety that the light of common sense struck me. If it was so unlikely to faint after a vasectomy, then accept this fact and look for another reason for the accident.

Research revealed that 30% of motor vehicle accidents in North America were caused by fatigue. If fainting is so rare after a vasectomy, then it only stands to reason that the accident was not caused by fainting. It was caused by falling asleep—something that happens all the time. The defendant's lack of memory of the drive from Vancouver supported this theory. He was just exhausted. His medical history also supported this view, as he suffered from hypertension and sleep apnea. Smoking marijuana to calm himself would also lead to drowsiness and sleep. His description of fainting was consistent with just falling asleep. Falling asleep while driving is negligence.

Further research regarding the cause of motor vehicle accidents in North America disclosed that 30% of accidents were caused by distracted driving. The defendant was smoking and on his cell phone. If falling asleep at the wheel was not the cause of the accident, then distracted driving certainly was. Distracted driving causing an accident is negligence.

My mediation brief certainly caused the insurance company to view Li jing's case in a totally different light. I was able to turn their expert report on its head and use it to my advantage. With the amount of sympathy that would be created for Li jing and her twin boys, given the tragic death of her husband, I couldn't imagine a Supreme Court judge not making a generous award for loss of financial support. After the favourable result of the mediation, it seemed clear that neither could the insurance company and their lawyers. The mediation lasted a full day, but led to an excellent settlement, subject to the approval of the public trustee and the court, as it would settle the claims of the two children, Yuanjun and Jian, as well as Li jing.

I didn't receive approval of the public trustee and the court until January 2020, which was the final year of my forty year career. I considered this my last big case. I felt a great deal of satisfaction as I sent the funds to the public trustee to be held in trust, along with interest that would be earned on the fund, for each of the boys until they reached the age of nineteen.

After our three-year battle, it was a great feeling to meet with Li jing to provide her with the settlement funds. She was now quite fluent in English, as she had been studying English almost every day for three years. Her confidence had grown as she contemplated her future. She wanted her twin boys to live and prosper in Canada. She had passed her driver's exam and drove her own car. She had excellent plans on how to invest the settlement funds and pursue a career in medicine. She had come a long way from that frightened little girl I had met in the boardroom three years before.

Even so, she was still the same person, as she repeated to me in that meeting, "Wang lei is still my best friend and lover." She showed me wonderful photographs of the boys at play in the park near their home. Wang lei would always be their father, and they would know everything about him, because, as she told me, she recounted stories and answered their questions about him every night when she put them to bed.

In China, the family is largely understood through Confucian thought. In Confucian thinking, the family contains the most important relationships for individuals and forms the foundation of all social organization. Although Li jing's husband was gone, the family maintained their relationship with him. The twin boys never said they did not have a father, as they understood they did. Li jing still felt she was married, and that a great reunion would occur in the next life.

It was a tragedy on Chinese New Year's Eve in the year 2017. The sorrowful and terrible events of that evening will never be forgotten by Li jing and her twin sons, Yuanjun and Jian—nor by me. Each year I think about the importance of Li jing's family, my family, and the undying love shared by all members of all families that link us all together in an unbreakable chain. The Chines New Year celebration is an important time for me to remember these cherished values. As I write these words, it is 2022, the year of the Tiger, a year with benefits both financially and romantically. It is an opportunity for bold changes for the better, including combatting any remnants of anti-Asian racism still existing in British Columbia. The colourful decorations of the Chinese New Year remind me that all colours are beautiful and needed in the exquisite mosaic of life.

CONCLUSION

Over the forty-four years of my career, these stories about prized animals, love triangles, tragic accidents, swindlers and thieves, disgruntled family members, and hardened criminals, paint a picture of the law, humanity, and the changing landscape of Langley. Just as the small town grew in size and political complexity, so too did I learn some of life's most joyous and painful lessons. Whether you win or lose a case, you always learn. I found myself questioning established "truths" with the voice of Grandfather Frog playing on a record in my head. What is an accident? Why did the bull lose his temper? How did the elephant tree lose its trunk? "Chugarum!" My clients expect and deserve the best I can give them and, I have found, that staying curious has helped me do just that. Asking the right questions and gathering the answers to create a story that achieves justice or closure for my client, has been my life's work and an invaluable source of fulfillment and creativity.

As Michael Morgolis states: "The stories we tell literally make the world. If you want to change the world, you need to change your story." Stories help us shape our perspective of the world and ourselves. From cautionary tales to absurd accounts, stories across all ages warn us and teach us how to laugh at ourselves, how to be a good friend and neighbour, and how to leave this life a better place for having lived well. The varied accounts of my clients, their backstories, passions, and injuries illuminate just how necessary establishing fair legal practices for all people are—regardless of sex, gender, sexual orientation, race, age, ability, religion, or creed. How can the stories we tell build a world where everyone is valued, equal under the law, and safe from prejudice, violence, and criminal manipulation?—Where all the animals in the "Hundred Acre Wood" or the "Smiling Pond" are celebrated for their differences and connected by their similarities. I wonder if my mother, with her ready smile and bright eyes, knew the world she was building for me all those years ago. I can still feel her tucked beside me on the edge of the bed and hear the rustle of the well-worn pages as each night the world was born anew.

ACKNOWLEDGEMENTS

Writing this collection of stories was a labour of love. After I finished a draft of each chapter, I would email the draft to my brothers and sisters and children, who provided great encouragement, helpful questions, and clever suggestions. Their dedicated readership, along with the unwavering dedication of my lovely wife, Beth, kept me motivated and reminded me just how exciting these cases were—and still are—even years later.

Thank you, Beth, for your patience in helping me with the things I find quite tedious, like compiling, formatting, editing, and typing. I'm an old dog, and new tricks don't come easily to me. Your compassion is truly a marvel, and I am so pleased that we chose each other as companions to journey with through life.

To my youngest daughter, Jane Conrad, who spent countless hours dreaming with me, brainstorming, editing, revising, and providing creative formatting and design ideas, I give my sincere gratitude. Shortly after completing the first draft of the manuscript, I was diagnosed with trigeminal neuralgia, a nerve disorder that causes excruciating pain to portions of the face. Through my treatment, surgery, and recovery, Jane took lead on the project, ensuring that my dream of publishing the book remained alive and well. She also took on the challenge of hand-drawing all the illustrations, which is very meaningful to me. My son-in-law, Joshua, was kind enough to lend his computer skills to scan the illustrations and digitize them with transparent backgrounds.

Thank you to the MyStory Publishing Team at FriesenPress under the direction of Benjamin Fligg. Your coordination, management, and constant communication kept me on track.

Lastly, I would like to thank my esteemed colleagues that I have worked with and learned from over the years along with all of the clients I have represented. What a grand adventure we have journeyed on together! I wish all of them well.

Printed in the USA
CPSIA information can be obtained
at www.ICGtesting.com
LVHW080247011223
765386LV00012B/255

9 781039 157279